MW00861258

Medieval Saints and their Sins

Medieval Saints and their Sins

A New History of the Middle Ages through Saints and their Stories

Luke Daly

First published in Great Britain in 2024 by
Pen & Sword History
An imprint of Pen & Sword Books Limited
Yorkshire – Philadelphia

ISBN 978 1 39905 062 3

A CIP catalogue record for this book is
available from the British Library

Typeset by Mac Style
Printed in the UK by CPI Group (UK) Ltd, Croydon, CR0 4YY.

Pen & Sword Books Limited incorporates the imprints of After
the Battle, Atlas, Archaeology, Aviation, Discovery, Family History,
Fiction, History, Maritime, Military, Military Classics, Politics,
Select, Transport, True Crime, Air World, Frontline Publishing, Leo
Cooper, Remember When, Seaforth Publishing, The Praetorian Press,
Wharncliffe Local History, Wharncliffe Transport, Wharncliffe True
Crime and White Owl.

For a complete list of Pen & Sword titles please contact

PEN & SWORD BOOKS LIMITED
47 Church Street, Barnsley, South Yorkshire, S70 2AS, England
E-mail: enquiries@pen-and-sword.co.uk
Website: www.pen-and-sword.co.uk
or
PEN AND SWORD BOOKS
1950 Lawrence Rd, Havertown, PA 19083, USA
E-mail: uspen-and-sword@casematepublishers.com
Website: www.penandswordbooks.com

To Lucy for her enduring patience while I lose myself in manuscripts, archives and the wonders of the medieval world.

'*Things temporal are all doomed to pass and perish…*'

The Decameron

Contents

Introduction: Faith, Pilgrimage, Saints

There are only a handful of words that have changed meaning as much as faith and religion across the ages. In today's often secular world, it has negative connotations of restraint, discrimination and harm. For those within LGBTQ+ communities, for instance, the church is somewhat the enemy to many for its views on homosexuality. Likewise, with the election of Donald Trump in 2017, often the 'religious nut' was synonymous with Trump supporters who would discriminate against African Americans, foreigners, Muslims, and even those who sought an abortion. In fact, often the idea of a 'crusade' was thrown around within the Trump administration. It is no wonder then, that so many people see that this current world has no place for 'archaic' institutions such as the church that are past their sell-by date. For me, however, I have a complex relationship with religion. I am faithful and believe in a higher power but an overwhelming number of questions forever inhibits me from truly defining what that means. As opposed to a concept instilled in me by my parents, my departure from secularity was a result of the vast number of years growing up in the Middle East and South East Asia where religion plays a more integral role in culture and politics than perhaps the UK. I'd like to believe, therefore, that my immersion in Christianity, Buddhism, and Islam has meant that I have been fortunate enough to have experienced some of the good that religion brings: community, passion, and, above all, devotion.

Some years ago, I embarked on a pilgrimage of my own to contemplate faith and attempt to even begin to understand the nature of religion. From Norwich, where I lived, I walked over several days to the medieval pilgrimage site of Walsingham. During the Middle Ages, this was one of the most popular pilgrimage sites in England and Europe, being visited by thousands who sought to pay homage to the house of Nazareth constructed by Richeldis de Faverches in 1061 as a result of a vision from Mary. Amongst the visitors were several high-profile kings and nobles including Henry II who visited twelve times, and Henry VIII who visited twice. Embarking on this journey was somewhat different to how the medieval pilgrim would have made it – for one, I had a North Face waterproof coat, a Vango backpack, and Google Maps to guide me. Nevertheless, I was sure to carry the iconic pilgrim staff to signify some sort of connection to the past.

On my journey, I was stopped by a vast number of people who sought to ask what I was embarking on and offered their support and well wishes for my journey. As I progressed, I stopped at various churches and sites including St Walstan's Well to embrace the 1,000-year-old tradition. Yet, it was not until reaching Walsingham that I began to understand what pilgrimage was truly about. The final mile of my journey was made without boots, a tradition that was said to be an act of penance and shed the sins of the pilgrim as they edged closer to their destination. Upon reaching the shrine I was in awe of its beauty. Within the church is a replica of the house in which Mary had given birth to Christ. Lighting a candle, I stood momentarily to quietly reflect on my journey and the journey of those who had come before me. Behind the shrine was a holy well which can still be drunk from today. As a sufferer of ulcerative colitis, a chronic disease, I thought I'd try my luck at seeing if the miracle stories were true. Safe to say I have not been affected by the debilitating illness since, but to the rational thinker these are mutually exclusive. Yet, it seemed as though I was not alone in this venture as, when sitting in the gardens of the shrine, I saw families, couples and individuals who seemed to share an affliction. Some were wheelchair-bound while others appeared to have learning or developmental difficulties – but all of whom were here to visit the shrine in hope of seeking relief. I sat and pondered on the many pilgrim miracle stories I had read at university while researching English cathedrals, many of whom travelled vast distances to sites like Walsingham to seek relief for themselves or loved ones. That evening, I stayed with a group of nuns at a former pilgrim hostel and despite not knowing who I was, I was taken aback by their care and kindness, and how they instantly cared for me as though I was one of their own. This was not the religion I read about in the headlines, the religion that sought prejudice, violence and discrimination against those who differed. What happened along the way for Christianity to become so disfigured?

The idea for this book began as a sort of throwaway concept for a fun *101 Weird, Wild, and Wonderful Saints of the Middle Ages* that was totally meaningless in conveying any purpose other than to talk about some interesting facts. While pitching the book, however, this question of purpose tormented my mind. One of the main reasons I have focused my research as a medieval historian on saints is that they appear as microcosms for the events, feelings, and certain themes happening at the time. In St Cuthbert, for example, we see an unusually high number of male pilgrims as a result of gender discrimination in Cuthbert's life that is upheld by the monks who then limit female access to the shrine. Likewise, in St Gerald of Aurillac, an aristocrat-turned-saint, we see many jostle with their thoughts about whether the church and state should become one and the same or whether these are definitively different institutions. As such, this throwaway idea quickly emerged into a wider retelling of the Middle Ages in order to understand medieval history, the ways in which saints influenced and were influenced by this history, and most importantly, how Christianity ebbed and flowed from the fifth to the fifteenth century to become what is is today.

What you may come to find is that, at times, Christian history is a very sad history that sees failures, suffering and paranoia take precedence due to various pressures. The hope, therefore, is that readers may then be able to understand faith (perhaps even their own notion of faith) and religion that may provide context to the current events we witness today – both good and bad.

This book is a pride and joy of mine; I had so much fun and learnt a great deal writing it. I hope sincerely that readers may find equal enjoyment in the following pages as we explore each century and the saints that underpin them.

Part I
New Beginnings

Chapter One

A Man Between Two Worlds

To pinpoint a specific moment in time when our dramatic epoch came into existence is one of the most difficult questions posed to the historian. Do we begin in 376, when tribesmen fleeing from Hunnic invaders entered the empire? Or 476 when the idea of the Western empire ceases to bear any practical significance? One may even argue that Rome never truly fell, but rather evolved into the Byzantine Empire which collapsed in 1453; or the Holy Roman Empire which was dissolved in 1806; or the papacy, which continues to this day. This is just the tip of the iceberg of problems involved in telling such a story, as while many histories of the Middle Ages begin with the end of a former world, one in which Rome falls to barbarians and a periodic collapse of civilisation ensues, the medieval world should be understood as being deeply connected to its predecessor. As such, the likes of Sallust or Suetonius are, for example, as influential to the twelfth century as the *Alexiad*. With this in mind, if we reframe our perspective around one of the greatest and well-known contemporary saints and church fathers of the fourth century, then we will be able to understand the transformative evolution between the classical past and medieval future. In light of this, rather than diving into the heart of the empire, our story begins on its outskirts, at Hippo in modern-day Algeria, where, in the face of violence and destruction at the hands of pagans, a theologian and philosopher was contemplating and constructing one of the most influential early medieval texts that would shape the future of Christianity.

Born in 354 to an aristocratic family in the dense forests and arid mountains of Thagaste, now Souk Ahras in Algeria, Augustine entered into a world which was a melting pot of culture, ethnicity and religion. His mother, Monica, was a devout Christian while his father, Patricius, was a staunch Pagan who only sought conversion to Christianity on his deathbed. This, combined with a hybridised culture of North African Berber heritage with Romanised administration, meant that Augustine stood at the conflicting intersection of theological and cultural tensions which would dramatically collide within his lifetime. Nevertheless, in order to understand the mind of Augustine and how he perceived the changing world around him, we have to look no further than to his early life to see the seeds of conflict being sown.

He admits in *The Confessions* that his early life was marked by pagan beliefs and sinful practices. His pious mother, who is the patron saint of marital hardships and victims of abuse, endured repeated violence from Patricius, who indulged in drink and promiscuous sexual pleasures. As such, Augustine grew up in a heavily divided household and claims to have inherited some of his father's habits. At the age of 17 while studying at Carthage, he drank, stole, enjoyed sexual exploits, and sought to indulge in his desires through his hedonistic lifestyle. He also read a great deal of Cicero, which he described as having a lasting impression and developed his enthusiasm for philosophy. Much to his mother's disappointment, however, Augustine also flirted with pagan beliefs and adopted Manichaeism, a highly influential belief system which arose from North Africa in the 270s and contained elements of Christianity and Zoroastrianism. The basis of this ideology was that the world was a battlefield between God and Satan, and humans are merely caught in between them and could only escape through meditation and asceticism. During his residency at Carthage, Augustine also fell deeply in love with a young woman. Being of a lower class, his mother discouraged the relationship and warned Augustine of his sexual desire and pursuit of sex outside marriage. Augustine continued despite his mother's disapproval, and his mistress gave birth to a boy, Adeodatus, in 372. Like Augustine, Adeodatus was regarded as extremely intelligent by his contemporaries.

Between 372 and 384, Augustine and his family moved from Carthage to Rome, and then on to Milan to teach grammar, philosophy, politics and Latin. During this time, however, he became increasingly disenchanted by Manichaeism, primarily due to its belief that humans were absolved from evil and simply lived alongside it. Instead, Augustine believed that if God gave humans the ability to decide their actions and deeds, otherwise known as free will, that evil was inevitable. There is no doubt that this conclusion was influenced by his abusive father and early life, but it is important to note that Augustine would have also been aware of, and influenced by, the emerging conflicts across the Adriatic and beyond the Balkans.

In the plains of modern-day Ukraine, Romania and Moldova, a mass exodus of fleeing refugees was gathering at the frontiers of the Empire's borders. The source of this crisis arose from a series of conflicts against the Goths and Alans by Hunnic tribes which led to their defeat and displacement. Travelling from the Steppe to the Balkans, the Huns were a mysterious nomadic tribe with little archaeological footprint but known to the Alans and Goths as unclean spirits and offspring of witches. Due to their enhanced tactics on horseback and incredibly deadly use of archery which could pierce armour at 100m, they slaughtered thousands and decimated the various villages of the Goths. In response to this, refugees fled their homes and sought out the Roman borders of the Balkans to be protected. For the Romans, however, the decision to act or not would be the flutter of the butterfly's wing which would cause the hurricane of their downfall.

In 376, the Balkans was thus caught in a migrant crisis along the river Danube. While it is difficult to know how many refugees there may have been, it can be said with a degree of certainty that numbers were in their ten-thousands. The task of dealing with this epidemic was given to the eastern Emperor Valens ('eastern' as the empire was so vast it was split and ruled by two emperors). Set with a moral and practical conflict between accepting thousands of foreign refugees or refusing them to be slaughtered by the Huns, Valens had to also contend with public order, food supply, and the potential for disease to run rampant. Favouring the idea of cheap immigrant labour and foreign military auxiliaries, Valens opted in 376 to accept only some of the Goths to settle in Thrace so long as military obligation was given. It was estimated that 15,000–20,000 Goths then crossed the Danube to be rehomed in an event which Valens believed to be a victory. Nevertheless, while this programme of resettlement for Goth refugees within the empire may have superficially seemed positive, exploitation and violence quickly turned it bitter, and questions of responsibility soon arose.

Although welcomed into the Balkans, this was partly through gritted teeth as previous wars fought between the Romans and Goths from 367 to 369 had left a lingering spitefulness. It may be suggested too that the economic sanctions levied on the Goths, combined with their losses from such wars, resulted in a weakened state which left them open to a Hun invasion. As such, the Roman officials coordinating this programme, Lupicinus and Maximus, took advantage of starving families by offering dog meat in return for sending their children to be slaves. Equally, alongside abusing the Goths, they failed to uphold Valens' condition that only the Goths were allowed in. Because of this, Thrace became a rich tapestry of thousands of different tribal inhabitants, most of whom were illegal. Although Valens believed that the infrastructure of the Romans could maintain these refugees, food supply quickly ran dry due to conflicts between the Romans and Persians in the East.

Starved, demoralised and angered, the Goths took it upon themselves to ease their struggle by undertaking a series of plundering skirmishes on Thracian estates. Overpowering the Roman armies stationed in the Balkans, the Goths and Alans combined forces to invade the surrounding areas, coming as close as the walls of Constantinople itself. Through corruption, neglect and exploitation, Valens had thus let a pressing migrant issue become a vast internal crisis which threatened the integrity of the empire. Attempting to rectify the situation, Valens marched at the head of an army to Adrianople where a large cohort of around 10,000 Goths had gathered under the command of Thervingian Gothic chieftain, Fritigern.

Although an encampment had been established on arrival, Valens, underneath the hot August sun, decided to push further outside of the fortified encampment to meet the Gothic army who were setting alight the surrounding plains. The Goths, attempting to outsmart the emperor, sent envoys to seek a truce while they secretly laid the grounds for a potentially devastating tactical trap. Exhausted and depleted after hours of unsuccessful negotiations, the Roman army decided to charge the Goth barbarians. During the violent and bloody battle, the Romans, who had believed the Goth army to be only 10,000 strong at best, quickly realised the extent to which they were wrong. Column upon column of barbarians set upon the depleted Romans successively for what seemed to be an eternity. Just as it was believed that enough Roman blood had been spilled, the trap that had been set during the negotiations was then released, and a hidden detachment of Goth cavalry, away from the Roman scouts, charged the closely packed Roman army and Valens was overwhelmed by Goth warriors. The wounded eastern Roman Empire, without its emperor, was now laid open to onslaughts of invaders.

While the frontiers of the empire were crumbling, the 380s would prove to equally push Augustine to his limits, and it was during this time that the spark for Christianity grew within him. While at Milan, Emperor Theodosius I, the successor to Valens, passed the Edict of Thessalonica in 380 which declared that Christianity was to be the only legitimate religion within the empire, gradually putting an end to the hybridised melting pot of theology Augustine had grown up with. Ambrose, the bishop of Milan, was a strong supporter of Theodosius and his tightening grip on pagan beliefs as a result of the migrant crisis. Though Augustine was not a particularly strong Christian, Ambrose played a strong role in leading him to re-evaluate his life and change his ideology. Augustine wrote, 'That man of God received me as a father would, and welcomed my coming as a good bishop should.' This bustling relationship, however, was cultivated in part through a series of devastating setbacks. The adoption of Augustine by Ambrose as a spiritual father was the result of Augustine's actual father passing. Around the same time, Augustine was then forced to forsake his beloved mistress of fifteen years (and mother of his beloved son) as Monica, Augustine's mother, betrothed him to a young girl of a higher class. Of this, he wrote that, 'My mistress being torn from my side as an impediment to my marriage, my heart, which clave to her, was racked, and wounded, and bleeding.' In 382, Theodosius tightened his grip further by issuing a decree that all Manichaean monks were to be put to death, further pushing Augustine away from his past philosophical and theological interests. In a time of desperate need during his crisis of belief,

Augustine writes in his *Confessions* that, at the age of 31 in 386, he heard a child's voice call out to him to 'take up and read'. Turning to a random page in St Paul's writings, he read Romans 13: 13–14: 'Not in rioting and drunkenness, not in chambering and wantonness, not in strife and envying, but put on the Lord Jesus Christ, and make no provision for the flesh to fulfill the lusts thereof.' This resonated with the sinful life that Augustine had lived until now, one which was marked by lustful desire, drunkenness, theft, fornication and immorality. As such, he writes in his Confessions:

> Belatedly I loved thee, O Beauty so ancient and so new, belatedly I loved thee. For see, thou wast within and I was without, and I sought thee out there. Unlovely, I rushed heedlessly among the lovely things thou hast made. Thou wast with me, but I was not with thee. These things kept me far from thee; even though they were not at all unless they were in thee. Thou didst call and cry aloud, and didst force open my deafness. Thou didst gleam and shine, and didst chase away my blindness. Thou didst breathe fragrant odors and I drew in my breath; and now I pant for thee. I tasted, and now I hunger and thirst. Thou didst touch me, and I burned for thy peace.

The Confessions of St Augustine, consisting of thirteen books written in the late 390s, though autobiographical, provides us with an incredible insight into the mind and contemplation of a man who finds God and Christianity in a deeply dark time, both in his own life, as we have seen, and geopolitically. As such, a reader may find incredible, and even somewhat relatable, discussions about anxiety, insecurity, free will and causality amongst other philosophical topics. Nevertheless, by 387, both Augustine and his son were baptised by Ambrose in Milan. In the following year, however, the final piece of straw which broke the camel's back occurred. While returning to Africa, both Augustine's mother and son, the loves of his life, successively passed away, leaving Augustine as the only remaining member of his family. It is reasonable to say that his fascination with contemplating evil on earth arose from the collapse of his beloved family unit within the greater setting of the crumbling empire.

The result of these tragedies was a complete surrender to Christianity. He converted the family home into a monastery, sold his patrimony, and gave his money away to the poor. In 391, he became an ordained priest at Hippo and began preaching thousands of sermons. He is known to have also preached against Manichaeism and other pagan beliefs he had once endorsed. That being said, the style in which he preached was heavily influenced by the ideas of Neoplatonism, a philosophical movement created by Plotinus (*c.*204–270), a follower of Plato. Neoplatonism distinguished the physical world from the intangible world of ideas, believing that evil could only reside in the physical world as it was imperfect, changeable and perishable. Therefore, the physical world was an imitation of the perfection of the eternal, a concept which Augustine continuously refers to within the City of God when reflecting on the crumbling empire.

While the stability of Augustine's life was deteriorating and leading him towards reforming his life, Emperor Theodosius, who had inherited the empire in a major crisis after a heavy defeat at the hands of heathen barbarians, was equally rectifying former mistakes. In order to recover a degree of stability, Theodosius implemented stern measures of conscription, punishments for desertion, and reinforced units with non-Roman auxiliaries – some of which were Goths. As a result of this, a series of minor successes were achieved, but a major life-threatening illness forced Theodosius to retreat and reduce the war's progress. Believing stability in the region was attained, he requested baptism and proceeded to move his court to Constantinople in 380. In the following year, Athanaric, a Gothic leader, visited the court and offered submission to the emperor. Though a propaganda victory, Theodosius saw that the Goths could not be completely defeated and exiled from the region. While minor victories continued to be achieved within Macedonia and Thessaly, an incursion of Sciri and Huns across the Danube threatened the stability of the Balkans once more. Negotiations thereafter took place in 382 to allow the Goths to settle in the region and provide military service for Rome. They were, however, able to remain autonomous under their own leaders which enabled them to remain strong and unified. Nevertheless, in 388, Theodosius was able to defeat the rival self-proclaimed Western Emperor Magnus Maximus at the Battle of Poetovio in 388. The recovery of the western lands following this battle made Theodosius the *de facto* ruler of the Western empire in 389, further aiding in installing a degree of stability into the empire. Theodosius thus became the last emperor to rule the Roman Empire as a whole.

Thereafter, in order to maintain public order, he adopted a moderate policy towards non-Christians. While he supported the preservation of temples, appointed pagans to high offices, and allowed pagan practices, he turned pagan holidays into workdays, banned animal sacrifice, divination and apostasy, and issued a number of laws against paganism. He is also responsible for abolishing the Olympic Games, believing that the worship of Zeus was a pagan abomination. Despite this, he took care to ensure the pagan population (which was still the majority by the fourth century) was not discontent with his reign. Archaeological evidence, as well as the hybridisation of language, culture and religion within society and individuals like Augustine, suggests that paganism was not the victim of a pious 'crusade' by Theodosius, but rather saw a slow decline over time. If Augustine's meandering between belief systems throughout his life is any testament to this, the relationship between paganism and Christianity within the empire even until the 380s can be understood through a lens of coexistence.

With the death of Theodosius in 395, the empire returned to its co-ruler split and Honorius was appointed as emperor of the western half while his brother, Acadius, ruled the east. From hereafter, the timer towards the collapse of the empire begins to accelerate rapidly. Honorius was young when he succeeded as Emperor, thus he relied on the military prowess and leadership of Stilicho, one of the most powerful men in the western Roman Empire and, like Augustine, a product of cultural and religious hybridity within the empire as he was part-Vandal and part-Roman. At the time of Stilicho's rise to power, the events of the Gothic migrant crisis were seemingly in the past. Yet the causes of the crisis were still prevalent and on the resurgence as the Huns were once again migrating in the 390s.

Though the fearsome Huns originated in Northern China, in over four decades from 380s to 420s, they had travelled over 1,700km in great numbers to Europe, scattering the various tribal inhabitants in the process. While in the 370s they had displaced the Goths, now, in the 390s, it was the Alans, Vandals and Burgundians. The Huns were not entirely a nuisance, however, as this time many opted to provide their military knowledge to Stilicho, who had various Huns within his personal bodyguards. Nevertheless, the great Hun surge during this period caused widespread panic amongst Romans and tribes alike. As such, between 405 and 410, the Roman borders were continuously battered by conflicts as well as migrant calamities. These forces were in no small number either; in 405 along the alpine border, a Gothic king called Radagaisus appeared with a migrant hoard of 100,000, a fifth of whom were warriors. Through a series of successful battles, he forced his way into Italy, prompting rampant panic in Rome. Stilicho, who was in command of the armies tasked at repelling these tribal invaders, had the manpower to do so but took far too long in gathering his hired Alan and Hun mercenaries, forces stationed in the Rhineland, and Italian armies. Six months after the initial invasion, the Roman armies under Stilicho finally assembled; in the meantime, Radagaisus was able to conquer and pillage as far south as Florence. Nevertheless, Stilicho was able to decimate their armies, capture Radagaisus, and free Italy from its periodic crisis. Although this was a victory, pulling resources and men from regions across the empire left large vulnerable gaps along the borders. Unlike a war with a single king whereby a relatively small area emerges as the battlefield, this war was being fought against multiple kings, across multiple battlefields, in multiple principalities. Within a year, in 406, Vandals, Alans and Sueve poured into the undefended borders of Gaul and Britain. In the process, hundreds of Christians and churches were attacked and ravaged by the barbarians; famine ensued and blood ran through the streets.

A contemporary to Augustine and fellow saint, Jerome (340–420), writes about the 'Fate of Rome' which gives us an idea of the general panic within the empire and details the sheer number of tribes entering the Roman borders:

> A few of us have hitherto survived them, but this is due not to anything we have done ourselves but to the mercy of the Lord. Savage tribes in countless numbers have overrun all parts of Gaul. The whole country between the Alps and the Pyrenees, between the Rhine and the Ocean, has been laid waste by hordes of Vandals, Sarmatians, Alans, Gepids, Saxons, Burgundians, Allemanni and – alas! – even Pannonians.

He continues by recalling the countless cities which have fallen to invasion or famine:

> The once noble city of Moguntiacum has been captured and destroyed. In its church many thousands have been massacred. The people of Vangium after standing a long siege have been extirpated. The powerful city of Rheims, the Ambiani, the Altrebatae, the Belgians on the skirts of the world, Tournay, Spires, and Strasburg have fallen to Germany: while the provinces of Aquitaine and of the Nine Nations, of Lyons and of Narbonne are with the exception of a few cities one universal scene of desolation. And those which the sword spares without, famine ravages within. I cannot speak without tears of Toulouse which has been kept from failing hitherto by the merits of its reverend bishop Exuperius.

What seemingly is most distressing to Jerome and contemporaries is that, unlike previous wars within their lifetime, this was being fought within their borders:

> Yet who will hereafter credit the fact or what histories will seriously discuss it, that Rome has to fight within her own borders not for glory but for bare life; and that she does not even fight but buys the right to exist by giving gold and sacrificing all her substance? This humiliation has been brought upon her not by the fault of her Emperors who are both most religious men, but by the crime of a half-barbarian traitor who with our money has armed our foes against us.

The so-called 'half-barbarian' being referred to here may be Stilicho who, as we know, was half-Vandal and hired foreign mercenaries to fight. Nevertheless, Jerome's writing emphasises the aura of fear from the Romans and contains a great deal of insecurity about the uncertain future of the empire. From this point onwards, the collapse of the Roman Empire began to exponentially increase. The Roman armies of Britain entered a state of mutiny, and in 406, two leading officers of the army, Marcus and Gratius, proclaimed themselves emperor before being murdered by their men. In 407, Constantine III gained control of the British armies and declared himself as leader of the Western empire, withdrawing all military forces to Gaul to aid in the war efforts. The following year, the Huns, whom this European crisis is attributed to, made a direct attack on the lower Danube. From hereafter, the empire as a whole was under attack.

A regular nuisance to the Romans and Stilicho was Alaric, King of the Visigoths. Unlike many other invaders, Alaric was a Christian and had led a warband of Goths and other tribes within the Roman army. Nevertheless, in *c.*395, he betrayed his Roman commanders to become king of a collective coalition of tens of thousands known as the Visigoths. In 401/02, and 403, Alaric attempted to invade Italy, only to be triumphed each time by Stilicho. Alaric, however, in 408, joined the mass onslaught of invaders in Gaul to get his piece of the pie. Coordinating an attack on Ravenna, he sent word to Honorius' court to negotiate the payment of 3,000lbs of silver in order for him to not invade. Stilicho, as Jerome tells us, gave in to his demands believing that his forces were already too far stretched. The senate, like Jerome, were deeply displeased by Stilicho's progress, and used his Vandal heritage in a racially charged campaign to accuse him of having an alliance with Alaric. Equally, Honorius cancelled the silver payments to Alaric, which resulted in an attack on Ravenna six months later.

Failing to eradicate the incoming plague of barbarians or defeat the disease of political opponents in the senate, Stilicho was unable to keep afloat. A coup ensued in 408 leading to several of Stilicho's officers being murdered, and three months later, Stilicho himself was captured, imprisoned, and executed for treachery. Alaric, after hearing that his strongest rival and obstacle to the rich spoils of Italy had perished at the hands of his own people, took advantage of the opportunity to strike. Within weeks, the Visigoths marched deep within Italy, and their numbers grew exponentially as the xenophobic campaign of the senate forced foreign Roman auxiliaries to switch their allegiance. For many, the abuse and violence towards foreigners and migrants within the empire transformed the expedition from guerrilla plundering to a war on racial oppression. As such, with a personal vendetta, Rome – the eternal city, the beating heart of the empire, and the centre of civilisation – became a fitting target to wound and shatter the institution that had abused and mistreated so many.

In November of 408, the city was under siege by Alaric. Holding the city ransom for all its gold, he halted the supply of food to its 750,000 citizens to starve them into submission. The impossible task of feeding these many mouths quickly became futile, and after just two months the court at Ravenna promised 5,000lbs of gold and 30,000lbs of silver to Alaric, along with other provisions, on the condition that he would withdraw and enable the city to continue its importation of food supplies. Now 24 years old and contending with the migrant crisis for most of his life, Honorius realised he had no other option but to follow the method Stilicho had once undertaken and had been put to death for. As such, he paid off Alaric. Meanwhile in Gaul, the usurper Emperor Constantine III was gathering support within the crippled Roman landscape. As St Jerome writes, economic strife, famine, disease and harsh conditions laid waste to the land, and meant that even if the barbarians could be overcome, the years to come would be marked by crises upon crises.

Accepting the terms and withdrawing from Rome, Alaric sought to gain a new proposition which would make him wilfully retreat from Italy altogether. Given that the four-decade long journey of the Goths to Rome was due to the loss of a homeland as a result of the Huns, Alaric pleaded with Honorius to allow him and the Visigoths to settle in south-east Europe, specifically within the plains and highlands along the Adriatic coast which today comprise Croatia and Slovenia. Another, more surprising condition of the settlement programme was that Alaric would be given high military office and become the successor to none other than Stilicho. This proposition of friendship, alliance and resettlement shows the true core belief of the so-called primitive barbarians which the records of history have placed on the various Visigothic, Alans, Gepids, Goth and Burgundian tribes. Rather than plunder and violence, at the end of the day, it was all about finding peace, stability, and – most of all – a home.

While this may seem a sensible solution to the problem of a migrant crisis, Honorius responded with outrage. He refused Alaric's offer and dared him to take what he believed was therefore his. As such, in 409, Alaric invaded and sieged Rome for a second time. Unlike the first siege, Alaric assumed a far more aggressive strategy. A Senatorial assembly which included Pope Innocent I, pleaded to Honorius to take Alaric's deal as Ataulf, Alaric's brother, was on his way with another army with the intent of joining the siege. Refusing, Alaric threatened Honorius with deposition and intimidated the senate into nominating an alternative emperor, Priscus Attalus, a pagan-Greek who had taken up Christianity later in life like St Augustine. Alaric subsequently embarked on a propaganda campaign throughout Italy whereby the inhabitants were to show support for Attalus, or fear being put to the sword. With the unstoppable force of Alaric, however, came the immovable object that was Honorius who, after all this, continued his staunch position of refusing Alaric's demands. To say this was a misjudgement is an understatement. In August 410, Alaric gave up on Attalus and the settlement programme and instead, charged for Rome. Within two days, on 24 August, the Salarian gates of Rome were opened by treacherous citizens, and a horde of barbarians sacked the eternal city.

This devastating news quickly spread through the Mediterranean, and over the next three years Augustine dedicated his time to producing *The City of God*, a highly influential twenty-two-book series (the first five being dedicated to the sack of Rome) which, as he describes, was to 'defend the City of God against those who prefer their own gods to the Founder of that City'. Though primarily about religion, beneath the moral preaching, readers can discover a theologian who was highly anxious and insecure about the future of his faith and nation. It must have been a daunting period for Augustine; his dedication to Christianity emerged from a period of great loss and desperation and now the very heart of the empire was being destroyed by a Christian leader at the head of a pagan army. His insecurities about the future of his faith are shown by his refusal to accept defeat. While St Jerome writes a chilling narrative about the attack on home soil, destruction of cities, and rampant spread of disease and famine, St Augustine downplays the impact of the migrant crisis and siege in Book II, saying, 'Let us help them [Augustine's critics] to recall the many similar and various disasters which overwhelmed the Roman State before Christ's incarnation.' In other words, commenting that Rome has suffered such attacks before, such as Caesar crossing the Rubicon, and it survived and endured – this event will be no different, and it certainly was not the fault of Christ. In fact, Augustine takes this postulation further in Book IV by commenting that Rome only endured this time because of Christ himself. This is a peculiar take on an event which many other contemporaries view as a devastating catastrophe. Nevertheless, it must be remembered that Christianity, though popular, was still relatively small in the greater religious melting pot of Europe, Asia and North Africa. As such, with critics attacking Christ for not protecting the eternal city against invading barbarians, Christianity was as under siege as Rome itself. This is why Augustine goes to great lengths and efforts to wield the narrative, a campaign which many may have witnessed or been aware of from the attack on the World Trade Centre on 11 September 2001.

I say this because the xenophobic campaign of the senate, loss of central political control, and an attack on home soil is what makes this event highly comparable to 9/11. The attack not only changed the identity of America on a global scale, but also had a significant impact on a domestic level. This was demonstrated by the racialisation of the Arab American and Muslim community expressed in the American public attitude. The Bush Administration constructed a particular narrative of 'good vs evil' – a theme which is highly prevalent in St Augustine's life and construction of *City of God* which arose from his former Manichaean and Neoplatonist beliefs. This is particularly important as Stuart Croft, in his book, *Culture, Crisis and America's War on Terror*, wrote that, 'crises often mark the origins of a particular discourse, and a discourse that emerges with credibility in a crisis – in a sense which gives that crisis meaning.' In this regard, the defence of the nation and 'good vs evil' narrative utilised by Bush with the aim of controlling the meaning and subsequent legacy of 9/11 may have been the same pursuit which Augustine sought to achieve in writing the *City of God* – with the legacy of Christianity in lieu of the United States.

The true mind and intentions of Augustine are, of course, unknown, which makes such a remark difficult to verify, but the emphasis on minor events while missing out others entirely shows that Augustine was carefully cherry-picking information and choosing his battles. To further absolve Christianity from being responsible for the sack of Rome, he repeatedly refers to an event whereby 'the enemies of Christianity were spared by the barbarians at the sack of Rome, out of respect for Christ.' During the siege, it is recorded by many contemporaries, including Orosius, St Jerome and Augustine, that many Roman citizens (both pagan and Christian) took refuge in Christian shrines, namely the Basilica of St Peter and Basilica of St Paul. Augustine repeatedly refers to this event to defend Christianity and say that these Roman pagans should be more grateful of their survival through the Christian God: 'The barbarians spared them for Christ's sake; and now these Romans assail Christ's name.' Following this, Augustine remarks that mercifully sparing the inhabitants within their church is an event unexampled in history. Historians have since shown that this observation by Augustine was not necessarily true as Alexander showed mercy to the inhabitants at Tyre, and Agesilus showed clemency after Coronea. It should also be pointed out that Augustine leaves out in his narrative that the Basilica Aemilia and the Basilica Julia were burnt. Nevertheless, it shows that in the years following the sack of Rome, the Christian Empire entered a crisis of belief with accusations against Christ that Rome had lost God's favour. In order to combat this, Augustine then refers to the fall of the 'conquered' Greek/ Roman gods which only survived through Aeneas, a man. As such, to put your faith in the old gods is 'to rely on defaulters, not divinities'. This is particularly interesting as while Christianity is not as endangered as the Hellenistic religion in Virgil's *Aeneid*, Augustine is playing the role of Aeneas in attempting to keep the fires of Christianity alight. This insecurity surrounding the threats against

Christianity is a theme which we will come to see throughout medieval history as new belief systems and events endanger its integrity.

This topic of 'good vs evil' is a prominent feature of *The City of God* but not necessarily in the same xenophobic outlet as Augustine's contemporaries. Instead, his perspective on this event is as a battle of faith rather than culture, race, or nationalism. As we saw with St Jerome, there was a racial undertone within his narrative when he described Stilicho as a 'half-barbarian traitor'. Augustine, however, criticises Romans as much as he does the Goths. In Book I, even though for the majority of his life Augustine was pagan, he attacks non-Christian Romans, saying that, 'many of these [pagans] correct their godless errors and become useful citizens. But many are inflamed with hate against it and feel no gratitude for the benefits offered by its Redeemer.' As such, the purpose of war is for 'God to correct and chasten the corrupt morals of mankind'. This is a highly aggressive religious attack which polarises the conflict into Christian vs pagan, as opposed to Roman vs various tribal communities. This is especially interesting because Alaric who besieged Rome was Christian, yet Augustine places the responsibility for evil and destruction equally on Roman pagans. He also combines all pagan faith systems, no matter now different, whether it be Hellenism or Manichaeism, under one group of evildoers. This scapegoat against the nonbeliever once again absolves Christianity and the institution of the Roman Empire by shifting responsibility and redirecting the narrative on to a question of faith and morality. It is therefore no surprise that readers will see that the once melting pot of faith and culture will now gradually become more polarised and segregated. The consequence is that this narrative and the sack of Rome played a key role in changing the fluidity of society into a binary format under Christianity.

It is for this reason that Augustine's *City of God* is unbelievably influential over the coming millennia, as each time Christianity endures turmoil, contemporaries refer to the defences and absolutions made by Augustine to justify the current threats. He would also come to influence St Thomas Aquinas and John Calvin in their theological contemplations and influence the political thought and order of kings and popes – especially in the relationship between church and state. As such, although Augustine died in 430 when the walls of Hippo were under siege from Vandal invaders and an epoch of empire and civilisation was collapsing beneath his feet, his *Confessions* and *City of God* stood as foundations of the new age we will come to know over the coming chapters. While many in the past have regarded this time as the Dark Ages, we shall see that the ideas and contemplations of Saints and Church Fathers like Augustine spur on a bustling theological and philosophical golden age.

Chapter Two
Rome Questions, Byzantine Answers

There is a theory within cosmology that describes a possible event whereby an imploding universe bounces back and reignites through a Big Bang into an entirely new expanding universe. While the science behind the 'Big Bounce' theory is far beyond the comprehension of this historian, the analogy it poses for our understanding is highly valuable. Within the previous chapter we, alongside Augustine, witnessed the pillars of Rome collapse beneath its feet. From this event, the following century saw the boundaries of the empire beginning to shrink and implode. Yet, while the flame of Rome may seem to have been extinguished, beneath the rubble a small flicker of antiquity endured which would give birth to a new era – the Age of Justinian, spanning from 482 to 602. A notable contemporary historian to Justinian, Procopius of Caesarea, wrote of his prominence as such: 'Then appeared the Emperor Justinian, entrusted by God with this commission to watch over the whole Roman Empire and, so far as possible, to remake it.'

It is for this reason that we continue our journey from the sack of Rome to the court of Justinian, as the sixth century was a historical milestone which marked a definitive transition between antiquity and the Middle Ages. Not only was this the dawn of a new age, it also marked the rise of a new culture which, despite being influenced by its past, was a new hybridity that sought to establish its own path, and shape what we came to know as the medieval era. While historians have regarded this age as 'the last of the Roman centuries' and contemporaries would have continued to call themselves 'Romans', a fusion culture began to emerge – one which borrowed from Christianity, Roman, Greek, and other local elements. This new civilisation was Byzantine, with its capital at Constantinople, and though it did not purposefully create a new medieval system, it prompted an evolution that would reform the old Roman institution. Nevertheless, in order to fully understand the sixth century, we must begin by outlining the volatile contours of the period since Rome's fall as the collapse of this institution left Europe in a fluid state, whereby the ripples of social mobility and opportunity were impacting lives across the continent.

The Age of Justinian was shaped by three major forces. The first and most important was Persia which, as we know from the previous chapter, was a constant pressure on the Roman borders. Over the century following the sack of Rome, Persia was able to expand into the Near East and Caucasus region at the expense of the Romans. Exponentially growing in power, this multi-ethnic empire would continue to be a threat throughout the Age of Justinian with tensions rising and conflicts between them becoming more frequent. Equally, the persistent attacks by Khusro I, the archenemy of Justinian, caused great amounts of damage to the rich Roman cities of the region. The loss of revenues from this, alongside the seizure of Roman property by the Persians, had a disastrous effect on the economy. Only in the seventh century would Emperor Heraclius finally repel the Persian invasion for good – only to then have to contend with the rising Muslim armies.

Aside from the pressing Persian matter in the East, the second force to mould the contours of Justinian's Age was the ultimate collapse of western Roman authority and rise of diverse barbarian kingdoms. The migrant crisis and 'barbarian invasion' of the former century resulted in an onslaught of warriors, traders and refugees pouring into the west from the Balkans and beyond. Over several generations, out of the ashes of the former empire, newly formed militaristic and aggressive kingdoms emerged. These kingdoms primarily evolved from the tribes who had contributed to the fall of the empire and had since become major European powers. By 527, when Justinian ascended to the throne, four major kingdoms were exercising power within western continental Europe: the Ostrogoths in Italy; the Vandals in North Africa; the Visigoths in Spain; and the Franks, who occupied the majority of Gaul as well as non-Roman lands beyond the Rhine River. Although the names of these tribes hark back to the atrocities Rome endured in the fifth century, by the sixth, their kings were maintaining a complex interrelationship and cooperative policy with their Roman populations. We must remember that while the institution of Rome had ceased, many Roman citizens continued to inhabit these lands. As such, varying degrees of civility can be witnessed as these new kingdoms interacted with their populations.

These kingdoms, however, prompted the rise of a religiously divided continent. Many of the new kings and settled tribes were Arian Christians, while the Roman citizens they ruled over were Chalcedonians, a branch of Christianity upheld by Justinian and the Byzantines that accepted and upheld the theological resolutions of the Council of Chalcedon in 451. This led to two distinct clergies and communities of faith forming and existing side by side, although the coexistence was not entirely smooth; in Vandal Africa there was occasional persecution of Chalcedonian Romans. Equally, despite efforts by John of Ephesus to convert thousands of nonbelievers to Christianity in Asia Minor and Syria, this only helped to build a superficial understanding of Christianity, leaving large numbers of peasants from across the Mediterranean world reverting back to worshipping the old gods. As such, in society, politics and religion, this new age experienced a complex internal evolution which, although being influenced by Rome, would be driven by Justinian's pursuit to achieve unity and create a 'Byzantine Commonwealth' in which Constantinople was the hub of a constellation of diverse ethnic Christian communities.

The third and final force which shaped this age was the emergence of confederacies of peoples who once again placed pressure on the borders of the empire. With such widespread social mobility causing tribes to form kingdoms, space was left for small pockets of nomadic groups to gather and form tribal confederacies:

To the north of the Danube, steppe nomads driven westward by Turks loomed. These people, the Avars, first appeared in the final years of Justinian's reign and immediately made an alliance to become another Byzantine pawn for the northern frontier. Among the Avar hegemony were Slavic communities who sought to cross the border and torment the regions of Greece and Thrace.

In North Africa, tribesmen collectively known as Berbers (the cultural heritage of Augustine) pressed north against the settled farmlands of Roman North Africa. Justinian's wars to reclaim areas of the former Roman Empire brought him closer to these tribesmen in 533 after overthrowing the Vandals, and though a series of fortresses were built along the North African coast to repel raiding parties, the Berbers would continue to be a problem until the seventh century.

To the south-east, on the cusp and fringes of the empire and borders with Persia, both sides endured frequent interactions and skirmishes from groups of Arabs. Though not a huge threat by this period, they were typically employed by both empires as pawns in the conflict. After accepting Islam, however, these peoples would utterly change the landscape of the Mediterranean world within a century.

And so, by 483 when a soon-to-be emperor was born to a peasant family in Thrace, the world was in an ever-changing state of social mobility and evolution. Born with the name Petrus Sabbatius, we know little about the childhood of Justinian aside from the prominence of his uncle Justin, a stalwart soldier who had risen to command the imperial guard during the reign of Emperor Anastasius. Being childless, Justin took Petrus under his wing by adopting him and bringing him to Constantinople where he received a good education in Latin, Greek, Theology and Philosophy. Departure from the old Roman ways in the forthcoming age can be seen in Justinian's distaste for Classics, being drawn more towards Christian Theology. Growing up he had a keen skill in intrigue and quickly learnt the politics of Constantinople which helped leverage his uncle to become emperor after the death of Anastasius in 518. In the following year, Justinian was bestowed several titles including Master of Cavalry and

Infantry at Court. By 527, he had become consul, patrician and 'Most Noble' of Constantinople. It was during this time that he met and married his beloved wife, Theodora, who would become a prominent advisor to Justinian until her death in 548.

History has been unkind to Theodora. She was born in 500 to a bear trainer and dancer – evidence of Constantinople's bustling entertainment industry primarily situated at the Hippodrome. Procopius, in his *Secret History,* wrote that Theodora followed her sister's profession by working from a young age in one of Constantinople's brothels, serving a variety of customers from all walks of life. It was said that her presence was avoided by all who wished to escape scandal or temptation as she was incredibly beautiful but equally as skilled in intrigue and gossip. After some time, sources describe that Theodora then travelled as a concubine of a Syrian official to North Africa. Maltreated, she made her way back to Constantinople but not before settling in Alexandria for some time. It is said that during this time she met Patriarch Timothy III who converted her to Miaphysite Christianity. This doctrine, which is held today by Oriental Orthodox Churches, affirmed that Christ was fully divine and fully human in one nature – a theory which opposed the Chalcedonian position that Jesus is one person in two natures. Nevertheless, from Alexandria, she travelled to Antioch where she may have met a close informer to Justinian. A relationship between her and Justinian grew, but when the question of marriage arose, Roman law prevented anyone of senatorial rank from marrying prostitutes. In 524, Emperor Justin passed a new law so that reformed women could marry outside of their rank if approved by the emperor – which enabled Justinian to marry his beloved Theodora. This law also passed that the daughters of these women could be free to marry outside of their rank, which secured the succession of Justinian and allowed the illegitimate daughter of Theodora to marry a relative of the former emperor Anastasius.

This marriage, however, was seen with controversy by many. Procopius, for instance, wrote slanderous pages about Theodora and her vulgarity in supposedly sleeping her way to empress. As such, these scandalous gossip and lewd stories that thoroughly defamed her have, for centuries, blacklisted her in the annals of history. Yet, despite being exploited by religious commentators, she stood strong with Justinian and faced opposition. Under her reign, rape was made punishable by death with the property of the offender being transferred to the victim. This law also extended to encapsulate anyone in society, regardless of position or rank. Equally, female inheritance was promoted, giving women physical social power; it meant that should a woman become widowed, she was able to claim the property and fortune of the family. Furthermore, she also empowered prostitutes by passing laws which limited the power of brothels and the exploitation of young women. Theodora thus revolutionised the social standing of women in this age through her command of the law, and therefore when we realign our perspective of history away from 'great men', we can empower those like Theodora who were saints in their own right.

Alongside his marriage to Theodora, Justinian rose to become co-emperor until Justin's death just four months later. Thus, by 528, a mere peasant and prostitute were crowned the rulers of an empire which dominated the Mediterranean – a testament to the social mobility of the period. Nevertheless, although Justinian had inherited the Roman throne and title of Augustus, his first act was to reform and renew the ancient law codes – an act which would set forth the departure from the classical world. Produced in *c.*530, the 'Corpus Juris Civilis' was a highly influential law codex which rationalised a thousand-years-worth of existing Roman laws. With a cohort of 2,000 Roman Jurists, contradictions and conflicts were eliminated, and any existing laws that were not included in it were repealed. Following its production, a digest was produced which commented, clarified, and expanded on the codex. These jurists also constructed a legal handbook, called 'institutes', that served as a guide and textbook for legal studies throughout Europe – the first of its kind in history. A prominent purpose in reforming these laws was that Justinian was able to promote a distinctly new Christian authority. Throughout the codex, there is a repetition and insistence that God entrusted the governance of the empire solely to the emperor, and that this law should attempt to establish the laws of Heaven on Earth. This insertion was the foundation of a concept many will know to be interwoven with the concept of kingship, one which arguably still underpins the monarch to this day. This was the medieval concept of Divine Right of Rule and would play a particularly prominent role when these laws were rediscovered in the twelfth century by Frederick Barbarossa (1152–1190) and be used against the papacy to reinforce imperial rights for the Holy Roman Emperor.

Justinian's pursuit for legal reform was accompanied by an equally strong approach to Christian unification. From the beginning of his reign, he sought to stamp out heresy and create a singular doctrine – Chalcedonian, named after the Council of Chalcedon in 451. To deviate slightly from our journey through the life of Justinian, the Council of Chalcedon is one of many examples of the councils put together throughout the medieval period to decide and agree upon questions in Christianity. While nowadays Christianity is a highly structured institution with a large degree of unity on its aspects of faith, once upon a time it was very fluid and scattered in its beliefs. Two prominent questions divided theologians and ecclesiastes across the continent. The first was how to calculate the date of Easter – should it always be celebrated on a Sunday? Or, should Christians follow the Jewish lunar month in which the Paschal Lamb was slaughtered? In order to answer this, a further issue then arose on deciding how to calculate when the Paschal moon appeared; the Celtic Church, Western Church and Eastern Church all observed it differently because of the conflicting calendars used. While this may seem like a small issue, it is one that continued until 1963 where the second Vatican Council finally stated that there was no objection to observing Easter on a fixed Sunday. A far more pressing and dividing issue, however, was understanding the nature (or natures) of Christ upon incarnation. Without getting too theological, if we agree that Christ is the son of God, what does it mean for him to be God and Man? Is he both? Or one? Or the other? This is what many councils throughout history have sought to answer and the Council of Chalcedon was a pivotal event in this controversy as it resulted in a schism which lasts to this day.

At the Council of Chalcedon were the Monophysites who believed in one nature, that Christ was purely divine and not human despite taking on an earthly form. Today, the Coptic and Armenian Orthodox churches and the Jacobite Syrian Church (also known as the Oriental Orthodox Church) follow this doctrine. Opposing this were the Chalcedonians who disagreed and stated that Christ had two natures – a fully human form and fully divine form. The Roman Catholic Church, the Eastern Orthodox Church, and most Protestant Churches currently uphold this doctrine. The Council of Chalcedon, which was attended by 520 bishops, therefore approved several earlier religious creeds, established definitions of faith and doctrine, and rejected Monophysite beliefs. The culmination of this division, as aforementioned, was that Justinian sought to achieve Chalcedonian unification throughout the empire and eliminate heresy and any deviations of Christianity.

In his early reign, all seemed to be going well with Justinian and his empire. Peace had been temporarily restored with Persia and his policies were running smoothly. Yet, in mid-January 532, that peace broke in what has been regarded as one of the most violent riots in Constantinople's history. An aspect of ancient Rome which endured into the Age of Justinian was the development of sporting factions who competed against each other in events such as chariot races. Typically, there were four competing factions; Blues, Greens, Reds and Whites, each one gaining their name from their coloured uniform. Often these factions became the focus of social or political issues as there was no distinct forum for such an outlet. In 521, during a riot comparable to modern-day football hooliganism, some members of the Blue and Green factions were arrested for a murder after a chariot race. While the majority of these members were executed for their crimes, two of them, a green and a blue, escaped and sought refuge in a church along with an angry mob. Threatened, Justinian changed the sentencing to imprisonment and sought to hold a chariot race in the following January.

Beneath this, however, were aristocratic political agitators who sought to use such an event to form a coup due to the high taxes levied in the city. Equally, civil reforms which limited the power of officials and aristocrats dispersed a cloud of betrayal across the Blues while the Greens felt that Justinian was implementing civil oppression. The culmination was a violent riot breaking out at the Hippodrome whereby urban rioters shouting 'Nika', or 'Victory' in Greek, revolted against the emperor. Fires destroyed the heart of the city, even reaching the palace gates.

A decision was presented to Justinian on whether to stay and endure, or flee instead. Opting for the latter, his influential and wise wife, Theodora, convinced him and his office to stay. Belisarius and Narses, two of Justinian's top generals, were able to restore order by massacring thousands of rioters in the Hippodrome. The victorious Justinian took this event and his survival as a sign of divine support, which only spurred on his already powerful religious zeal. Following this devastating event, multiple building projects took place to rebuild the areas of the city which had been destroyed. Taking the opportunity to demonstrate his dedication to God, Justinian embarked on several prominent building projects. The most prominent of these was the creation of the world-famous Hagia Sophia which replaced a much earlier church that was destroyed in the fire. It is perhaps ironic that this palace which Justinian built to stand as a testament to Christian reform is now a holy Mosque. Nevertheless, with a heart overpouring with zeal, he girded himself with the ecclesiastical sword and embarked on a vast military campaign westwards against anti-Christians.

Justinian's first target was the great Vandal kingdom at Carthage. Motivated by heresy, Justinian sought to overthrow the Arian Christians in the region and further spread his Chalcedonian doctrine. This conquest also enabled him to expand his territory and influence in the region by conquering a major centre of trade and commerce. In doing so, this would also fulfil his policy of remaking the former Roman Empire.

The Byzantine army of 15,000 men, led by the general Belisarius, sailed to North Africa and laid siege to the city of Carthage in 533. The city was heavily fortified and defended by a large garrison, but Belisarius was able to breach the city walls and capture it after a prolonged battle. The conquest of Carthage was a major victory for the Empire and allowed Justinian to extend his control over a significant area of North Africa. It allowed the Byzantines to gain control of important trade routes in the region and gave them a strategic foothold in North Africa. However, the conquest of Carthage was not without its costs, as the Byzantine Empire had to devote significant resources to the campaign and suffered heavy casualties. Nevertheless, fuelled with divine favour, Justinian turned towards the ancient capital of Rome – his next target.

The Ostrogoths were a Germanic people who migrated into the Roman Empire in the fourth and fifth centuries. They came into conflict with the Romans and were eventually allowed to settle in the area of Italy as *foederati*, an allied barbarian tribe that was granted land in exchange for military service. In 493, Theodoric the Great became the king of the Ostrogoths, and he set out to conquer the remaining Roman territories in Italy. Over the next few decades, he was able to defeat the other barbarian groups in Italy and establish the Ostrogothic kingdom, with its capital at Ravenna. The Ostrogoths maintained control of Italy through a combination of military force and diplomacy. They had a strong army, led by Theodoric and later by his successors, and they were able to defeat the Romans and other barbarian groups that challenged their rule. At the same time, Theodoric sought to integrate the Ostrogoths into Roman society and maintain good relations with the Byzantine Empire. Nevertheless, in 535, Justinian sent an army again under the command of his general Belisarius against the Ostrogoths. The Byzantine army was able to make some initial gains and capture Sicily quickly, but the war was soon slowed by a series of costly sieges and battles. In 540, Belisarius was able to capture Ravenna, capital of the Ostrogothic kingdom, and Theodoric's grandson, Totila, was killed in battle the following year. The Ostrogoths, however, continued to resist and, under the leadership of their new king, Teia, they were able to regain control of much of Italy. In 552, Justinian's forces, now led by another general, Narses, were able to defeat the Ostrogoths once and for all at the Battle of Taginae.

This was perhaps a sign of times to come as although Justinian had thus far ruled successfully, during the arduous twenty-year struggle for Italy the 540s would prove to be a difficult decade for the emperor. In an event that many in the twenty-first century have become familiar with, The Plague of Justinian was a pandemic that struck the Byzantine Empire, as well as many other parts of the Mediterranean world, in the sixth and seventh centuries. Recent epidemiologists have concluded that the disease is believed to have been caused by the bacterium *Yersinia pestis*, a cousin of the later bubonic plague 'The Black Death'. The first outbreak of the plague is thought to have occurred in the early 540s, and was named after Justinian simply as it occurred within his reign and because the plague had a significant impact on the empire and its history. The plague is believed to have originated in the region of Egypt and spread westward along trade routes, eventually reaching the Byzantine capital, Constantinople, in 541. It is estimated that the plague may have killed as many as half of the city's population and also spread to other parts of the empire, including the provinces of North Africa, Italy and the Near East. The plague continued to erupt periodically in the Byzantine Empire and other parts of the Mediterranean world for the next two centuries, causing widespread death and suffering.

Alongside the Italian campaign, pressures of a Persian war front, and the devastating plague (all of which diminished the resources of the Byzantines), Justinian's policy of Christian unification also began to crumble beneath him as a result of The Three Chapters Controversy. This theological debate centred around the writings of three theologians who had been condemned for their beliefs by the Council of Constantinople in 543. These three theologians were Theodore of Mopsuestia, Theodoret of Cyrrhus, and Ibas of Edessa. The controversy arose because some church leaders believed that the writings of these men contained teachings that were at odds with the teachings of the church. In particular, they were accused of supporting the heresy of Nestorianism, which held that the human and divine natures of Jesus Christ were separate and distinct. In response to these accusations, the Council of Constantinople issued a condemnation of the three theologians and their writings, known as the 'Three Chapters'. This decision was met with resistance from some church leaders, who argued that the theologians were being unfairly condemned and that their writings should be considered valid expressions of Christian doctrine. The controversy continued for several years, with different factions within the church supporting one side or the other. Eventually, the controversy was resolved at the Second Council of Constantinople in 553, which affirmed the condemnation of the Three Chapters and reaffirmed the teachings of the church on the nature of Christ. The Three Chapters Controversy had a significant impact on the development of Christian theology and the relationships between different branches of the church. It also highlighted the ongoing struggles within the church over issues of doctrine and authority. Ultimately, rather than reconciling Chalcedonian and anti-Chalcedonian Christians while maintaining support from the western clergy, Justinian's alienation of the west by undertaking the role of a priest rather than emperor left a bitter taste between Constantinople and the papacy.

The final decades of Justinian's reign continued to be disappointing. In 548, Justinian's beloved wife Theodora passed away and with it, the dome of the Hagia Sophia cracked and partly collapsed – a symbol of Christianity's splintering and partial downfall through Justinian's policies. Alongside this, in 559, Slavic raiders from the Balkans raided and pillaged through Thrace and up to the gates of Constantinople, which reignited the same fear and paranoia as from those witnessing the fall of Rome at the hands of similar barbarians. Earthquakes struck the empire, civil disturbance continued to rock the capital, and ambitious men sought the throne. Religiously, an independent anti-Chalcedonian clerical hierarchy emerged and the rift with the west deepened as bishops at the Fifth Ecumenical Council condemned the Three Chapters.

On 14 November 565, Justinian fell ill with a fever and passed away at the age of 83. The exact cause of his death is not known, but it is believed that he may have died from a combination of old age and illness. He was known for his ambitious attempts to reconquer the territories that had been lost to the barbarian invasions, as well as for his efforts to codify Roman law and create a unified Christianity. While the earlier years of his reign were underpinned by eagerness and hope, by the end it was anger and frustration. Despite this, we now turn to the saint of this chapter, Gregory the Great, to explore how Justinian's policies, beliefs and pursuits rippled through time and influenced the lives of those to come for decades.

Gregory was born towards the end of Justinian's reign in Rome, which had been recently reconquered by the Byzantines from the Ostrogoths. What is particularly interesting about Gregory's family which, like Augustine's, was wealthy and of a degree of nobility, is that it contained a prominent ecclesiastical dynasty. When historians discuss nobility, bloodlines and family connections are often discussed in conjunction with their prominence. Adela of Blois, for example, was the daughter of William the Conqueror, mother of King Stephen of England and Bishop Henry of Winchester, wife of Count Stephen, and sister to King Henry I of England (to name just a few of her connections) – a very powerful bloodline. While Gregory may not have had noble veins, he certainly had Christian fervour coursing through them. His father was a senator and prefect of the City of Rome but also Regionarius of the Church; his mother and two aunts (Trasilla and Emiliana) were saints; and his great-great-grandfather was supposedly Pope Felix III. As such, Gregory's family was one of the most distinguished clerical families of the period. Despite this, Gregory was born in the epicentre of geopolitical upheaval. From 542, the Plague of Justinian swept through Italy – wiping out up to a third of the population in some regions and leaving thousands destitute. Following this, the Gothic Wars endured and turmoil on Italian soil persisted through the 540s. In 546, Totila led his forces on a campaign against the city of Rome, which was then under the control of the Byzantine Empire. The Sack of Rome was a devastating event for the city, as Totila's forces were able to breach the city's defences and plunder its wealth. The sack lasted for several days, during which time the Ostrogoths looted and destroyed many of Rome's most important buildings and landmarks. The damage to the city was so severe that it took many years for it to recover. Later, Totila went on to recapture almost all of the lands previously seized by Justinian in his zealous campaign. The 550s for Gregory were equally as relentless; he bore witness to the continued Gothic War as well as a Frankish invasion in 554 and the Schism of the Three Chapters in 553.

Growing up in the Age of Justinian and witnessing the turmoil of Italy had a lasting impact on the young Gregory – both in a spiritual and emotional way. At school, he was well educated and read Latin but refused to read or write Greek, the lingua franca of Constantinople. He gained a keen interest in politics and religion, and became Prefect of Rome at only 33. Like Augustine, the death of a beloved family member had a profound impact on his faith. Following his father's passing, he converted the ancestral home in Rome into a monastery dedicated to St Andrew the Apostle (later being rededicated to Gregory following his death). A painting commissioned by the monks and hung at the home a few years after Gregory's death portrayed him as rather bald with a tawny beard and a face that was an intermediate between his mother's and father's. He had long, curled hair on the sides, his nose was thin and straight and his forehead was high. Above all, he had beautiful hands with which he wrote poetic theological axioms such as, 'In that silence of the heart, while we keep watch within through contemplation, we are as if asleep to all things that are without.' Contemplation was key to Gregory's devotion, but equally as important was poverty. From losing his home and becoming a refugee at a young age to the plundering of Rome by Totila, appreciating and acknowledging poverty while rejecting greed was a key pillar of Gregory's ethos that he took incredibly seriously. When a dying monk was seen to have stolen three gold pieces, Gregory ensured the monk died alone, and then threw his body, with the coins, on to manure as punishment. He said, 'Take your money with you to perdition.'

Gregory also firmly asserted that punishment for sins could occur during one's life – no doubt a remark reflecting the Byzantine downfall that followed Justinian's zealous micromanagement of Christian doctrine and controversial marriage. Perhaps this bitter statement was also influenced through frustrations incurred during his office as Apocrisiariate. In 579, Pope Pelagius III appointed Gregory as Apocrisiariate, an ambassador to the Imperial Court of Constantinople on behalf of the papacy and western world. Most notable was his appeal to the emperor (Tiberius Constantine at this point) for military aid against a Lombard invasion. Tiberius, however, was more concerned with the eastern war front to pay attention to such trivial skirmishes and thus denied such aid. In 584, during the reign of Emperor Maurice, another attempt was made to send a relief force to Italy. Maurice, opting for diplomacy over war, was able to strike an agreement with the Franks to fight against them instead – only partially solving the issue.

It was clear to Gregory that the Byzantines were far more occupied with the eastern front and the crisis with the Avar and Slav tribes to pay any attention to Italy. This in itself is important, as Rome was seemingly fading as a priority. Although recovering and remaking the former classical empire had once been a priority of emperors following the fifth century, as they entered the seventh century and the rapidly changing world, the Byzantines were forever straying from their predecessors. As such, Gregory was a man stuck between two worlds, not only teetering on the borders between the Germanic and Roman, but above all between the ancient and medieval.

One element of continuity was the ongoing debate involving the nature of Christ. Gregory was deeply involved with this theological debate throughout his life, and had a bitter theological conflict with Eutychius, the Patriarch of Constantinople. As Gregory could not read the untranslated Greek exegeses and commentaries on the Bible, he had to rely on pure scripture. This worked in his favour when he cited Luke 24:39 to support the Chalcedonian argument. This passage, which states, 'Behold my hands and my feet, that it is I myself: handle me, and see; for a spirit hath not flesh and bones, as ye see me have,' seemingly confirmed that Christ's body was corporeal and palpable after his resurrection. In support of Gregory, the emperor burnt Eutychius' writings.

The culmination in all this was that Gregory ascended to the papal throne following the death of Pelagius from a plague outbreak in the city. In 2013, a *Guardian* news article reported that Pope Benedict XVII said, when being appointed as pope, that it was a 'great burden' and he did not want the job. Likewise, Justin Welby, upon being elected as Archbishop of Canterbury, simply said, 'Oh no.' Even Pope Francis, the current pope when writing this book, followed suit by saying that, 'Anyone who wants to be pope doesn't care much for themselves. God doesn't bless them. I didn't want to be pope.' It is interesting, therefore, to see that this is seemingly a historical tradition as Gregory, upon becoming pope, issued a series of letters disavowing any ambition to the throne of St Peter, instead stating that he preferred the quiet life of a monk and did not wish to carry the weight of the papacy on his shoulders. It is important to note, however, that at the time the papacy was not the all-powerful institution we are more familiar with in the eleventh, twelfth, or thirteenth centuries. Instead, the papal power in the west was limited: Gaul's episcopy was drawn from territorial families; Visigothic Iberia was simply disconnected from Rome; and the Italian *de facto* lands were constantly under attack. As such, Gregory had a huge role to fulfil and, despite his conflicts with the Byzantine regime, it is here that those seeds which Justinian had sown in his age a century earlier come to fruition.

In a religious sense, Gregory vastly expanded upon Justinian's superlative piety through the production of one of the most influential works of Western literature. Known as the *Dialogues*, this work of religious history and biography is a collection of four books about the lives of various Italian saints, including St Benedict, as well as spiritual contemplation. On the topic of St Benedict, who was a close contemporary of Gregory, the second book of the *Dialogues* provides the earliest and most authoritative account of the saint that we possess and was thus incredibly treasured by the Benedictines of the Middle Ages. Indeed, it, together with the Rule of St Benedict, is our only source for the story of his life and the understanding of his character. Nevertheless, in discussing the lives and histories of saints, Gregory also provides us with an insightful and vivid picture of religious life in Italy during the sixth century, especially during the invasion of the Lombards, a 'barbarous and cruel nation', according to Gregory, who, 'drawn as a sword out of a sheath', wrought such unimaginable destruction and havoc in the peninsula that many truly believed that 'the end of all flesh was come' (a somewhat more pragmatic approach to the looming darkness over Italy that Augustine repudiated in *The City of God*). Yet, in a Christian sense, the nuances contained in the theological contemplations of the fourth book are, without a doubt, the basis of inspiration for many medieval authors we shall come to know in the following chapters. The *Dialogues* were among the most popular readings of the Middle Ages, and early translations exist in almost every European language. In the fourth book, we find the first rudiments of the medieval conception of the three states of souls in the afterlife. Gregory's story of the vision seen by a certain soldier is the genesis of the imaginations of Hell, Purgatory and Heaven, which inspired so many imitations throughout the Middle Ages, from Venerable Bede's *Legends of Fursaeus and Drythelm,* to the twelfth-century *Visions of Tundale*, Alberic of Monte Cassino, and Edmund of Eynsham, which culminate in the *Divina Commedia.* We know that Dante, for instance, knew the *Dialogues* well and utilised them often in his writing, and Gregory's earlier work, the *Moralia*, or *Exposition of the Book of Job*, is referenced in many passages of the *Divina Commedia.*

Furthermore, the far-reaching shadow cast by Justinian is equally discernible in the legislative behaviour of Gregory. The greatest definitive achievement of Justinian's reign by far is his law code, the *Corpus Iuris Civilis.* Aside from his *Moralia* and *Dialogues*, Gregory is equally known for his 800 letters which spanned his episcopate. From religious contemplation to social commentary, these letters offer an unrivalled insight into the world of a sixth-century Roman bishop. What is clear from a comparative exploration of the letters and law codes is that Christianity was emerging as a state religion, and one whereby the bishop's role in society was fundamentally, and more importantly, intermeshed within the civic sphere – a concept which was widely practised in the successive medieval centuries. Justinian's primary goal was to form a united Christian doctrine throughout the empire and Europe. This central thesis is one which Gregory sought to adopt and thus re-energise Christianity in Europe through the conversion of non-Christian peoples. He believed that the best way to convert pagans was through peaceful means, such as preaching and missionary work. He also believed in the importance of education and the use of local customs and traditions to help convert people to Christianity. The targets of this campaign were the various Anglo-Saxon kingdoms in England.

St Augustine of Canterbury was a Benedictine monk who was sent by Pope Gregory to convert the Anglo-Saxons to Christianity. While there was an element of Christianity in Britannia during and following the Romans, in the eyes of the papacy it was not the right version and wasn't being practised in the right format. Thus, Augustine arrived in England in 597 and established his base in Canterbury. Through his preaching and missionary work, he was able to convert many of the Anglo-Saxons, including King Ethelbert of Kent, who gave Augustine land to build a monastery and a church. This monastery became the centre of Christianity in England, and Augustine is considered as the 'Apostle to the English'. Canterbury then became a base of operations for missionaries to convert regions of Germany and the Netherlands. These efforts were largely successful, and many of the Anglo-Saxons converted to Christianity during Gregory's pontificate. Yet, Gregory, like Justinian, was equally as averse to heresy. We see in Gregory's correspondence to subordinate bishops, for example, that there were multiple occasions when heresy was at the forefront of religious policy: once for 'pagans and heretics' amongst the Lombards in Italy; once for Sicilian 'worshippers of idols'; three times in Sardinia; and once in Corsica for those 'worshipping idols.' As such, both monarch and pope saw the role of the episcopate as a means of enforcing the Christian faith within the empire and beyond its borders.

Likewise, it is unquestionable that Gregory, like Justinian, wanted his bishops to be active participants in civic life. With empowerment, however, came regulation, and just as they wanted their clergy to help reform and regulate their subjects, Justinian and Gregory also realised that their authority demanded regulating subordinate bishops. This was the role of the Roman bishop outlined by Justinian and undertaken by Gregory. One such legislation emerged against purchasing ecclesiastical office, a nuance of the time, with five separate laws across a thirty-seven-year period being issued. Likewise, simony, the sin of buying or selling religious privileges (a crime we will explore further in later chapters on the twelfth and thirteenth century) was an issue that struck to the very core of Justinian and Gregory. From the sheer number of references to this crime, twenty-nine in total, we can clearly see that just as Justinian never gave up on the hope of eradicating simony, nor did Gregory. It is not surprising that Gregory's concern focused significantly on simony given its pervasiveness within the Merovingian church. As such, we see five letters sent to bishops on the topic, as well as eight sent to four different Frankish monarchs – all of which asked them to organise councils to prevent simony in their kingdoms. Both Gregory's hatred of simony and his recognition of its prevalence throughout Northern Europe is plainly expressed:

> For I have learnt from certain reports, that in the lands of Gaul and Germany, no one obtains holy orders without handing over a payment. If this is so, I say with tears, I declare with groans that, when the priestly order is rotten on the inside, it will not be able to survive for long externally.

In quoting the relevant laws, the legislative weapon wielded by Gregory was underpinned by his awareness of the Justinian law code and the policies of his age. In nurturing the ideology of Gregory, Justinian, by extension, provided the necessary tools for medieval Christianity to flourish. From its rich liturgical and artistic heritage, its theological insights, to its distinctive approach to spiritual life, the enduring contributions of Byzantine Christianity to the broader Christian tradition have been an important source of inspiration for Christians across almost every monastic community for centuries.

The Age of Justinian did not entirely diminish with the end of his reign. Following Justinian was his nephew, Justin II. His reign from 556 to 578 is categorised by various losses. Not only was there a long and expensive war with Persia, resulting in a substantial loss of Roman territory and revenues, but the Lombards also invaded and seized Italy, and the Slavic and Avar tribes gained a foothold in the Balkans. Justin's successor, Tiberius Constantine, who ruled from 578 to 582, maintained the war with Persia and failed to retake Lombard Italy. Nevertheless, Tiberius did implement further administrative reforms by introducing exarchs, a new local administrator, in the remaining Roman lands of Italy in 584. The Balkan crisis, however, worsened when aggressive forces of Avar tribes skirmished against the Roman defences that were weakened by the Persian Front. Sirmum was captured by the Slavs and their resettlement within the region continued. After Tiberius' death, he was succeeded by his general, Maurice, who ruled from 582 to 602. As Tiberius had depleted the treasury, Maurice was forced to limit expenditure and military pay, which further impacted Roman morale and disfavour. Out of all the aforementioned successors, however, Maurice was the most religiously active, but his aim was to maintain a tolerant posture between Chalcedonians and anti-Chalcedonians. Towards the end of his reign, the geopolitical climate of Persia began to change when a new king, Khusro III, sought peace and Roman support. Maurice was also able to reassert control over the Avars in the Balkans within a decade. As with all good things, they eventually come to an end. In 602, Maurice ordered his troops to camp north of the Danube during winter and, though strategically sound, his undernourished and underpaid troops rebelled. One soldier, Phocas, led a band of mutinied Romans to Constantinople where he murdered Maurice and claimed the throne. This ended the age of Justinian and began a decade of misrule.

Chapter Three

Caliphs, Iconoclasts and Usurpers

Across Europe and the Mediterranean, it seemed as though a degree of stability was finally achieved. The various tribes around the Danube were tamed, Christianity had a foothold in England and was quickly spreading through the north, and many of the newly formed kingdoms were centralising and flourishing. History, however, is rather unkind as an idle empire is the devil's workshop. As such, while theologians were occupied with discussions on the true date of Easter, a warm and dusty wind was rising in the south that would become a torrent of force which would rapidly shape the future of Europe and Christianity to this day.

Within the inhospitable deserts and arid mountains of the Arabian Peninsula was the home of a rich cultural heritage, situated on the crossroads of trade and religion, and whose story can be traced as far back as ancient Assyrian inscriptions. These people, known as Arabs, were first described as a group of tribes, uniquely rooted in nomadism and with an ability to command and withstand the harsh desert conditions of the Peninsula. In the centuries that followed, these tribes began to diversify and each develop their own customs, beliefs and practices. A rich literary tradition and culture emerged that was steeped in poetry, storytelling and Bedouin lifestyle. Through their positioning on the intersection of three continents, Arabs were able to establish themselves as keen traders who interacted with civilisations across the known world from Egypt to Rome, and even as far as the Indian Subcontinent and China. Despite all this, Arabs were detached and autonomous from one another. That is until a merchant of the Quraish tribe was able to ignite a fervorous light within the hearts and minds of those scattered across the desert to unite and assert their influence beyond Arabia.

Muhammad, peace be upon him, was born in the year 570 and was a contemporary of the aforementioned Gregory the Great. As a young man, he laboured as a merchant across the region and developed a reputation for honesty and integrity. It was during this time that he met his first wife, Khadijah, a wealthy widow who was allured and impressed by his character and business acumen. Muhammad , however, was displeased by the moral and spiritual decay that he saw around him. Equally, he bore witness to the aftermath of Justinian who, as we know, sought to unify his people through faith and Christianity. Often

Muhammad would retreat to a cave on the outskirts of Mecca to meditate and reflect. It was during one such visit, when he was 40 years old, that he received the first of many revelations from God through the Angel Gabriel. At first, he was hesitant to share the message with others through fear of isolation from his tribe, but as the revelations continued, Muhammad knew it was his mission to preach the word of God to the Arabs. His message was monotheism, social justice, compassion, as well as a call for the end of the mistreatment of the poor and vulnerable. One of the most prominent doctrines was iconoclasm – that is, to inhibit the worshipping of idols, statues, paintings, etc. He and his early followers experienced widespread persecution to begin with from powerful elites in Mecca (a separate story which will be explored in the following chapter) who saw him as a threat to the ingrained traditions. As such, in 622, he was forced to flee to the nearby city of Medina. This journey, known as Hijira, heralded a turning point in the history of Islam and marks the beginning of the Islamic calendar. Upon his arrival to Medina, Muhammad was able to build a community of believers who aided him in preaching his message of compassion and justice. Alongside this, he also established a new political order based on consultation and consensus whereby all members of the community had a voice in the decision-making process – a proto-democracy as it were. Until his death in 632, Muhammad and his followers grew in strength and numbers. In 630, they returned to Mecca triumphantly and established Islam as the dominant religion in the Arabian Peninsula. More than this, he did the impossible by uniting the Arab tribes into a state that was centralised around its language (Arabic) and faith. In doing so, within a century through military conquests, missionaries and merchants, Islam became one of the most rapidly growing religions ever seen in history.

Following Muhammad's death, a caliph, or 'successor', was selected to inherit the task of continuing to expand Islam and establish its prowess in the Peninsula. Abu Bakr, a close friend of the Prophet, was chosen and with it, the Rashidun caliph dynasty was born. Abu Bakr and his successors Umar, Uthman and Ali were democratically selected through a process of Shura, or consultation. They embodied the ideal of Islamic leadership and under their rule, in no less than three decades, Islam grew beyond the borders of modern-day Saudi Arabia to include Iran, Iraq, Syria and Egypt, as well as parts of Turkey and Libya. Nevertheless, aside from a spiritual leader, the caliphs were military commanders and political administrators who were responsible for governing the newly conquered territories. In 661, power was transferred to the Umayyads. While their dynasty originated in Mecca, they would rule over the Arab Empire till the 760s from the great Syrian city of Damascus.

The Umayyads led a rather controversial rule which adopted a secular view of government and thus focused primarily on a militaristic and political usage of Islam. They retained their control through vast military strength as well as political manoeuvring. One such way of consolidating their power was to adopt a Western feudal tactic and divide the empire into governing provinces, essentially dukedoms, which were to be ruled over by an elected governor. These governors would exercise a variety of powers including tax collection and law enforcement. To further the message of social justice proclaimed by the late Prophet, the Umayyads implemented a system of taxation based on wealth rather than religious tithes or family heritage – reflecting the systems we are more familiar with today. Equally, the Umayyads were patrons of free thought, liberal arts and philosophy as they oversaw the translation and interpretation of ancient Greek and Persian texts into Arabic and later Latin – a pursuit which would later lead to the Renaissance of Europe. Vast building projects also took place such as the great marble Umayyad Mosque in Damascus which took influence from former Roman basilicas and was unlike any seen in the empire – likely the largest in the world at the time.

The ability of Muhammad to unite the Arab tribes through a union of faith and politics quickly began to break down and create tension. To put it simply, Jesus was a spiritual leader and it would not be until centuries later that Christianity took a place alongside monarchy. Even now there was still a distinction between church and state. Islam, on the other hand, was somewhat different as the Prophet, and by extension, the caliph, was a union of the two. This quickly created a succession crisis amongst those from various backgrounds who believed in alternate legitimate heirs to the throne of Islam. The Abbasids, who would come to depose the Umayyads, affirmed through bloodlines that they were the rightful heirs of Muhammad as they were descendants of Abbas ibn Abd al-Muttalib, one of the youngest uncles of Muhammad and of the same Banu Hashim clan. Other later contenders include the Fatimids who were a Shi'a Muslim dynasty that traced their lineage back to Fatima, the daughter of the Prophet Muhammad, and his cousin and son-in-law, Ali ibn Abi Talib, who the Shi'a believed should have been the first caliph of the Muslim community. As such, what once united the Arab peoples quickly separated them into a distinct variety of empires. This crisis is the origin of the Sunni–Shi'a split which was to cause a rift in Islam that endures in today's world.

Returning to the Abbasids – they were far more spiritual than their predecessor and embraced Muslims, non-Muslims, Arabs, and foreigners alike in an attempt to form an empire based on justice and equality. The capital was also moved from Damascus to Baghdad as the site was located near both the Tigris and Euphrates rivers, making it an ideal spot for food production to sustain a large population. Equally, the city stood at the crossroads of three continents: Asia to the east, Europe to the north-west, and Africa to the south-west. This was embodied by its diverse inhabitants of Turks, Arabs, Persians and Europeans. Within the grand walls which encircled the settlement were a vast variety of markets that housed exotic spices, perfumes and luxury goods from across the known world. Baghdad quickly became a hub of cultural, scientific and commercial activity which attracted the greatest minds of the age to its House of Wisdom. Perhaps one of its greatest achievements was implementing a system of meritocracy over bloodlines and ancestral heritage.

Unlike the Umayyads, the Abbasids took a far more spiritual understanding of Islam and were thus great supporters of Sufism, a mystical and spiritual form of Islam which emphasises a personal experience of the divine, and aims to cultivate a relationship with God through practices and disciplines. Moreover, Sufism had a profound influence on literature, art and culture which saw the continuation of the translation and analysis of ancient texts to advance science, philosophy and mathematics. Altogether, Arabia was thriving and the process from tribe to empire which took Europe half a millennium to achieve was achieved by the Arabs in no less than a century. This meant that tension and conflict began to stir on its borders, however, as Europeans became uneasy at the sight of this new superpower.

The seventh and eighth centuries saw a rapid expansion of Arab conquests into Europe. In the western half of the Mediterranean, Arabs were able to establish sustainable states on the European shores of Sicily and Spain.

With its ancient Greek and Latin heritage, Sicily has always served as a bridge between the two cultures. While Latin influence, particularly clerical links, persisted in Gregory the Great's era, it appears that the island became more and more Greek in terms of language, government and religion in the seventh and eighth centuries. Nevertheless, pressure on Sicily first arose in 642 when Mu'awiyah, the ruler of Syria who would go on to become the first Umayyad caliph, sent the initial raid to various towns along the North African coastline. Larger-scale raids followed in 667 and in 693/4. Umayyad armies captured the highly prized city of Carthage which they formed into a new province that is now modern-day Tunisia, and established Qayrawan as its capital. Due to Sicily's new position as the front line for the Mediterranean, the straits were frequently raided in the early seventh century. These were initially just raids in pursuit of loot, but it appears that in 740, the Arabs were attempting to invade Syracuse in order to establish a more long-term occupation similar to that of Carthage.

Berber rebellions in North Africa during the mid-740s distracted the Arabs from Sicily until the early ninth century where, under Harun al-Rashid, a force of 10,000 foot soldiers invaded the island. In the first campaign, Mazara was seized in the south-west relatively easily. Syracuse, however, was well defended by the governor and as such, the army was forced to over winter which resulted in hundreds of deaths from various diseases. This may have been the end of the Arab conquests if not for a vast cohort of reinforcements which advanced to siege Palermo in 831. By 832, Sicily was conquered by Muslims and, with the Vatican only 200km away, things were beginning to look uneasy for Christendom.

Elsewhere in Europe, the Muslim conquest of the Iberian peninsula was well underway from 711 to 716. As Muslim armies moved west across the coast of North Africa they recruited various Berber tribes to inflate their numbers. For the Berbers, such an opportunity to join a conquering army and gain vast weights of booty was enough to instil vigour for battle. After reaching Tangier in modern-day Algeria by 703, it seemed as though crossing the narrow Straits of Gibraltar to the fertile lands of southern Spain would be a logical target.

Until now the peninsula had been ruled over by Visigoth kings from Toledo. As with all cases in medieval history, the eighth century was tainted by a Visigoth succession crisis which swelled instability in the region. According to Arab sources, when King Witiza died in 710, his sons actively urged Arab armies to invade and depose the newly elected King Roderick. As such, Berber chief and governor of Tangier, Tariq Ibn Ziyad, led the first Muslim invasion into Spain. Sources on the size of the Arab force vary but it seems as though it was no more than 7,000, of which the majority were Berbers. Despite leading a Visigoth army against Basques in the north, word of a Muslim force heading to Seville forced Roderick to divert his troops immediately south to face them. At Medina Sidonia, towards the end of July in 711, a fierce battle took place in which Roderick was decisively defeated and killed in battle. Following this, Tariq unleashed an unrelenting force and took the prominent and powerful cities of Cordoba and Toledo with ease within a year. Meanwhile, another commander, Musa Ibn Nusayr, set out with an Arab army of 18,000 to get his share of the profits of conquest. Rather than joining Tariq, he went on to Seville and Merida which fell in 713. Only later did the two forces combine and lead an extensive and devastating warpath in the north, seizing Zaragoza, Ebro, Leon and Astorga.

After being forced to leave Iberia at the request of the Umayyad caliph, Musa left his son, Abd al-Aziz, in charge of the conquered territory. From here, his son led Muslim expeditions into Murcia, Barcelona, Girona and Narbonne. By 716, almost all the peninsula was under Muslim control and Visigoth aristocrats were incorporated into the new elite. The sons of Witiza, who had urged for an invasion, retained a vast amount of their personal wealth and became keen advisors of Muslim governors. Sources also describe some Visigoth elites converting to Islam, as was the case with a Visigoth noble in upper Ebro by

714. Only in Asturias were there glimpses of a resistance movement among the Basques. Nevertheless, from here, the province of Al-Andalus was born.

From 714 to 741, the succession of governors ruling from Cordoba, the capital, was relatively stable. Within the province, a vibrant cosmopolitan society was formed which produced significant advances in science, philosophy and arts, and Arabic became the standard scholastic language – all of which aided in furthering the policies of the Umayyads and Abbasids. Links to the Umayyad caliphs in Damascus, however, were tenuous and there are a lack of sources which would hint at any revenue being exported from the new province to the capital. Still, the key to Al-Andalusian control was conquest, therefore the governors led frequent raids into northern Spain and southern France including Pamplona, Bordeaux, Langres and Sens.

This all came crashing down in 732 with the Battle of Poitiers (also known as the Battle of Tours). With the rapid growth of Muslim control, the Arab armies were an unprecedented threat for the Frankish kingdom. Seeking to expand their faith and territory, a force led by Rahman Al Ghafiqi set its sights on the Frankish kingdom. As such, the stage was set for one of the most significant battles in European history. At Poitiers, the Frankish army, led by the legendary tactician and warrior Charles Martel, came to blows with the Arab army numbering in tens of thousands. The battle raged on for hours and saw Muslim cavalry clash with Frankish foot soldiers who formed an impenetrable shield wall. Despite their advanced skills and technology, which had forced the Franks into a defensive tactic, Charles Martel was able to rally his troops into a daring charge which sent the Muslim army into a full retreat. This crushing Arab defeat at the hands of Charles Martel hindered the Muslim war campaign from pushing any further into the West, and by extension, Christendom. Following the battle, the Muslim conquest of the West would be confined to Iberia where civil war would ensue. Despite this, the peninsula would remain under Islamic control for the next 700 years, although the resounding victory at the Battle of Poitiers is a highly celebrated event in European and Christian history. Elsewhere in the Mediterranean, others were not as lucky.

By the eighth century, the Byzantines were thrown into a crisis of faith. In the early 600s, Emperor Heraclius was faced with a grim situation. By 611, the Persians were advancing into Asia Minor while the Avars were once again attempting to launch an assault on Constantinople. In a sort of proto-crusade, Heraclius plastered iconography of Christianity on banners and ships to invoke the power of Christ in his campaign to repel the invading armies. A crushing blow was to come in 614 when the Persians seized Jerusalem, and with it the relic of the True Cross which was brought back to the Persian capital along with the Patriarch of Jerusalem and other noble prisoners. Following this, in 626, the Avars and Persians joined forces to besiege the great city of Constantinople for ten days. Eager to lay waste to the jewel of the empire, the Avars attacked the walls while the Persians held the eastern shores of the Bosporus. Although the odds were stacked against them, Heraclius was able to utilise the infamous weapon of Greek fire to destroy an Avar fleet which broke the siege and freed the city from the grasp of its enemy. Attributing the success to the Virgin Mary, Heraclius pressed further into the Persian heartland which, with the aid of a Persian revolt against Khusro, allowed peace to be negotiated and the former Byzantine territory to be returned to its rightful owners. The True Cross was recovered and it appeared as though Christianity was saved.

The events of the former decades, however, raised similar questions about the power of faith that Augustine had once rebuked after the Fall of Rome. Before he was rebelled against and murdered, Khusro had capitalised on the former schism created by Justinian between the Chalcedonians and Monophysites. Meeting with Monophysite leaders as well as Nestorians (another Christian sect) it was agreed that if support for Persian invasion was given, the Nestorians would retain their position in Sasanian territory while the Persians would support a Monophysite uprising in Armenia, Syria and Egypt. As such, although the Persians had been defeated, such sentiments remained and if Heraclius was to secure his empire, he would have to support the Monophysites. The answer was Monoenergism, a supposed union between Monophysites and Chalcedonians which stated that Christ, although having two natures, possessed only a single divine-human activity. Such a compromise achieved a degree of success in Armenia and Egypt, but Syrian Monophysites would not shift and demanded a full rejection of Chalcedonian beliefs. Rejection of Monoenergism not only came from Monophysites, however, as various churchmen across the western half of Christendom spoke out and petitioned to Pope Honorius I to protest this new union of doctrine. One such man was Abbot Sophronius who, with such determination to overturn Monoenergism, became Patriarch of Jerusalem in 634 to preach about the heresy of the doctrine. Meanwhile, and to complicate the picture further, a newly refined sect of Monoenergism, called Monothelitism, had emerged from supporters of the union. As such, Christianity was divided and in crisis as several doctrines clashed and conflicted one another. With this backdrop, the Arabs then entered the scene.

Palestine and Syria were the first to receive raids from Arabs in 633. In 636, despite Islam being in its infancy, a Muslim army routed the Byzantines at Yarmuk. At the same time, Umayyad forces seized Damascus and Heraclius was forced to retreat from the peninsula. Once again, a crushing blow was given in 638 when Patriarch Sophronius surrendered Jerusalem to the caliph. Following this, the ancient city of Alexandria fell and the Persian Empire altogether collapsed at the hands of the Arabs. Heraclius died and a succession crisis ensued with a series of short and contentious reigns. The victor, Constans, became the sole emperor in 641. While the stability of the Byzantines was fading, Egypt was slipping away from their grasp, Armenia was being heavily raided, and Anatolia was being besieged by Muslim forces. At sea, a series of naval raids took place whereby Arab fleets attacked Rhodes, Crete and Kos. From one defeat to the next, opposition to Monothelitism grew as Maximus the Monk, a close companion to Patriarch Sophronius, led a religious campaign to embrace a form of Orthodoxy. One such supporter of this was Patriarch Pyrrhus of Constantinople who, along with Maximus, travelled to Rome to prepare for a synod at the Lateran Palace under the newly elected Pope Martin I. The exarch of Ravenna, Olympius, ordered the arrest of Martin for allowing such a synod to take place and compelled bishops to oppose the pope. Martin, Maximus and Pyrrhus were arrested and exiled to Thrace. Martin was later executed for his continued efforts to preach against Monothelitism. At this time, Constans, feeling the pressure of his divided empire, attempted to abandon Constantinople and move the court and capital to Syracuse in Sicily. But in 668 he was assassinated by his chamberlain.

The empire that Constantine IV inherited was in ruin. It was only the beginning. In 674, Muslim forces made a serious attempt at besieging and blockading Constantinople which, although eventually defeated, lasted four years. At the same time, a new tribe, the Bulgars, migrated into the Danube and became a long-lasting threat to the capital. To deal with the religious division, Constantine saw unity with the West as being more important than a union with the Monophysites – of which most of the former territories were lost to the Umayyads. As such, with the assistance of Pope Agatho, they called for an Ecumenical council to denounce the former Monothelitism. Known as the Sixth Ecumenical Council, it condemned various Monothelitists and aimed to restore a degree of stability to Christendom.

In the following decades – from 680 to the early 700s – more and more of the Byzantine Empire fell to Muslim invaders. Meanwhile, succession crises and murder became staple undertones of Byzantine rule. As such, the empire was once again slipping away as it had done in the fifth century and in order to recover, they saw that 'desperate times called for desperate measures'. Has God given up on the Christians? Why was Islam flourishing so rapidly? What was it that they do that we do not? – All questions asked by churchmen in the face of political and religious instability. The answer they fell upon was iconoclasm.

It was seen that the prestige of Islamic successes in the seventh and eighth centuries motivated Emperor Leo III to adopt the Islamic position of rejecting and destroying devotional and liturgical images in 726 – a policy known as iconoclasm. The way in which the Byzantines would implement iconoclasm, however, was slightly different to Islam. Muslims would extend their iconoclastic reach to reject images not only including religion but also living people and animals, which contrasted the Byzantine approach that focused primarily on the iconography of Christianity such as relics.

Within the schisms we have seen, Christianity by the sixth and seventh century had developed into a theology that was founded on the worship of saints and was likewise influenced by a hierarchy of sanctity with the Trinity at its apex and humanity at the base. In order to obtain a blessing or divine favour, Christians would pray to intermediaries such as holy images, icons and, most importantly, relics. Increasingly, debates over icons began to emerge when images in the form of mosaics or paintings, which did not fulfil the religious specifications to make them relics, gradually started to take on spiritual significance. From 570 onwards, the boundary between Acheiropoieta, 'man-made' relics, and legitimately acclaimed Christian relics began to blur, with the most famous examples of Acheiropoieta taking spiritual significance being the Image of Camuliana from Cappadocia – a Greek palladium relic, said to have come from Athena, which had been attributed as the saviour of Constantinople in 626 when it defended the city from a Persian–Avar siege. As society began gradually channelling their faith into icons and relics rather than the church, Christianity witnessed a shift in authoritative power from church men to relics.

In the summer of 722, however, judgement took the form of a submerged volcano west of Thera which erupted violently and caused widespread damage to local areas. Seeing this event as a direct sign from God, Leo III removed the icon of Christ which hung over the main entrance to the palace at the Chalke Gate. Following this, Leo set forth on a warpath. He ordered the destruction of iconophile (supporters of icons) texts, and it is suggested that books with missing reports and pages were to be presented to the Second Council of Nicaea for review. Despite this, there were many who did not approve. Between 720 and 730, a series of letters were produced by the Patriarch Germanos pertaining to Constantine the bishop of Nakoleia, and Thomas of Klaudioupolis. These letters oppose the iconoclastic policies of the church and Leo III stating that, 'Whole towns and multitudes of people are in considerable agitation over this matter.' As such, there was a clear outrage by the general population as well as iconophile clergy who opposed Leo III. In a sort of Stalin-esque regime, Germanos was quickly replaced with the iconoclastic Patriarch Anastasios in an attempt to circumvent opposition and create a unified embrace of these Islamic practices.

While there was a degree of opposition, the policy of iconoclasm continued long after Leo III's death in 741. Emperor Constantine V succeeded the throne and maintained a staunch iconoclastic position. Throughout his reign, he had vast military successes against the Bulgars (which may explain why the maintenance of iconoclasm continued as it fulfilled Leo IIIs efforts to reclaim divine favour). Perhaps what is most significant of Constantine's reign is the Council of Hieria where the Epitome of the Definition of Iconoclastic Conciliabulum announced that, 'We declare unanimously […] if anyone ventures to represent the divine image [or] endeavour to represent the forms of the Saints in lifeless pictures […] he is an adversary of God.'

In Leo III's reign it is understood that there was a factional divide within the church, yet during Constantine V's reign there was a seemingly unanimous support of iconoclasm by the 338 assembled bishops at the council – most probably as those assembled were iconoclastic supporters anyway. Evidence of resistance can be most famously found in the writings of John of Damascus, a Syrian monk who greatly opposed iconoclasm. Noteworthy here is that John lived outside of Byzantine territory, as St Stephen the Younger details areas where iconophiles were forced to flee from persecution: Cherson, Crimea and the Greek-speaking regions of southern Italy. At that time, it seems as though a forced unity of Christianity could only be achieved through an authoritarian dictatorship centred around censorship.

The harsh iconoclastic policy seems to have died alongside Constantine in 775, since his son, Leo IV, who only reigned for five years, attempted to mediate between the iconophiles and iconoclasts. Despite this, the most significant event attributed to his reign (in terms of iconoclasm) is detailed by eleventh-century historian George Kendrenos who wrote that Leo IV discovered two icons hidden underneath the pillow used by his wife, Irene, and subsequently launched an investigation where two courtiers were tortured for being responsible and Irene was shunned for violating the law and faith. Not only was there a division of Christian doctrine within the empire but clearly also within the royal household.

Theophanes the Confessor details in his commentary of 790 that after Irene came to regency on behalf of her son Constantine following Leo's death, she attempted to assert her right as an iconophile emperor. She tried to use law to besmirch the image of her iconoclast father-in-law, Constantine V, by attacking the reputation of him and the children of his third marriage to Eudokia – as while the church declared that second marriages were permissible if no children from the first survived, having a third marriage was undesirable. By reducing the power of her opponents, she was able to attempt to reverse the harsh policies of iconoclasm through the support of monks, painters, venerators and ecclesiasts who refused to support the destruction of icons. With the election of iconophile Tarasios as the Patriarch of Constantinople, she was able to initiate the Seventh Ecumenical Council which was later held in Nicaea in 787. The council included papal representatives, and its decrees affirmed the veneration of icons and declared iconoclasm as heresy.

Irene's reign ended what is known as the 'First Iconoclastic Period' and the veneration of icons lasted until 814 when the 'Second Iconoclastic Period' began with the reign of Leo V. It seems that like Leo III, Leo V's motivation for iconoclasm was due to military failures against the Arabs. Henceforth, he began to toy with the idea of reviving iconoclasm, reportedly remarking that, 'All the emperors, who took up images and venerated them, met their death either in revolt or in war; but those who did not venerate images all died a natural death.'

As a result, Leo V strongly felt that this would once again win the divine favour of God and lead to military successes, and so in 815 the revival of iconoclasm was rendered official by a synod held in Constantinople.

The Second Iconoclastic Period was shorter than the previous one and only lasted twenty-eight years. Equally, the second period was in no way as violent and dramatic as the first as represented by Michael II who succeeded Leo. Michael was far more diplomatic than the likes of Constantine V as he encouraged reconciliation with the iconophiles, stopped persecution, and allowed the exiled to return. This may have been because no one was as extreme in their iconoclastic views as those in the first period. As such, it was very unstable and weak from the offset which is why it soon failed. Theophilus, who succeeded Michael, was equally as diplomatic and only in 832 did he issue an edict forbidding the veneration of icons.

The tyrannical period of iconoclasm, however, reached a crushing defeat at the hands of St Theodora, the Triumph of Orthodoxy. Despite growing up in a family of traders and military officials, in 830 she was selected by Euphrosyne, the wife of Constantine who was besmirched by Irene, to be the bride of the young emperor. As such, she was quickly surrounded by staunch and powerful iconoclasts. Evidence is difficult to find on whether he knew that Theodora was an iconophile, but she secretly venerated icons throughout her husband's reign. Like Irene, stories of the empress detail that she also kept venerated icons within her chamber in the palace and that a servant witnessed and reported her to the emperor. Sources suggest that Theodora stated these were merely 'playing dolls' which have themselves, ironically, become relics held at the monastery of Vatopedi on Mount Athos. Following her husband's death, Theodora, the empress regent, had to contend with one of the most impactful events of Christian history when Rome was attacked by Arab forces in 846. Though the city itself was saved, the Vatican was pillaged which signalled a direct attack on Christendom. Equally, from Sicily, Muslim armies began to venture into Southern Italy to expand their empire. Despite these setbacks, Theodora hoped to demonstrate that a faith revolving around icons could uphold the empire as it once did in the time of Justinian.

As such, Crete was the first of her goals as it had been lost to Arab invaders some decades before. In 843, with a force headed by Niketiates and Theoktistos, she successfully laid siege to Muslim fortresses and periodically regained the island for the empire. The following year, an army of Arabs launched a counter-attack, killing Niketiates. It appears as though the defeat left the veneration of icons unchallenged, as it was overshadowed by a general degree of stability being reached. Save for some minor raids in the east and the losses of Sicily, the remaining years of Theodora's reign saw a flourish of military successes and peace. In 846, Theodora repelled a Bulgarian army in Macedonia and Thrace, forcing the Khan into a peace treaty. And following attacks in Asia Minor, she launched a series of raids in retaliation along the coastline of Egypt in 853 and 854. One such attack resulted in Byzantine raiders burning the city of Damietta, and later, in 855, the city of Anazarbus was sacked with 20,000 prisoners being taken and forced into Christianity or execution. Such victories and power impressed even the Arabs.

But her achievements in domestic policy were as successful as her foreign policy. After her husband's death, she pounced on the opportunity to make vast religious changes. She firstly claimed that, upon his deathbed, Theophilos had repented and rebuked his iconoclastic stance in order to seek salvation. Gaining considerable support from iconophiles, the empress regent assembled a collection of lay officials and courtiers to condemn iconoclasm. Since almost all the bishops within the empire had to submit to iconoclasm, although religious policy would usually have been decided through them, Theodora understood she had to think creatively and carefully about how to traverse the path ahead. She met with Theoktistos, Niketiates (before his untimely death) and her two brothers at the home of Theoktistos and reinstated the Second Council of Nicea from 787, which condemned iconoclasm.

With widespread support, Theodora moved to the offensive and replaced John VII, the Patriarch of Constantinople, with the more iconophile Patriarch Methodios I. John did not go willingly and attempted to stir unrest against the empress by claiming a self-inflicted wound had been caused by imperial guards. Equally, while in exile, he attempted to coerce a servant into removing the eyes of a venerated idol. Nevertheless, Theodora remained headstrong and to show the prowess of her faith she had John whipped over 200 times. Then, in an event which echoed the 'Night of the Long Knives' in Nazi Germany, Methodios had every bishop in the empire deposed for having opposed the Second Council of Nicea. With iconoclasm on the retreat, Theodora led a congregation to the Hagia Sophia where, in 843, the restoration of icons was celebrated with great grandeur. One such symbolic action during this time was the restoration of icons to the tomb of Constantine V, the champion of iconoclasm. Equally, the tomb of Irene, the former empress and iconophile, was moved to the Church of Holy Apostles where it was revered as the resting place of another iconophile hero. The day has since been celebrated as the Feast of Orthodoxy.

This did not come without a degree of resistance, as the Paulician heretics, a sect of dualist Christians who rejected the material world, rebelled in eastern Anatolia. Theodora, however, with her might and power ordered an army to convert or execute every Paulician in the empire. Thousands were killed and many others escaped across the borders.

By the end of her reign, she had accomplished that which no former emperor had achieved and gained the upper hand over the rapidly expanding Abbasid caliphate and Bulgar tribe. As such, it was clear that the adoption of iconoclasm was not achieving the aim of divine favour that the Muslims seemingly enjoyed. Thus, Theodora, in her religious zeal in putting an end to iconoclasm for good, was subsequently known as the 'Triumph of Orthodoxy'. Hymns attributed to the saint describe how she stood as a defender of the faith:

> As a right worthy namesake of gifts bestowed of God, and a divinely-wrought image of holy wisdom and faith, thou didst make the Church to shine with godly piety; for thou didst demonstrate to all that the Saints in every age have shown honour to the icons, O Theodora, thou righteous and fair adornment of the Orthodox.

She was highly regarded by future generations as a formidable leader who was able to re-establish control both domestically and externally. Her legacy, however, lay in the restoration of icons. As iconoclasm was too weak to be restored to the extent it formally was, Theodora would be heralded as the saviour of the church and become canonised later as a Saint with her feast day on 11 February.

Altogether, the Byzantine Empire was located at the crossroads of Christian, Jewish and now Islamic worlds whose interactions played a significant role in shaping the development of Byzantine Christianity. With this in mind, the first and second iconoclastic eras stood as crucial milestones in the history of Christianity. In the face of Muslim invasion in the East and West, both militarily and religiously, the eighth and ninth centuries were key periods in the defence of the faith. Without the likes of Theodora, with whom the most powerful empire may have religiously fallen into disrepair, and Charles Martel who halted the progression of Islam into western Europe, the world may well have looked very different to what it does today. Ultimately, the east and west Christian worlds would periodically unite, showing their own strength through the unified invasion of the Islamic world in 1095 that we shall come to see in the following chapters.

Chapter Four

Heresy on The Fringes of Christendom

While triumphs in the east and west of the Christian Empire had hindered the Muslim advance, other kingdoms and empires on the frontiers of Christendom were not as fortunate. Much of our narrative thus far has focused predominantly on the chronology of events within the Mediterranean – be it with an Iberian, Byzantine, or Italian focus. This allows us, especially when framing our perspective around religion, to understand through our saints the local impacts of those, like Justinian, who sought to command and wield Christianity. This chapter is a brief distraction from this theme and aims to understand the consequences of a nation whose history dramatically changed as a result of its contentious relationship with the Arab expansion into the horn of Africa. With this in mind, we turn towards a short history of a kingdom whose once great and bustling narrative became scarce through being encompassed by the torrent of Islam.

Described by third-century Persian prophet Mani, the Kingdom of the Aksumites, now modern-day Ethiopia, was one of the four greatest powers in the known world at the time and rivalled the likes of Babylon, Rome and China. Undoubtedly, alongside its imperial expansion, the profound Aksum trade and naval power which interacted with Egypt, southern Arabia, Europe and Asia is why Mani attributed such great prominence to the Aksumites. The empire flourished in the fourth and fifth centuries under the banner of Christianity and Roman influence. Roman historian Rufinus writes in his *Ecclesiastical Histories* of the colourful circumstances of Ethiopia's conversion to Christianity under the Emperor Ezana:

> The boys [Aedesius and Frumentius] were found studying under a tree and, preserved by the mercy of the barbarians, were taking to the king [King Ella Amida of Ethopia]. He made one of them, Aedesius, his cupbearer. Frumentius, whom he had perceived to be sagacious and prudent, he made his treasurer and secretary. Thereafter, they were held in great honour and affection by the king.
>
> The king died, leaving his wife and infant son [Ezana] as heir to the bereaved kingdom. He gave the young men [Aedesius and Frumentius] liberty to do what they pleased but the queen besought them with tears,

> since she had no more faithful subjects in the whole kingdom, to share with her the cares of governing the kingdom until her son should grow up.
> [Thus] Frumentius held the reins of government in his hands, God stirred his heart and he began to search out with care those of the Roman merchants who were Christians and give them great influence and urge them to establish in various places religious buildings to which they might resort for prayer in the Roman manner. He himself, moreover, did the same, attracting them with his favour and his benefits, providing them with whatever was needed, supplying sites for buildings and other necessities, and in every way promoting the growth of the seed of Christianity in the country.

Frumentius proceeded to travel to Alexandria to the Patriarch Athanasius to urge him to send a worthy man to be bishop of this newly emerging Christian kingdom in Africa. Seeing Frumentius as the best option, Athanasius declared, 'What other man shall we find in whom the Spirit of God is as in thee,' and consecrated him there and then. Frumentius is considered a saint within the Ethiopian church and is also known as Abuna Salema Kesate Berhan, the first bishop of Ethiopia. Following the official conversion, several Christians, known as Tsadkan or Righteous Ones, arrived from the Roman Empire to assist in spreading the Gospel. The greatest development in Ethiopian Christianity, however, was the arrival of the Nine Syrian Saints in the latter half of the fifth century. They are thought to have been monks and priests expelled from the Byzantine Empire following the Council of Chalcedon in 451 but were received by Emperor Ella Amida II with open arms and are glorified in the Ethiopian church calendar. These saints, of whom only two or possibly three were actually from Syria (others may have been from Constantinople, Cilicia, Cappadocia and Rome), were active in translating the Bible and organising Christian communities.

From thereafter the kingdom flourished and large discoveries of Christian Aksum coins in India show the extent of international trade participation. A major hoard of mid-fourth century Roman and Aksum coins, for example, were found at Matara, India, and reciprocally a collection of Central Asian Kushan coins were discovered in the Debre Damo monastery in Tigray, Ethiopia. Thus, the circulation of coinage between Europe, Asia and Africa demonstrates an economic union paralleled with the modern-day European Union which was accessible only through subjugation and conversion to Christianity. The fourth-century Emperor Mehadeyis further developed Aksum coinage by issuing bronze and copper coins inscribed with the Ethiopian vernacular, Ge'ez, translation of Emperor Constantine's coin inscription, *In hoc signo vinces* meaning 'By this cross you will conquer', which further reflected the Aksumite pursuit to align themselves closer to Christianity. Coinage from the fourth and fifth centuries demonstrates an attempt to create an affiliation between the Aksum Empire and Christendom, and undoubtedly an advantage of this was the inclusion in the economic empire that Christianity had established.

Although Christian Aksum continued to flourish through the fourth and fifth centuries, it was with Emperor Kaleb, also known as St Elesbaan, that we see the impact of Justinian's new Christian world order on the geopolitics of the Mediterranean and the final period of Aksumite expansion under the banner of Christendom.

St Elesbaan was an Ethiopian saint who is considered to be the founder of the Zagwe dynasty, which later ruled Ethiopia from the twelfth to the thirteenth century. The story of St Elesbaan's life is steeped in legend and mystery, and there is much debate among scholars about the historical accuracy of the accounts of his life. According to tradition, St Elesbaan was born in Axum, the capital of the ancient kingdom of Axum. He was the son of the king of Axum, apparently a cruel and unjust ruler. Despite his father's tyranny, St Elesbaan is believed to have been a kind and just prince, beloved by his people. When he grew older, he is said to have risen up against his father's oppression and overthrown him, becoming the king of Axum himself. As king, St Elesbaan seems to have been a wise and just ruler, who worked to improve the lives of his people, building many churches and monasteries and encouraging the spread of Christianity throughout his kingdom.

In Hejaz, the capital of Yemen, Judaism had become the state religion adopted by Himyarite King Dhu Nuwas (with Jewish traditions tracing back to the time of Queen Sheba and King Solomon). In the mid-520s he had organised a massacre of the Monophysite Christian community of Najran. This attack rippled through the Christian world, being recounted by contemporary scholars such as Procopius. Urged by the eastern Roman Emperor who was seeking new allies in South Arabia and Africa to fight the Persians, Elesbaan sent an expedition in 525 to overthrow the king and defend Christianity. He was defeated and in desiring to learn the reason for his defeat, Elesbaan, inspired by a revelation from above, visited a recluse named Zenon. He revealed to the emperor that he had acted unrighteously in his desire to take revenge, for the Lord has said, 'Vengeance is mine, I shall repay!' (Hebrews 10:30). The holy ascetic urged Elesbaan to promise that he would devote the rest of his life to God (if he wished to escape his wrath for his self-willed revenge), then he would defeat Dhu Nuwas. St Elesbaan made that vow to the Lord, and in the 520s he and his army confronted the enemy. This time, he defeated, captured and executed Dhu Nuwas. According to Roman Martyrology, after Elesbaan defeated the enemies of Christ, he abdicated and sent his royal diadem to Jerusalem to be hung near the Life-Giving Tomb of Christ.

The successful campaign deposed Dhu Nuwas and recognised Sumyafa Ashwa as the new Christian king of Yemen. But in the subsequent four years Aksumite rule in Yemen witnessed rebellion and rivalry. Sumyafa was overthrown by an Aksumite general, Abreha, who sought political power and consolidated himself as an independent sovereign. In *c.*547 Abreha subdued the tribes controlling Mecca, and extended his rule over Saba, Himyar, Hadhramawt and Yamanat, as well as other coastal and highland regions.

Stuart Munro-Hay observed that the result of Elesbaan's ambitious expedition was a weakening of Aksumite authority, over-expenditure in money and manpower, and loss of prestige as the empire began to divide. In fact, following his abdication the deterioration of coinage across his successors' reigns over the next century shows a decline in the Aksumite empire as a whole. Changes in climate led to infertile fields and deforestation around Aksum, and Persian trade expansions meant markets and merchants shifted away from the empire.

Despite the many legends and traditions surrounding St Elesbaan's life, it is difficult to separate fact from fiction. Nevertheless, he is revered as a saint and hero in Ethiopia, and is considered to be one of the most important figures in the country's history. It is to be noted that today St Elesbaan is not officially recognised by the Catholic Church or other mainstream Christian denominations but only within the Ethiopian Orthodox Church. Nevertheless, sixteenth-century Cardinal Caesar Baronius added him to his edition of the *Roman Martyrology* despite his being a Miaphysite. Once again, we see the long-lasting effects of Justinian's battle with heresy take form a millennium after the Miaphysite–Chalcedonian councils.

Christianity had thus brought great riches to the area, but by the seventh century, Aksum was becoming increasingly isolated from its Christian allies, and while being an ally of Christ was incredibly beneficial during this period, becoming an enemy was more than a mistake. According to an eighteenth-century Chinese biography of the Prophet Muhammad which drew upon earlier Arabic manuscripts written in the fourteenth century, Aksum Emperor Saifu in *c.*570 sent gifts to Muhammad's family upon sighting a star that announced his birth, and again when he was 7 years old. Islamic traditions are thus favourable to Ethiopia; Muhammad grew up with an Ethiopian nurse, and in Mecca there was an Ethiopian Christian community which consisted of merchants, craftsmen and soldiers who Muhammad interacted with. In fact, Muhammad in response to persecution by the Quraish clan who controlled Mecca, advised his followers, 'If you were to go to Ethiopia, it would be better for you until such a time as Allah shall relieve you from your distress [...] it is a friendly country.'

In *c.*616, Aksum received seventeen Muslim followers at first, with more arriving in the following year seeking asylum, all of whom were accepted and provided for by Emperor Armah. According to a later Islamic source, Armah was so impressed by the refugees' new faith that he himself allegedly became a secret convert to Islam from Christianity. Upon Muhammad's request for these followers to return, only sixteen did. It is detailed in Ethiopian tradition that the rest settled at Negash, in eastern Tigray, which a subsequent Muslim community continues to inhabit to this day. The most notable influence is that the Qur'an contains over 200 words that derive from the vernacular Ge'ez language. Detailed in the Qur'an is an indication that upon Armah's death Muhammad performed Salat al-Janazah, an Islamic funeral ritual carried out if a Muslim died in a place with no Muslims to pray for them. This is a strong justification for the theory that Armah converted to Islam during the period in which he sheltered Muslims in Aksum. Eighth-century Arab historian and hagiographer, Ibn Ishaq, reported that Christians rebelled and accused him of renouncing their faith, and as a consequence of this, Europe refused to acknowledge Emperor Armah's bestowed Arabic name Al-Najashi. Ibn Ishaq's report is noteworthy as the renunciation of Christianity in favour of Islam would have been deemed heretical.

As Aksum increasingly lost control of its former prominence and empire, Ethiopia turned its back on Christendom and allied itself with the emerging Islamic religion. It is significant to note that while there is seemingly an abundance of contemporary sources on the Aksumite empire during the fourth, fifth and sixth centuries, upon researching the seventh century it is witnessed that the kingdom enters a 'Dark Age' whereby contemporary sources such as the *History of the Patriarchs of Alexandria* cease to reference the Aksumites. Archaeological evidence from the city of Aksum suggests that it saw a population decline, the disrepair of large buildings and potentially ceased to be the capital by the mid-seventh century, as evidenced by the ninth- and tenth-century Arab sources which described Armah as ruling from a capital called Ku'bar. As the Rashidun caliphate established themselves, Aksum no longer had trading dominance in the Red Sea, nor did it have access to the trade union with Christendom which further isolated it from its once strong allies.

While in the later Aksumite era the decline of Christianity was set into motion, the establishment of a Judaic Zagwe dynasty and the later Solomonic dynasty would consolidate the end of the Christian nation and solidify the anticipated 'betrayal' of Christendom. In *c.*1137, Mara Takla Haymanot established the Agaw Zagwe dynasty. The Zagwe can be characterised by being shrouded in a degree of mystery as they were only loosely in contact with Christendom via the Patriarch of Alexandria. Much to the distaste of Christendom, Zagwe Ethiopia continued to develop a strong relationship primarily with the Ayyubid dynasty and later Mamluks. It is noteworthy to compare the Aksumite 'Crusade' of Yemen to the First Crusade of *c.*1095, as while the Byzantine emperor called upon his brother to protect Christianity in *c.*520, there is no reference of a call to arms made in the eleventh century to Ethiopia, which is significant in understanding the extent to which the kingdom had been isolated from its former Christian ally. When he reconquered Jerusalem in *c.*1189, Saladin granted Ethiopians special privileges in holy places and protection of pilgrims en route, thus demonstrating the extent of the relationship the Zagwe dynasty had with Islamic powers. The cultivation of trade and relations between the Islamic world and Ethiopia were uninterrupted by the call of the First Crusade, perhaps due to the Muslim Ethiopian merchants trading along the Red Sea who were instrumental in gaining positive political favour with Egypt.

A further contribution to the Zagwe's stray from Christianity is the religious instability within the kingdom. The only significant contemporary source of the Zagwe is a letter received in *c.*1150 by Pope John V, the Patriarch of Alexandria, from Mara Takla Haymanot, who requested to have a new *abuna* (bishop) because the current one was too old. The true reason for Abuna Mikael's replacement was because he refused to endorse the new Judaic dynasty since he remained Christian. The letter also represents the diverse religious melting pot that the eleventh- and twelfth-century Ethiopia had become as while the ruling kings were Judaic, the northern regions of Ethiopia remained Christian, the highlands retained a pagan populous, and the coastal regions were predominantly Muslim. Further dissonance emerged when the Ethiopian Church adopted Islamic and Judaic traditions in the twelfth century. The church placed heavier emphasis on the Old Testament and adhered to certain practices found in Judaism. Ethiopian cuisine also follows dietary rules found in Jewish Kushrut and Kosher dietary laws by not mixing dairy products with meat. As with Islam and Judaism, the Ethiopian church separates men and women while praying within the site of worship, and all worshippers must remove their shoes. Thus, most probably due to cultural assimilation through the diverse religious groups within Ethiopia, the church had adopted a wide range of non-Christian traditions. This, once again, reiterates the narrative that this once staunch Christian kingdom was establishing its independence and betraying Christendom in favour of their Islamic enemies.

The Zagwe dynasty was relatively short-lived as it was overthrown in *c.*1270, a century and a half after coming to power. While fighting the Zagwe in a mid-thirteenth century rebellion, Yekuno Amlak overthrew the ruling dynasty with the aid of the Muslim Sultanate of Shoa which established Amhara and Shoa as independent kingdoms. The remnants of Christian Ethiopia were overthrown by a joint Judaic and Muslim revolt. Yekuno Amlak thus established the Solomonic Dynasty and claimed Ethiopia to be the resting place of the Judaic relic, the Ark of the Covenant, as well as the alleged home of Queen Sheba, as written in the Gospels of Matthew and Luke. In *c.*1272, Amlak sent a delegation of Muslim merchants to Egypt to request a new *abuna*, as was tradition, from the Sultan. In a letter accompanying the delegation, Amlak assured the Sultan that 'he protected all the Muslims within his territories'. Acknowledging that Louis IX of France had launched the unsuccessful seventh crusade against the Ayyubids and Mamluks a few decades in earlier in *c.*1248, and in *c.*1270 launched the eighth crusade against the Hafsid dynasty, means that this undisguised pursuit of an alliance with Egypt showed a defiance to western Christendom.

Yekuno Amlak, and the Solomonic dynasty, thus concludes the narrative needed to understand the tempest of Ethiopian history which revolved around religion. There is a prolific correlation between the popularisation of Ethiopian demons in western art, and the betrayal of Ethiopia characterised through its transformation from a strong Christian Empire into a weaker Judaic kingdom with robust Islamic alliances. Equally, the schism involving the Coptic patriarchs of Alexandria further separated Ethiopia from the papacy. The schism represented the separation of the Catholic Church from the Orthodox Church as a culmination of theological and political differences. For example, western Monophysites deemed eastern Miaphysitism theology as heretical due to their theological differences. Furthermore, due to the Latin-led crusades, Egypt and the Coptic patriarch of Alexandria were not politically aligned with France or the papacy. During the Fatimid caliphate rule over Egypt in the eleventh century, the Coptic patriarch of Alexandria changed the Coptic Christian language used to write theological texts to Arabic, much to the distaste of the papacy who continued to endorse the use of Latin. This schism is why there is a lack of contemporary sources on the Zagwe and Solomonic dynasties; although the Orthodox patriarchs of Alexandria remained in full communion with the eastern Roman Empire and the papacy, the Coptic patriarchs were deemed illegitimate.

It would not be until the legend of Prester John swept across Christian Europe that contact with Ethiopia would be re-energised. The story of Prester John is a medieval legend that tells of a Christian king of the East who ruled over a Christian nation, surrounded by enemies of various religious beliefs, mostly Muslim, who he is always at war with. The legend of Prester John was based on a letter that circulated in the twelfth century and claimed to be from the king himself, describing his kingdom and the wonders that it contained. The letter was widely believed to be genuine, and sparked a series of expeditions to find the fabled kingdom. The letter describes a place of great wealth, with a golden palace and vast treasures, precious stones and many wonders, including a fountain that provided a cure for all illnesses, and a palace made of crystal and guarded by giant griffins. The kingdom was said to be located perhaps in either India or Ethiopia. This inspired several European explorers, including Marco Polo and his father and uncle, to search for this kingdom in Africa and Asia, but it was never found. Despite this, explorers and missionaries found the Ethiopian kingdom where diplomacy was subsequently restored.

From the sixth century until the thirteenth, Ethiopia witnessed a great deal of religious instability and contention. What was once regarded as a strong ally to Christianity and a prominent empire equal to the likes of Rome had deteriorated in the wake of Islam. The kingdom's embrace and alignment with the new religion quickly isolated it from its former Christian partners, and thus the genesis of betrayal had begun. The schism of the patriarch of Alexandria, alliances with the Ayyubids and Fatimids, and the establishment of Judaic dynasties all contributed to the further collapse of diplomatic relations between Ethiopia and western Christendom. The result of this was the European perspective that Ethiopia was embracing heresy and had become an enemy. From hereafter, especially in art and literature, the nation was categorised amongst the 'monstrous races' of Saracens and Jews.

The *Song of Roland* (*c*.1040–1115), for example, which was based on the Battle of Roncevaux Pass in 778 and is a *chanson de gesta* that describes the heroism of Roland, Charlemagne's nephew, reveals such feelings. The battle had previously been detailed in the *Life of Charlemagne* by eighth-century Frankish Scholar Einhard who stated that, 'In the Pyrenean mountain range [Charlemagne] had to experience a brief taste of Basque treachery.' While Einhard specifies the ambushing army was Basque in his historical chronicle, the *Song of Roland* differs and instead writes, 'For with your own eyes you can see the Saracens. Proclaim your mea culpa; pray for God's mercy,' and further states, 'his uncle Marganice [...] He it was who held Carthage and Ethiopia, an accursed land. The black people are in his domain; they have big noses and wise ears.' The anonymous author of the *Song of Roland* had therefore altered the historical narrative with a racial and religiously charged bias to instead present the battle as a reflection of the First Crusade which had taken place during the poem's construction. The poem, as a result, was Christian propaganda that depicted a legendary martyr fighting in the last stand to protect Christianity from the Frankish enemies of the Crusades. Political history, therefore, provides the contextual knowledge to understand why changes within literature and art occurred. As such, to understand the artistic motivations behind the symbolic religious depictions in, say the twelfth or thirteenth century, the religious complexities on the fringes of Christendom that were sown during the Age of Justinian are crucial. All that said, returning to Elesbaan back in the sixth century, this story demonstrates that although within the borders of the empire, Justinian and Gregory were attempting to building a strong and unified Christian Empire, on its frontiers where religion was a contentious mixing pot, support for border allies to establish and uphold Christianity pushed certain nations to their limits and, with the rise of Islamic expansion, forced the hand of many leaders to defend their faith or else fall into despair.

Chapter Five

Martyrdom and Paganism

Edmund the Martyr was a young king of East Anglia in the ninth century. He was a wise and just ruler, loved by his people for his fairness and compassion. But his reign was short-lived, as in the year 869, aged just 29, he was called upon to defend his kingdom and faith. The Vikings were ruthless conquerors, known for their brutality and savagery. When they invaded East Anglia, they were determined to subjugate the people and plunder their riches. King Edmund, however, stood in their way, and after a fearsome battle, they captured him and brought him before their leader, Ivar the Boneless. Ivar was a formidable warrior, with a reputation for cruelty and ruthlessness. He demanded that Edmund renounce his Christian faith and swear allegiance to the Viking gods. But Edmund refused, declaring that he would die before betraying his beliefs. Enraged by Edmund's defiance, Ivar ordered his men to tie the young king to a tree and torture him. They beat him until he was bloody and bruised, but still he refused to renounce his faith. In a final act of torture, he was scourged against the tree before being pelted with projectiles 'like the bristles of a hedgehog', shot with arrows and pierced with javelins. As his head was cut off, a bright light shone from his neck, and a heavenly choir of angels was heard singing his praises.

Just south of Hoxne village, near Diss in East Anglia, is a stone cross which was erected at the alleged site where Edmund was tied to an oak in 870. Edmund, however, entered the realm of sainthood when his people went searching for his body and decapitated head. Allegedly, the latter was discovered between the paws of a wolf who willingly gave back the head. Upon doing so a spring broke through the soil where the head had lain. Today, just north of Abbey Farm on the site of a Benedictine monastery, is a deep moat surrounding an island which is said to have been the very same spring. It is also recorded that 'the occupiers of the field have never been able to divert' the spring and many miracle stories show pilgrims drinking the water to be healed. Nevertheless, it is also recorded in legend that the head perfectly reattached to the body when reunited.

This legendary tale about the Anglo-Saxon martyr reveals a vast array of details about the ninth century. Firstly, the supernatural and mystical elements of the story of Edmund alongside the veneration of the site where he had defended his faith is something which we have not necessarily seen as of yet within our journey through sainthood. As we have seen with Augustine, Gregory, Theodora and Elesbaan, their roles as saints were as icons and role models to others – through how pious, just and pure-hearted they were.

An element of mystery can be seen in a miracle involving Gregory the Great whereby a woman began to chuckle at the bread used at Mass during a communion from St Gregory. She believed it was absurd for people to believe that the bread she cooked represented Jesus' flesh. This was the situation in the St Gregory the Great account from the *Golden Legend*:

> It happened that a widow brought hosts every Sunday [for the priest] to [celebrate] Mass with … when Saint Gregory [was about to] give to her the holy sacrament in saying, [he said] May the body of our Lord Jesus Christ keep you into everlasting life … this woman began to laugh at Saint Gregory, and he withdrew his hand, and placed the sacrament upon the altar. And he asked her, before the people, why she laughed, and she said: Because that the bread that I have made with my proper hands, you call the body of our Lord Jesus Christ.
>
> Saint Gregory put himself to prayer with the people, for to pray to God that hereupon he would show his grace for to confirm our belief, and when they were risen from prayer, Saint Gregory saw the holy sacrament in figure of a piece of flesh as great as the little finger of an hand, and by the prayers of Saint Gregory, the flesh of the sacrament turned into appearance of bread as it had been before, and therewith he gave communion to the woman, which after was more religious, and the people more firm in the faith.

Similar to many other Eucharistic miracles, this one involved a person or perhaps a priest whose faith was waning and who was given evidence of Jesus' presence in the host. The idea behind such a miracle is that God permitted this to strengthen everyone's faith and to demonstrate that he is actually present in the host at Mass. All that said, however, it is a relatively symbolic miracle which aims at teaching about faith as opposed to the mystical and absurd legend of Edmund and his head.

Alternatively, St Augustine, for example, acknowledged critiques of the practices of the Eastern hermits in the Egyptian desert in *The Ways of the Catholic Church*. According to some, their extreme asceticism and seclusion 'were no longer useful' for the church or society. Augustine encouraged continence of the heart and poverty of spirit in reaction to this while residing in the context of a town like Hippo. His monastic group at Hippo maintained their communal living while also fulfilling their pastoral duties. 'The love of neighbour was merely another expression of the love of God,' according to Augustine. Even if doing so interfered with a desire for introspection and academic pursuits, he considered the call to serve in the church as a necessity that must be answered. Known as The Rule of Saint Augustine, it was carried by small groups of hermit monks and nuns into the sixth century but never quite truly took off – that is until much later in the eleventh century when rapid reform occurred and the veneration of Augustine and adoption of his rule spread quickly through a religious renaissance. Nevertheless, as with the other saints, their capacity for mystical legends is limited and rather their stories are steeped in historical evidence.

The point here is to show that the ninth century marked a turning point in the role of saints in Christian society. From the redemption of the faith after iconoclasm, saints like Edmund represent a seedling in the ecosystem of sainthood that will soon burst into vibrancy in the Golden Age of the eleventh, twelfth, and thirteenth centuries – closely reflecting the image of the saint which we imagine today. This will all be explored in greater detail in the following chapters, but for now, we turn to the next significant aspect of Edmund's story.

As of now, we have primarily focused on the Mediterranean, Arab Peninsula and North Africa for our narrative (with a little bit of the Horn of Africa sprinkled in). Nevertheless, from Chapter 2, the borders of Christendom have been slowly expanding and solidifying throughout Northern Europe and across modern-day France, Ireland and England. Just as the rise of Islam had threatened the fabric of Christendom in the south-east and south-west, a new foe from the fjords of Scandinavia was on the move. It began as a nuisance but over a period of 120 years rapidly changed the landscape of western Europe forever.

To understand why Edmund was tied to a tree and tortured into renouncing his faith, we have to travel back to the previous century to understand how these Arctic barbarians popped into existence. It would be expected that the influence of environmental and demographic determinism would be negligible as these factors represent a gradual and subtle change over many centuries. Nevertheless, prevailing evidence illustrates that while these changes were not observed by Scandinavians, they provided the foundation to which state formation, technological development and economic stability within Viking culture could form. The success of Viking conquest and expansion was dependent upon large populations. Such rapid growth occurred during a period of prolonged warm climate in the North Atlantic known as the 'Medieval Climate Optimum'. Occurring between *c.*900 and *c.*1300 (though on the rise from the eighth century), summer temperatures were approximately 1.5–2°C higher than the present. Temperatures in the North Sea also increased by an average of 1.5°C, and temperatures escalated 4°C within the Scandinavian fjords. The result of this, as evidenced by pollen analysis from agricultural regions in Scandinavia, demonstrates that the heatwave resulted in more land being cultivated and an increase in cereal production. Ester Boserup's agricultural intensification theory stating that population drives the intensity of agricultural production would indicate that the increase in cultivation and yield is thus a result of population growth. This theory complements the archaeological evidence of urban expansion, that black-earth sites with massive occupational layers demonstrate a rapid development of urban centres over time. Sites such as Hedeby, Ribe, Birka and Åhus, founded at the beginning of the Viking age, all show rapid expansion as population and industry grew. In fact, archaeological records have indicated that the population density rose from 0.1 persons per square km during Neolithic Scandinavia, to four persons per square km in the Viking age. As such, it becomes apparent that there is a +4 per cent growth rate per year between *c.*400 and *c.*700. Such a rapid growth led to the consequences outlined by the Malthusian Theory. This theory dictates that the population will grow exponentially alongside the arithmetic growth of food and resource supply. At the point in which the exponential overtakes the arithmetic, a crisis will ensue unless demands are achieved. The combination of population growth and climate changes led to the demand for resources, land and food which prompted Scandinavians to mitigate this via wealth-based raiding across Europe.

A question that scratches the heads of historians is why the Vikings chose to raid rather than conventionally expand. The answer becomes clear when understanding that the Viking age was caused by this demand for resources. Early Viking activity was primarily wealth-based to acquire the necessary supplies to relieve demands in Scandinavia. The cleric Dudo of Normandy records that:

> These people who insolently abandon themselves to excessive indulgence […] once they have grown up, the young quarrel violently […] about property, and if they increase too greatly in number, and cannot acquire sufficient arable land […] a large group is selected to be driven away to foreign peoples and realms to fight.

While being a religiously charged and biased account, this does show recognition that wealth-based raiding was used to relieve the pressures of overpopulation. Clearly, by the eighth and ninth centuries, demands and pressures were at an all-time high, which provoked regions to shift methods to fulfil such demands. But what if the necessity for this was, in the short-term period at least, caused by growing pressures on their borders from solidifying empires? Historian, Bjørn Myhre has noted that within the history of Scandinavia is an example of 'changing cultural and political relations on the borders of an empire' that meant the development of the Viking age was a consequence of the empires in post-Roman Europe. During this century, nations across the continent advanced in state formation, centralisation of power, and establishing an economy leading to the foundation of multiple empires. Such empires include the Frankish Empire encapsulating central Europe; the Abbasid caliphate spanning the Middle East and Northern Africa; and the eastern Roman Empire extending over the Balkans, East Asia and West Africa. Did such empires influence and pressurise the Vikings into constructing their own empire?

Previously, Norway had never been united under a native king; however, thirteenth-century Icelandic literature attributes the ninth- and tenth-century migration period to the attempt by Harald Finehair to extend his power over the whole country. While the famous battle of Hafrsfjord is traditionally seen as Harald's final effort to unify Norway, it is believed that his rule extended only over western and southern areas in the Bergen region. Though he was unlikely to ever have had control of the whole nation, it is still important to recognise the attempt to establish a unified nation and empire by an individual. Denmark provides compelling evidence that external pressure influenced political efforts. Situated along the border with the Frankish Empire, Denmark was the first nation in Scandinavia to centralise its power. Harald Bluetooth originally ruled Denmark, yet in *c.*970 he unified parts of Scandinavia by claiming subjugation and kingship over Norway. Bluetooth also developed political connections with Normandy through Richard I, the Count of Rouen. The accumulation of evidence surrounding Harald's external political alliances, as well as his internal expansionist pursuits, demonstrate that external influences and pressures did motivate some Viking kings to follow suit in state formation, centralisation of power, and expansion. Noteworthy, however, is the notion that state formation could only have occurred so rapidly and successfully because climate conditions and population growth combined to produce the circumstances necessary for establishing a stable economy, developing infrastructure, and acquiring new territory. Moreover, this theory only describes the motivations behind state formation in Denmark; the state formations of Sweden and Norway occur after Denmark and as such were potentially encouraged by Denmark's advancements rather than pressures from external empires.

Whatever the case may be as to how the Vikings came into existence – most simply it was through a multifaceted web of reasons – once they were on the scene, they were deadly foes of Christendom. The predominant reason behind this was ideological. Norse mythology is one of the few known world mythologies to include the pre-ordained and permanent ruin of all creation and all the powers that shaped it, resulting in the psychological implication that, as a Viking, your fate is already decided and thus your actions do not matter. Honour, warfare and fatalism were deeply interwoven beliefs stemming from cultural traditions of duty and predestination in Norse mythology which amalgamate into a highly militarised Viking age. Historians have pointed towards evidence of the extreme risk Vikings took on journeys and conquests, which were rife with shipwrecks, disease, violence and death, as a sign of this ideological fearlessness. Even in their worshipping practices we find undertones of death, magic and a deeply interwoven connection between man and god. One of the greatest sources of this can be found within the observed worshipping practices of the Swedes from Adam of Bremen. He writes:

> That folk [Swedes] has a very famous temple in Uppsala, situated not far from the city of Sigtuna and Björkö. In this temple, entirely decked out in gold, the people worship the statues of three gods in such wise that the mightiest of them, Thor, occupies a throne in the middle of the chamber; Wotan and Frikko have places either side. […] If plague and famine threaten, a libation is poured to the idol Thor; if war, to Wotan, if marriages, to Frikko.
>
> […] It is customary also to solemnize in Uppsala at nine-year intervals a general feast of all the provinces of Sweden. From attendance at this festival no one is exempted. Kings and people all send their gifts and, what is more distressing than any king of punishment, those who have already adopted Christianity redeem themselves through these ceremonies. The sacrifice is of this nature: of every living thing that is male, they offer nine heads, with the blood of which is customary to placate the gods of this sort. The bodies they hang in the sacred grove that adjoins the temple. Now this grove is so sacred that each and every tree in it is believed divine because of the death or putrefaction of the victims. Even dogs and horses hang there with men. Furthermore, the incantations customarily chanted in the ritual of sacrifice of this king are manifold and unseemly; it is better to keep silent about them.

As such, the mentality of Vikings simply separated them from other kingdoms and instigated an age where the boundaries of exploration, conquest and trade were pushed by a mentality geared for war and predestined death. This all came into fruition in 793 when the infamous story of the Lindisfarne attack unravelled. The *Anglo-Saxon Chronicle*, a chronological account of the Anglo-Saxon age, provides vivid details about the attack:

> This year came dreadful fore-warnings over the land of the Northumbrians, terrifying the people most woefully: these were immense sheets of light rushing through the air, and whirlwinds, and fiery dragons flying across the firmament. These tremendous tokens were soon followed by a great famine: and not long after, on the sixth day before the ides of January in the same year, the harrowing inroads of heathen men made lamentable havoc in the church of God in Holy-island, by rapine and slaughter.

This was just a small taste of what was to come. From 793, a series of small Viking fleets led hit-and-run attacks on poorly defended (or entirely undefended) coastal monasteries and towns along the coast of England and modern-day France. Two areas of the Carolingian Empire came under attack at this time. The first was Frisia where Danish raiders had made their way south along the Frankish coast, the second was Aquitaine, which suffered a series of attacks from Norse invaders well into the ninth century. In Aquitaine, a particular account written by Ermentarius details how monks would periodically abandon their monastic community because of the relentless attacks – only to return in the autumn when the volatile sea conditions made Viking attacks difficult. He writes in the 830s that the island monastery of Noimoutier was deemed to be so unsafe that it was entirely abandoned.

In Frisia, however, the attacks were far worse. The trading centre of Dorestad was the first to be sacked in 834. The *Annals of St Bertin* reported that 'they ravaged everything, killed some of the men, carried others off as captives, and burned down part of the emporium'. In the following three years, the port was continuously ravaged by barbarians. Louis the Pious made strenuous efforts to defend the coast by building a fleet alongside small ring fortresses with garrisons but the Viking attacks were relentless. Yet what is particularly notable about the raid of 834 on Dorestad is its seemingly perfect timing in conjunction with regional political instability.

The Frankish Empire, also known as the Carolingian Empire, was a powerful European state that existed from the eighth to the tenth century. It was founded by the Frankish King Charlemagne, who united several Germanic tribes and expanded his kingdom through a series of successful military campaigns. Charlemagne was the son of Frankish King Pepin the Short. He became king in 768 after the death of his brother Carloman. Charlemagne was a skilled military commander and expanded his kingdom through a series of successful campaigns. He conquered the Lombard Kingdom in Italy, subjugated the Saxons in Germany, and defeated the Muslim Moors in Spain. He was also a patron of the arts and education. He established schools and libraries throughout his kingdom and invited scholars from all over Europe to his court in Aachen. He also promoted the spread of Christianity and was crowned Holy Roman Emperor by Pope Leo III in 800. After his death in 814, Charlemagne was succeeded by his son Louis the Pious, a devout Christian and a patron of the church. He continued his father's policies of promoting education and culture, but he struggled to maintain the unity of the Frankish Empire. He had three sons: Lothar, Louis and Charles the Bald. In a crisis of succession, each was given equal portions of the empire which led to a bloodthirsty and devastating power vacuum over territory. The year 834 was marked by a failed revolt by Lothar as well as his exile to Italy. Not only did this cause instability and weakness within the empire but West Frankish sources even claimed that Louis encouraged Viking attacks on his father's land to undermine his power and allow Lothar to seize it. According to such sources, Lothar was to reward them with grants of land on his accession in 840. This spiralled out of control as the return of fortuitous raiders to Scandinavia prompted and encouraged others to follow in their footsteps.

Across the Channel, raids on England were sporadic but deadly. Following Lindisfarne, Monkwearmouth was raided in 794 but it was not until the 830s that the raids escalated rapidly. Sheppey was the first to be sacked in 835, and in 836 King Egbert of Wessex fought off an attack at Carhampton and Hingston Down. Despite the *Anglo-Saxon Chronicle* regarding these raiders purely as 'Danes', it was likely that it was Norwegians who used parts of Ireland as a raiding base that were tormenting the English coastline.

From 841 to 875, a second phase of attacks occurred with a heightened increase in number, scope and scale. An account from an incursion on the Seine describes such a devastating attack:

> The Northmen appeared on 12 May, led by Oskar. They set fire to the city of Rouen on 14 May and left on 16 May. On 24 May they burned down the monastery of Jumieges, on 25 May the abbey of St Wandrille was ransomed for 6 pounds [of silver], and on 28 May monks arrived from St Denis and redeemed sixty-eight captives for 26 pounds. On 31 May the pagans made for the sea, and although Vulfard, a royal vassal, opposed them with an army, the pagans were not at all prepared to fight.

As if they were a ghost in the night, these attacks were characterised by their swiftness as Viking raiders left as quickly as they had arrived after plundering, burning, killing and enslaving the inhabitants. In this time, it was almost impossible for local armies to be mustered or defences be raised. Raids of this nature endured through the early 840s on both sides of the Channel with London, Rochester, Southampton, Quentovic, Nantes, Hamburg and Paris being victims of the Viking invasion.

A sudden change occurred in the winter of 843 when a Viking fleet landing on an island off the coast of Southern Aquitaine 'brought houses from the mainland, and decided to spend the winter there as if in a permanent settlement'. From hereafter Aquitaine was hardly ever free from a Scandinavian presence, with fleets camping on the Loire almost every year. Likewise, in England, the *Anglo-Saxon Chronicle* recorded a similar change in tactics as 'the heathen for the first time remained over the winter' in 851. Though not staying for long, this prompted a much larger army, known as the 'Great Heathen Army' to camp in Thetford, East Anglia and remain for many winters within England – eventually settling and establishing what is known as Danelaw. Such an army signified the exponential increase in the size of raiding parties since the former attack on Lindisfarne. Despite the *Anglo-Saxon Chronicle* reporting 3 ships in 798, this quickly grew to 9 ships in 835, 13 in 820, and up to 25–35 in 836. It is equally recorded that Ragnar's fleet on the Seine in 845 numbered 120 ships, and the fleet that stormed Canterbury and London in 851 contained 350 ships. Not only were there increased numbers, but also the number of raids at any given time increased. One larger group of Danes that was raiding Frisia in 850 divided into three, with one group occupying Dorestad, another invading Flanders, and the third wintering on Thanet in Kent. As such, Viking armies were continuously evolving and changing size, leadership, and often target, as Viking raiding parties were even known to attack each other when their paths crossed.

Nevertheless, as the Vikings' prowess grew, so did their ambitions and expeditions. One striking example of such adventures occurred in 844 when both Frankish and Arab sources reported a fleet of Viking raiders that had previously sacked Nantes and Toulouse making their way into Islamic Iberia at Lisbon and Seville before being defeated by an Umayyad army. Another army, after leaving the Loire in 858, ventured to the Mediterranean to raid along the coast of Spain and North Africa. They also sacked various places along the coast of Southern France and Northern Italy, where they looted Pisa and other towns. Such a development also showed that the Vikings were penetrating further inward, as before 840 only coastal sites were targets, while by 865, Fleury, Orleans, Tours and Nantes were all victims of raiding.

With such a rapid expansion in the size of armies alongside the extended periods of stay, the Vikings at this point began to become increasingly interwoven with the internal politics of the kingdoms they were raiding. As mentioned, one form of this was through the exploitation of political disputes such as that of the War of the Three Brothers. In fact, they capitalised on all three of the contenders of the Frankish throne, often joining forces with Pippin II, Lothar, Bretons and Aquitainians. In England, however, their influence was far more than a 'mercenary for hire'. Rather here the Vikings were able to install puppet kings to the various kingdoms operating within the island, such as Ceowulf, 'a foolish king's thane', in Mercia in 873, but also in Northumbria and East Anglia. Unlike the Arab invasion, which was rebuked at the borders of Europe, the pagans were beginning to infiltrate Christian society. Certain Viking leaders were even adopted into Frankish and Anglo-Saxon politics through cash, land, or both. A former king of Denmark, for example, was known as 'a most Christian leader' and died defending the island of Walcheren from a Viking attack in 837. Nevertheless, such successes to overpower paganism with Christianity were limited. Rather a payment of tribute, a time-honoured tradition since the Fall of Rome, was opted for instead. Evidence has shown the money paid to the Vikings in the ninth century totalled 30,000lb of silver which equates to 7 million silver pennies. It is also noted that the overall output for Frankish mints in the same period was 50 million coins and that the Viking tribute is approximately 14 per cent of this. Despite such a tactic being looked down upon by many, it seemed to have worked well with the raiders who were, in essence, in search of booty. Evidence also shows that the Anglo-Saxon and Frankish kingdoms were able to afford such prices, even if it took a while to gather the funds. The church deeply resented such practice as the defence of the realm was determined to be a secular responsibility, not that of the church.

From accumulating such vast wealth in the region, the year 867 ushered in a new stage of Viking raids – expansion into England and Francia. The *Anglo-Saxon Chronicle* details the following: 'In this year Halfdan shared out the lands of the Northumbrians, and they proceeded to plough and to support themselves.' This is a milestone in Scandinavian history as the previously unique culture and society of the Vikings now aimed to align itself more with its European neighbours. Despite originally searching through the English countryside for rich pickings, the 'Great Heathen Army' is also seen to emulate Halfdan by settling in Mercia in 877, and East Anglia in 879/80 and 896. Of course, this was not a unified shift as raiding parties still tormented both sides of the Channel for plunder and blood. One such contemporary detailed the bloodthirst of these pagans:

> The Northmen never stopped enslaving and killing the Christian people, pulling down churches, demolishing fortifications and burning towns. And on every road lay the corpses of clergy and laity, noblemen and commoners, women, youngsters and babies. Indeed there was no village or highway where the dead did not lie, and all were filled with grief and torment as they saw the Christian populace being destroyed to the point of extinction.

The response to the Heathen Army settling, expanding and raiding was varied amongst opposing rulers. In England, Alfred required several years of reform, development and learning in order to devise an effective strategy to expel these foreign pests. The 878 battle of Edington was the result of such vigorous opposition as opposed to the common pay-off tactic; this year was marked by the establishment of various fortresses along the south coast alongside the development of a standing and naval fleet. By 892, the Vikings discovered that their previous freedom to roam the seas and land was now incredibly restricted around the English Channel by local armies.

In Francia, the presence of the Heathen Army was still strong, so much so that the stability of the kingdom and fate of the Carolingians under Charles the Simple was dependent upon the strength of opposition against the Vikings. Earlier in 885/6, the former king, Charles the Fat, was deposed after his failure to repel the invading armies from Paris, only for the city to be saved by its Count, Odo, who later would be called to replace the king due to his defence of the besieged city. Thus, with the new army, Charles the Simple used a combination of pay-offs and attacks to repel the invaders from 892. Despite sources being limited in the following decade, Charles did secure a victory in 911 at Chartres. A treaty was drawn up with the Viking leader, Rollo, at the mouth of the Seine after recognising his power and utility as a strong presence in the region. Rollo was baptised and pledged allegiance to Charles which ushered in a transformation from pagan to Christian, and from Viking to Norman; this treaty would establish Normandy and the dynasty that would eventually lead a conquest into England in 1066. From hereafter, the barbarians were integrated into civilisation.

Despite Christianity taking a foothold in Scandinavia by the end of the ninth and tenth century, throughout this whole narrative Christianity was repeatedly threatened. As such, during this time there was a burst of Christian theology (particularly in Francia) whereby some contemporaries aimed to defend the faith while others sought to condemn Christians for their sins. If we hark back to the fall of Rome as seen with Augustine and the many other times Christianity has been under threat for that matter, widespread panic ensued when defeated at the hands of non-Christians, especially when, as with this example, said attack was directly on the church. The majority of sources on Viking attacks inherently were from clerics, monks, bishops and other ecclesiastical officials. As such, there was a deeply religious paranoia that reverberated across Anglo-Saxon England and Francia during the eighth and ninth centuries that began with the attack on Lindisfarne. Upon hearing about the sack of the monastery, the renowned scholar Alcuin of York was at the court of Charlemagne. He stated in a letter to Higbald, the bishop of Lindisfarne:

> When I was with you, the closeness of your love would give me great joy. In contrast, now that I am away from you, the distress of your suffering fills me daily with deep grief, when heathens desecrated God's sanctuaries, and poured the blood of saints within the compass of the altar, destroyed the house of our hope, trampled the bodies of saints in God's temple like animal dung in the street ...

Alcuin believed that this terrible incident was God's retaliation for the people's sins, as he continued to write:

> What security is there for the churches of England if St Cuthbert with so great a throng of saints will not defend his own? Either this is the beginning of greater grief or the sins of those who live there have brought it upon themselves.

Such invasions, therefore, became quickly associated with the notion of divine punishment for the sins of the Frankish people. A vast number of sources, for example, denoted the Vikings as 'pagani' and the Franks as 'christiani'. Various theological conclusions hereafter became popular. Many contemporaries sought to perceive the Vikings as the rod of God's wrath sent to punish sinners in a fulfilment of the prophets' warnings, while others simply denoted the heathens as the people *of* God's wrath and thus were presented with an anti-Christian crusade. Nevertheless, what was clear is that the church had to be defended by the *milites Christi* who were called to take up arms through prayer and proclamation of the Gospel to expel these demons.

In regards to the former theological argument that this was a punishment from God, this was the focus of the Synod of Meaux and Paris in 845/6 which concluded:

> Wherefore, because obedience did not follow God's commands, as was necessary, the Lord sent 'from the north', from which, according to the prophet, 'evil shall break forth', apostles befitting our merits, namely those cruel and most savage persecutors of Christianity, the Northmen, who, coming as far as Paris, showed what God commanded.

It appears from this Synod that there were three predominant elements: the Franks failed to live as God commanded; the prophets warned of their disobedience; and the assertion that the Vikings had consequently been sent from God. In terms of what the specific sin was – it came in a variety of forms. Carefully drawn-together parallels by the bishops of Pitres in 862 suggested that the pillaging of the land was happening as people had lost the fruits of faith, hope and love; people were being murdered as they had slain with the sword of sin; churches, monasteries and holy sites were being burnt because the fires of iniquity were bursting within; the relics of former saints were being destroyed and stolen as the Franks had expelled the Holy Spirit; and finally monks, clerics and bishops were being forced to flee as they had failed to subdue evil. Alongside this, specific allegations against individuals were set forth by contemporary authors. Charles the Bald in 853, for example, was accused by Audradus Modicus as being the sinful cause of the recent attacks on Tours for his appointment of a Lotharingian to the see of Chartres earlier that year. Equally, in the Middle Kingdom, Regino of Prum linked the various woes endured in the 880s to the attempt by Lothar II to divorce his wife and marry a concubine twenty years earlier. Kings were not the only ones to be accused, as the deaths of Robert of Anjou and Ramnulf of Poitou while fighting the Vikings in 866 were attributed by Archbishop Hincmar of Reims to their acceptance of lay abbacies in Tours and Poitiers. As such, the idea of sinful punishment became a sort of scapegoat whereby the failures of certain Franks, no matter how far in the past nor how relevant it was to the present, would be connected to being punished by God.

Frequently, many contemporary sources discuss a type of prophecy that warned the Franks of the Vikings. First mentioned by Alcuin in his letter following the attack of Lindisfarne, the verse from Jeremiah 1:14 was commonly used out of context: 'Out of the north shall evil break forth.'

Others also comment on the attacks in reference to the history of Israel as described by the Old Testament which demonstrates the various and differing approaches to scripture from Carolingian clerics. Particularly, an exegesis of Lamentations 4:12 is given in reference to the events of 845 when Ragnar entered the seemingly impenetrable city of Paris: 'None of the kings of the earth would believe, nor could any of the inhabitants of the world accept that the enemy could enter the gates of Jerusalem.'

Another school of thought was that the Vikings were sent to chastise the faithless Carolingian Franks. In the *Annals of St Bertin* around the year 881, King Louis III is seen to flee despite no one pursuing him. Yet, as the *Annals* describe: 'God's judgement thereby revealing that what had been done by the Northmen had not been accomplished by man's strength, but by God's.'

That being said, it should be noted that it was not only the Vikings whom the Franks believed they had received from God. Elsewhere, as already touched upon, the Muslim raids in the south were equally a nuisance and were also received as God's displeasure. Still, it shows how deeply emphasised the sinfulness of people was within the church.

Alternatively, perhaps despite being a century or two early for the 'Call to Arms' by Pope Urban II, the Vikings were embarking upon a pagan proto-crusade. Historians have identified a variety of features within Viking behaviour and their expeditions that would seemingly constitute there being a deliberate attack on the 'Christian' element of the Vikings' Christian enemies:

1. The destruction of churches and monasteries
2. Attacks on altars and reliquaries
3. The murder, torture and enslavement of monks
4. The pagan practice of ritual sacrifice

The focus of a pagan-derived crusade occurs from strongly Christian perspectives rather than pagan fanatics, yet it offers an insightful look at how contemporaries interpreted the events happening around them. Many of the above can be fairly easily dispelled through evidential reasoning. The argument that the Vikings were regarded as 'pagani' by contemporaries is limited when noting that the *Annals of St Bertin* describes the Scandinavians as 'Northmanni' 116 times and 'Dani' 36 times, but 'pagani' only 9. Likewise, the *Annals of Xanten* and *Annals of Fulda* have similar figures. Equally, 'pagani' was also used to describe any kind of 'barbari'; Muslims in the south, Slavs in the east, as well as the invading Magyars were all denoted at times as 'pagani'. It simply denoted the self-consciousness of the Franks as a Christian Empire against otherness. This idea even extended to the Byzantine Empire whose Orthodoxy and gradual separation from western Europe was becoming more distinct. Liudprand, bishop of the Holy Cremonese church, provides one of the more humorous and emotive descriptions of such tensions and distinctions between the east and west when he was sent on an embassy mission to Constantinople in 968. He says:

> We arrived in Constantinople on the day before the nones of June (968) and, as an insult to you [Emperor Otto I], we were received in a shameful way, rudely, and shamefully handled. We were closed into a certain mansion, quite big and open, which neither protected from cold nor kept out the heat. It added to our disastrous position that the wine of the Greeks was undrinkable for us because of their commingling pitch, pine sap, and plaster in it.

Exhausted, thirsty and cold, Liudprand's expedition further worsened upon meeting the emperor's brother; it is here we truly see the tensions between the two empires:

> For he [the emperor's brother] called you [Otto] not 'emperor', but rather, out of disdain, 'king' in our tongue. When I answered this by saying the meaning was the same even if the signifier is different, he told me I had come not for the sake of peace but to squabble.

This was only the beginning, as we see that upon meeting the Byzantine Emperor Nicephorus the reason behind the poor treatment of Liudprand and his embassy becomes clearer. Nicephorus says:

> We should have, indeed we wished to, welcome you kindly and magnificently; but the impiety of your lord does not permit it, a man who arrogated Rome to himself with a hostile occupation, who took it by force from Berengar and Adalbert [Former kings of Italy] against all law and custom, who killed some of the Romans by the sword, others by hanging, deprived others of their eyes, consigned still others to exile, and on top of that attempted to subdue his power at the cities of our empire by murder and arson.
>
> If they were powerful, if they were emperors of the Romans, why were they leaving Rome to the power of the whores? Were not some of the most holy popes expelled, others so cast down they did not have enough to pay their daily expenses or for charity? Did Adalbert not strip the churches of the most holy apostles with his robbery? Which of you emperors, led

> by zeal for God, bothered to avenge such an unworthy crime and return the holy church to its proper condition?

It is no surprise perhaps that Liudprand considers Nicephorus to be a monster when he later says that:

> He did not permit it when I wanted to respond to this and throw out a counter-argument worthy of his inflation; instead he added, as if to insult us: 'You are not Romans, but Lombards!'

In return, Liudprand says the following, which truly underpins the separation and evolution of western Europe from its predecessor:

> The annals recognise that fratricidal Romulus, from whose name they are called Romans, was born to a whore, that is, he was generated in defilement; and he made a refuge for himself where he welcomed defaulted debtors from foreign climes, runaway slaves, murderers, and people who deserved death for their crimes, and he attracted such a throng of people that he called them Romans.
>
> We, that means Lombards, Saxons, Franks, Lotharingians, Bavarians, Swabians, Burgundians, so disdain them that we utter no other insult than 'You Roman!' to our enemies when aroused, and we understand that single term, the name of the Romans, to include every baseness, every cowardice, every kind of greed, every promiscuity, every mendacity, indeed every vice.

It goes without saying that this was a defining moment at the court of the emperor. Nevertheless, the interaction tells us so much about how the Christian Empire viewed itself as distinctly separate and nuanced from any pre-existing culture group. Here we see the culmination of the centuries of history, as the East and West had vastly different attitudes regarding the former Roman Empire. Although the Byzantines were becoming more distinct over time, as we saw with Justinian, there was still a Roman link between the old and the new that would endure. In Europe, this link was Christendom and thus the Roman past was held with a bitter taste. Thus, in this rather long-winded detraction from the Vikings, the Franks and the Christian Empire were surrounded, quite literally, by this notion of otherness and 'pagani' – Vikings to the north, Muslims to the south, and the newly divorced Byzantines to the east.

Though the concern of the Vikings to protect and propagate their religion in the same way as the Muslims, for example, is limited, to say the Scandinavians targeted attacks on churches and monasteries to weaken Christianity is an overstatement when you consider the immense wealth the Frankish church held in the ninth and tenth centuries: inventories of ecclesiastical treasures, gold- and silver-gilded crosses, reliquaries, lamps, ornaments, gems and offerings would cumulate in vast amounts of wealth. The accounts of the Abbey of St Riquier in 831 note that the offerings to the tomb of the saint were no less than 300lb of silver per week. No wonder the Vikings swarmed to such sites. Nevertheless, the Synod of Savonnieres in 859 showed that it was not only the Vikings who attacked such sites. They accused Bretons of violating churches and stealing sacred vessels and church treasures. Similarly, Lothar I is said to have sacked and burnt churches in the West Frankish kingdom during the War of the Three Brothers. In short, the religious motivations for Vikings to seek conquest are scarce and rather such a notion only represents the paranoia of the churchmen and Christian Empire in seemingly being surrounded by opposing ideologies.

This, therefore, speaks of a wider understanding about the Viking age, as the majority of sources are tainted by a Christian perspective. While this does distort the picture to a degree, it is crucial in examining the paranoia of Christendom. In spite of such attacks and the introspective look at their sinfulness, is it no wonder why in England, for example, faith is reinforced and defended through the use of martyrdom? Unlike the aforementioned saints such as Gregory or Augustine, Edmund was not a particularly zealous figure, rather his death occurred through a requirement to defend his realm. Nevertheless, his timely veneration in conjunction with such a prominent obsession with sin harks back to the idea of Christ as the original martyrdom. Without getting too theological, God declared that 'without the shedding of blood, there is no forgiveness' in Hebrews 9:22 as through the shedding of blood, redemption for one's sin is provided. The Law of Moses then further built upon this by providing a way for people to be considered 'sinless' or 'right' in God's eyes – the offering of animals sacrificed for every sin they committed. These sacrifices were only temporary, though, and were really a foreshadowing of the perfect, once-for-all sacrifice of Christ on the cross (Hebrews 10:10). Christ, then, was martyred to absolve the people of their sins and stand as a symbol of such. With sin being at the forefront of the church, here we see the beginnings of a transformation whereby saints, rather than being a feature of Christianity, became a tool – or Swiss-army knife – used by the church to maintain order. Returning to St Edmund, we quickly see this become apparent in the construction of his hagiography. A hagiography consists of biographies of saints, martyrs, and other holy figures that describe the lives of these figures (known as a Vita), their miraculous deeds (known as Miracula), and their enduring influence on their respective religious communities (Translatio).

Hagiographies typically follow a similar and formulaic structure, with an opening section that describes the life and upbringing of the holy figure, followed by a section that details their miraculous deeds and their religious teachings. The final section focuses on the death of the saint and their continuing legacy. They often also contain a mix of historical fact and mythological embellishment, with the goal of inspiring readers to lead more virtuous lives and emulate the examples of the holy figures they describe. For example, some hagiographies may describe the saint performing miracles or having visions, while others may describe the saint overcoming personal struggles or facing persecution for their religious beliefs. Archdeacon Herman, a character we will return to later when understanding more about how the church appropriated their saints, writes the following in the hagiography about Edmund:

> Remaining, by God's grace, the defender of East Anglia, Edmund provided unceasing support all over that region. For we believe he merited this privilege from the Almighty: that none other than God should succeed him in those parts. For England at that time was divided under the rule of many kings, the lion's share having fallen to one called Aethelred in Wessex. Even then, it persisted in the Christian faith, except that the eastern parts had been shattered in by the onslaught of pagans. During Aethelred's reign this frenzied storm of paganism, hateful to God, struck time after time with all its might. During his reign, God intervened, and the wicked, piratical race of Danes was dispersed, diminished, and cut off in their invasion, for the time had come for God to display His vengeance through St Edmund and to reveal the saint who enjoyed His favour.

Written in the 1090s, we see here how Herman really exaggerates the divine aid given to Edmund despite the fact that the battle was a crushing blow and successes against the Vikings were limited in this period. This emphasis is evidence of Edmund's story being used as a tool for absolution. Herman refutes the contemporary notion that the Vikings were the wrath of God by flipping the story so that Edmund was God's vengeance and saved Christianity. It is a tool that harks back to the time of Augustine when he used and exaggerated the example of the Romans taking refuge in the church and being saved as a sign of God's protection as opposed to the fact that the empire around them was crumbling. Is it no coincidence that between the eighth and ninth century the number of Christian martyrs that are venerated doubled? Likewise, across the whole medieval period, the number of martyrs peaks in the ninth century during the onslaught of the Vikings. With the threat of paganism on home soil – as is especially the case with the establishment of Danelaw in England – Christianity was thus once again called to defend itself from accusations in the midst of death and murder at the hands of foreign demons. Martyrs of the ninth century served a purpose and therefore stood as a symbol of absolution from the paranoia that medieval culture was underpinned by sin. The success of this utilisation would lay the groundwork later used by churchmen during the golden age of monasticism to appropriate, capitalise and wield the narrative on their saints in order to seek various ulterior gains.

Part II
The Golden Age

Chapter Six
Secularity vs Sanctity

When asking anyone what comes to mind when they think of the medieval era, many will describe a picturesque (and somewhat violent) scene involving knights, princesses, pageantry, and, of course, castles. Despite venturing through five centuries thus far (half of what is considered the thousand-year span of the medieval era), it is doubtful that many would note Byzantines, Arabs and Huns. The question is, therefore, when did all this come about? Historians disagree on a plethora of things about the Middle Ages, yet there appears to be, in some sense, a degree of consistency that the tenth century, specifically Francia, endured a transformation, even a mutation, in culture, power and society that introduced what many know as the feudal system. This chapter is to explore this transformation and seek to understand its impact on saints, their cults, and their role within the church.

Firstly, the term 'feudalism'. Although the term itself is derived from the Latin word *feodum* meaning 'fief' or 'landholding', it was only in the eighteenth century that the term was first coined. Montesquieu, in his book *The Spirit of the Laws* published in 1748, first used the term to describe the system of government and social organisation that prevailed in medieval Europe. He described feudalism as a system of reciprocal rights and obligations between lords and vassals. According to him, the feudal system was characterised by a complex network of relationships between the king, the nobles, and the peasants. This, however, is rather problematic as it attempts to oversimplify what was a highly complex and, at times, fluid structure. This framework is therefore inadequate to capture the changes that occurred in the preceding centuries. Rather than a linear progression from a 'pre-feudal' to a 'feudal' society, there was a more complex process of social and political transformation that was the 'feudal revolution'. This revolution was characterised by three interrelated changes: the fragmentation of political power; the emergence of a new class of regional lords; and the development of a new social hierarchy. These changes were driven by a combination of external pressures, such as Viking invasions and Arab raids, and internal developments, such as the breakdown of the Carolingian Empire and the rise of local elites.

One of the most significant aspects of the feudal revolution was the fragmentation of political power. This occurred as a result of the collapse of the Carolingian Empire and the emergence of local lords who were able to carve out their own territories and assert their own authority. This fragmentation, however, was not a simple process of decentralisation, but rather involved the creation of a new kind of political structure based on a system of overlapping and nested lordships. The system was characterised by a complex web of relationships between lords and vassals that were based on personal ties of loyalty and service rather than formal legal structures.

The emergence of a new class of regional lords was another key aspect of the feudal revolution. These lords were not simply traditional aristocrats but rather represented a new kind of elite that was characterised by its wealth, military power and territorial control – the knight. At Conques in Rouergue, for example, the monks recalled how Count Raymond III (961–1010) had insisted against their will on building a castle, declaring that his intention was 'to subjugate by his violence [*violentia sua*] and submit to his lordship those who neglected to render their due submission to him'. Thus, the new system of power was underpinned by castles and violence. This new class of lords was able to assert its authority over a wider range of people and resources than had been possible in the past, and played a key role in shaping the political and social landscape of medieval Europe.

Finally, the feudal revolution led to the development of a new social hierarchy, in which social status was increasingly defined by the possession of land and the ability to extract resources from it. This hierarchy was based on a system of reciprocal obligations between lords and vassals, in which the lords provided protection and support in exchange for the vassals' loyalty and service. This system created a new kind of social order that was based on a more horizontal distribution of power than had been possible in the past.

Though a later example, Abbot Suger's *The Deeds of Louis the Fat* in the twelfth century is integral in understanding the practicalities and realities (and complexities) of the newly formed feudal system and the impact of the new warrior class. Suger, being a close confidant of King Louis of France, also provides one of the most detailed descriptions of what the newly emerged image of French kingship was, specifically through two overarching themes: 1) administrator of the kingdom; 2) a protector of the poor and churches.

Suger conceived that as an administrator of the kingdom, the king was responsible for the defence of the nation against foreign and domestic enemies. Domestic threats during Louis's reign are a particular point of interest as they provide insight into Suger's perspective of the twelfth-century feudal structures, as well as the relationship between the king and those within the hierarchy of feudalism. The concept of suzerainty is best exemplified through the example of the Auvergne campaign. In the first campaign against Count William VI in *c.*1122, Count Fulk of Anjou, Count Conan of Brittany, the Count of Nevers, and many other magnates owed their feudatory and allegiance to Louis VI. Equally, during the second expedition in *c.*1126, Louis's suzerainty is demonstrated by his host which consisted of the 'Count Charles of Flanders, Count Fulk of Anjou, the count of Brittany, a host from Normandy that owed tribute to the English King Henry, some barons, and enough of the magnates of the kingdom to have conquered even Spain'.

In this passage, Suger regards Louis as the highest feudal lord in France to which barons, counts and magnates owe their direct feudatory and allegiance. The intervention of William, Duke of Aquitaine, however, shows the complexities and paradoxes of this perceived suzerainty. After seeking peace, the duke met with Louis, and Suger details that the duke said, 'For even as justice demands the service of a vassal, so it also demands a just lordship. The count holds the Auvergne from me, which I in turn hold from you.' Notably, Suger details that the duke 'addressed him as his lord', once again highlighting Louis's supreme suzerainty. In this campaign, Louis is extending his jurisdiction over a sub-vassal who does not have direct feudatory from him. As Louis holds suzerainty over the duke and his lands, by extension this means he holds suzerainty over the sub-vassal. This prompts the notion that land-based fief is regarded as more important than personal relationships. To Suger, as Louis is the king of Francia and all the kingdom's land, his land fief prompted an authority and obligation which personal ties could not, which is why he intervened against a sub-vassal with whom he had no diplomatic or personal connection.

This passage and campaign demonstrate the confusing and paradoxical feudal system of the twelfth century, as the lines which defined the hierarchy and the nature of feudal relationships were becoming blurred. Suzerainty and feudal relationships became a primary tool for Louis and his government, and Suger thus understood feudalism through the notion of Mouvance. In *The Deeds*, Suger denotes the term 'feodum' to the select principalities and vassals whom Louis had overlordship of. In *c.*1109, Suger writes to the envoys of Henry I of England that:

> Your efforts have gained for you the duchy of Normandy by the noble leave of the lord king of the French. [...] the duchy was given in vassalage as fief by that same munificent right hand.

Further, he held that:

> Louis, king of the French, conducted himself toward Henry, king of the English and duke of the Normans, as toward a vassal, for he always kept in mind the lofty rank by which he towered over him.

According to Suger, royal policy focused on strengthening ties between the king and his great vassals, even though according to the Auvergne campaign, Suger also perceives physical land-based fiefs as being stronger than personal ties. Louis's ability to administer justice, however, was strengthened by the aid of bishops and vassals, as exemplified in the campaigns against Henry I of England (*c.*1109–1118) and Emperor Henry V (*c.*1124). The twelfth century saw a shift in power which placed great vassals almost equally among the king, resulting in a relationship and service that was mutual rather than owed. Suger subscribed to this concept as shown through his interactions with Count Theobald in *c.*1137. Theobald's brother, Stephen, had ascended to the English throne and as count, Theobald held Auxerre, Maligny, Ervy, Troyes and Châteauvillain as fiefs from Duke Odo II of Burgundy which placed him as a strategic asset.

Suger, in an attempt to admit Theobald to the king's entourage, continuously referred to him as Palatine, and writes, 'For it was our intention to bind that man to the lord king by an oath of fidelity since he excelled all in the kingdom in his faith and oath and legitimacy of his decrees.' This scenario demonstrates that Suger saw personal relationship as a strong approach to feudal relationship, even though this contradicts the previous example of land-based fief at Auvergne.

What do these conflicting concepts on the nature of feudalism mean for Suger's perception of kingship? A possible theory is understanding that within the pyramid of feudalism, fief was the base, the king was the summit, and what connected the dots in between was personal relationship. This results in the concept Suger presents: that a king ruled over his people because he ruled over the land. These contradictions, however, show that structures of feudalism were fluid and Suger was able to influence and wield these concepts to the scenario presented. In simple terms, Suger himself defined what feudalism meant in a situation, which is why his concepts contradict over time. In the example of Theobald, Suger saw personal relationship as the effective feudal tool to secure strategic alliances, while at Auvergne, the land-based fief was able to create a chain of authority that personal relationships could not. What is certain is that although the nature of feudalism was fluid, Suger placed his king at the summit of this hierarchical pyramid.

Suger also defines kingship as 'namely safeguarding the churches, protecting the poor and the needy, and working for the peace and defence of the kingdom'. Suger reiterates this throughout his life as he writes that the king 'attacked the count of Clermont and his allies' because he was told 'about the savage attacks on churches' by those who 'encouraged him to avenge the poor and the imprisoned'. This concept is a notion of kingship that Suger shares with his contemporaries. Another text of this century, *The Murder of Charles the Good*, by Galbert of Bruges provides a close copy of Suger's statement when he writes about Count Charles of Flanders: 'He had presided over the kingdom for seven years like a father and protector of churches of God, generous towards the poor.'

This is one of the great contradictions of Suger; on one hand Suger upholds the Mouvance concept that 'The king holds from no one' as he is the summit of Suger's political and feudal hierarchy, on the other Suger also upholds that the king must be 'safeguarding the churches' and thus does not hesitate to present Louis VI as a vassal of the Abbey of Saint-Denis. In the dispute between Adam of Saint-Denis and Burchard of Montmorency, 'news of the conflict, when it reached him, bothered the lord Louis and made him angry' resulting in Louis as king-designate waging war on Burchard on behalf of Saint-Denis. Furthermore, when Louis assembles his host against the threat of Emperor Henry V, Suger writes that, 'He then took from the altar the standard belonging to the county of Vexin, which he held as a fief from the church.'

Thus, in the same way Louis's vassals hold land as a physical fief from him, he held this standard as a fief from Saint-Denis. In Suger's mind, therefore, this responsibility of the king to protect the church was to be exercised on the behalf of his abbey. This clearly contradicts Suger's Mouvance concept that 'The king holds from no one' as he is presented as being a vassal of Saint-Denis and the church. This exception extends further than just the church as Louis is also presented as a subject of his land, vassals and people, according to Suger. He writes about Louis before he was crowned, stating:

> A hundred complaints against this forceful and criminal man [Count Ebles of Roucy] had been tearfully lodged with the lord king, but the son heard only two or three before he angrily assembled a medium sized host.

While there is an argument that this is an example of Louis's virtue being greater than his father's, thus making him a greater king, it also demonstrates that Louis is subject to the people. Lastly, in the dispute between Count Matthew of Beaumont and Hugh of Clermont, Hugh immediately went to the king-designate and 'defender of the kingdom' Louis to ask for his help against Count Matthew. Louis 'extended his hand in alliance, promised to give aid, and sent away the man who hope had made joyful; and this hope did not disappoint him'. Once again, this blurs the lines of feudal hierarchy as the king is subject to his vassals, church, people and kingdom and thus this creates a paradox within feudalism, prompting questions about who is truly subject to whom.

What is certain, however, is the emphasis on a connection between the king, crown and land by which the king was not only a feudal lord, but a monarch of the whole kingdom. Suger particularly demonstrates this in the account of the threat made by Emperor Henry V when he writes that Louis:

> Sent forth a mighty call for all France to follow him. The customary fighting spirit of France became angry at this unaccustomed brazenness of its enemies. Stirring itself on all sides, it sent forward select forces of knights, [...] From all directions we gathered together in great strength at Reims. Numerous hosts of knights and foot soldiers came into view.

The assembly of magnates under the king's call to arms evokes a great national spirit. In the wake of a potential threat to the kingdom of France and to the French, all nobles owed their service to the king. Suger's idea of national kingship reiterates the idea that he is the summit of the French political pyramid. However, this concept also relates to domestic defence as Louis is the defender of the poor and churches which is why, for example, Louis intervened against a sub-vassal at Auvergne. Suger's letters provide particularly noteworthy evidence about to whom *fidelitas* was owed. He instructs the bishop of Chartres that his fealty is owed 'to the king and the kingdom', and archbishops and lay vassals owe their fealty 'to the king and crown'.

Combining the role of king with the crown and kingdom demonstrates that Suger seemingly merges the obligations of Louis as a monarch and feudal lord. Furthermore, evidence shows Suger consciously incorporating the concepts of the crown and kingdom into feudal culture. In fact, in *c.*1149, Suger made fidelity to the king and realm a customary condition which bound the concept of the realm with the crown.

In light of this, the church was forced to rapidly change in order to adapt to the new threats of power that arose. As such, a movement that originated in Aquitaine called the 'Peace of God', would create a transformation of its own. With the growth of the new feudal system that was underpinned by the violence and authority of the new warrior class, the church of the tenth century had to protect ecclesiastical property and non-combatants (namely women, merchants, pilgrims and priests) from internal threats as much as external.

The Peace of God movement emerged from a combination of factors. The first was due to an incredibly weak civil authority in France as a result of the new warrior class who were growing in number, building castles, and violently pillaging each other's territory. This was especially seen in the Loire Valley and Aquitaine with the introduction of the motte and bailey castle (at the time many were basic wooden structures as opposed to vast stone fortresses). Unlike England which, in the tenth century, consisted of multiple kingdoms that were somewhat centralised under an overlord who retained a degree of control over his neighbours, France was so vast and sparse that royal authority lacked any true substance south of the Loire. Of the French kingdom, Aquitaine was the largest duchy and William the Great (993–1030) ruled in Poitiers with a great support for the Peace movement and thereby assisted in creatively implementing it into his domestic policies with regional churches. As such, the foundation of transformation lay in a combination of weak civil authority and a pursuit for domestic peace.

The second factor was these regional churches, in particular monasteries, who had gained vast amounts of asset wealth in the tenth century. Cartularies of the period reveal that monastic communities such as St Julian of Brioude, St Gerald of Aurillac and St Martial of Limoges had holdings scattered throughout the duchy that were difficult to defend. As we have seen from the Viking raids, these were easy targets for wealth-hungry aggressors and so with the rise in the warrior class, the church was often under direct attack. As such, churchmen saw that they had to band together, using all the tools at their disposal, to overcome this. As Ademar of Chabannes indicates in a pre-NATO protocol: 'Who offends one saint offends them all'.

A third, and very important, factor was saints themselves, or rather their popularity in Aquitaine and southern France. Bernard of Angers (see also Chapter 10) describes the nature of saint worship in the southern regions:

> It is an old usage and custom in the whole region of Auvergne, in Rouergue or Toulouse, and in the whole country round, that each should set up according to his ability for his saint a statue of gold or silver or any other metal, in which the head of the saint or some other part is preserved with reverence.

Though statue reliquaries go back to the Carolingian period, they did not become truly appreciated until the last half of the tenth century. Nevertheless, with such beauty came popularity and thus in turn, more adoration in the form of gold and gems from pilgrims and churchmen alike. At St Martial of Limoges, for instance, a large gold image was made in 952 which was seated on an altar and blessed people with its right hand as it held the Gospels in its left.

As much as heavenly harmony was at the forefront of hearts and minds, apocalyptic terror, the fourth factor, was equally as prominent. With the year 1000 looming, southern France was supercharged with a sense that the world and society would come crumbling down in a scene from Revelations. Historians have shown that in the decade before the year 1000 (as well as 1028–1033 which was a millennium after Christ's death), peace gatherings with the presence of miracle collections were numerous. Returning to Ademar, he emphasised that the peace and harmony witnessed by the many saints of Aquitaine in heaven was very different to the violence endured on earth. As such, salvation was key and in order to find this salvation, saints were crucial.

Perhaps one of the most important factors is the fifth one. In order to uphold peace, an oath was taken in the presence of relics. This act separated the Peace of God movement from earlier Carolingian practices. Previously, it was the power of the king which gave enforcement to peace and this, to a large extent, remained. Nevertheless, with the sanctified movement, spiritual weapons were now utilised as saints thereby became powerful enforcers of God's rule. This oath, however, was just the beginning of the connections between the heavens and earth as saints and their followers became intrinsically connected – almost symbiotic. Mass was another key connection that was utilised in the evolution of worship. Tropes became a creative outlet for churchmen and studies have shown that Aquitaine was key in being one of the earliest and most important religious centres of troping in Christendom. Manuscripts and liturgical works of art depicted saints as citizens of Christ who were venerated by the songs of their pilgrims, and presented them as great throngs in heaven who aided in conquering death. One such way to invoke the aid of a saint in death was to be buried near him. This was customary with many of the great nobles and aristocrats of the time. In fact, the first Christian Duke of Aquitaine, Stephen, who was converted by St Martial, was buried near that saint. Symbolism was therefore the key to the heavenly gates and saints evolved to become an intermediary between the heavens and earth. Having your prayers answered by Christ was far too hopeful and beyond anyone's scope – but to pray to a saint ... that was realistic. Saints were therefore intermediaries between heaven and earth as well as defenders of the faith and the faithful.

While this, for a time, was the answer to the growing problem of the emerging warrior class, the practicalities were somewhat different. Christ did not return with the turn of the millennium and this energy for the Peace of God movement then somewhat dwindled as fears subsided. Nevertheless, the role of the saint had forever changed and with it, new forms of worship took hold within the discourse of faith. With wealth and power being interwoven with sainthood, however, issues then arose when sainthood was infiltrated by the wealth and power of these warriors.

> I am undertaking, venerable father [Father Abbot Aymo of St Martial at Limoges], as best I can and with much trepidation, the little book which you recently urged me so strongly to write concerning the life and miracles of a holy man Gerald. On the one hand I fear to be presumptuous in undertaking something beyond my capacity; on the other hand, in not doing it I fear greatly to be contumacious by being disobedient. I undertake the task, however, relying on the obedience and the goodness of Christ, and I beseech you to implore His mercy, that for the love of His servant

> Gerald He would deign so to guide what I say, that it may not be entirely unworthy of the man He has seen fit to glorify, and that to me it may not be a cause of transgression.

The above is taken from the dedicatory epistle of the author of *The Life of St Gerald of Aurillac*, Odo of Cluny, who is seemingly conflicted in constructing a hagiography on the life of this saint. In fact, he continues in the prologue by stating:

> Many doubt whether the things that are said about the blessed Gerald are true, and some think that they are certainly not true but fantastic. [...] For I too, formerly, hearing the fame of his miracles, was nevertheless in doubt.

There is no doubt that the medieval era is underpinned by Christianity, faith and belief – the stories of St Cuthbert that we shall discover in the following chapter will show the extent of empowerment through divine power in post-Conquest England amongst his followers. But it should not be stated that people blindly followed God. There are plenty of examples, as with the one we are to explore, where doubt and persuasion play a pivotal role in the belief of sanctity. And so, with the fears surrounding the new feudal class, there was anxiety and scepticism towards the veneration of these aggressors.

Count Gerald of Aurillac (855–909) was born into a Gallo-Roman noble line that included Cesarius of Arles among its ancestors. Abbot Odo of Cluny reported how William, Duke of Aquitaine, had pleaded with Gerald to forgo the *militia regia*, the feudal service rendered directly to the king, and pay homage to himself instead, 'for the sake of love'. Gerald objected, likely choosing to devote his fealty to the more distant liege, the king in Paris, having recently taken on the title of *comes*, an official within government. On the other hand, his friend Geusbert, the bishop of Rodez, convinced him against joining a monastic order on the grounds that, given his social standing, he could accomplish more good by remaining in the world as a layman. Nonetheless, despite everyone's opinions Gerald committed his life to God, gave away his possessions, took a personal vow of chastity, and prayed the breviary every day while keeping his tonsure concealed under his customary cap. On his property of Aurillac, where he was buried after passing away on a Friday, 13 October, most likely in 909, he established a church and an abbey. Today, Cézens or Saint-Cirgues may be the location. His wider adoration was established by Odo of Cluny's recognition of his local cult. St Gerald is revered by the church and his adherents as a magnificent example of a celibate Christian aristocracy.

All that said, Gerald is rather out of place when comparing him to former saints featured in this book. He was new and unique; he was an aristocratic warrior, a great lord, and a man of the world as opposed to a saint in ascetic withdrawal. Odo also believes this too with his doubts about the saint as we have seen. Nevertheless, through his local veneration, Odo had been convinced enough and now had the task of trying to produce a hagiography that would convince others. That being said, doubts about Gerald's sanctity are prevalent throughout the life of the saint [*Vita*] as written in his hagiography. One concern for Odo was that he did not personally know Gerald. This, interestingly, seems to be a common objection amongst Continental writers as in 836, Lupus of Ferrieres was incredibly anxious about writing a *Vita* on St Wigbert as he had died almost a century before. That being said, the main issue for Odo was not so much the gap of time between their lives, but rather Gerald's life itself.

Gerald appears to have been a controversial figure with some scoffing at the idea of him becoming a saint while others misappropriate him. Odo writes that, 'Some men, trying to excuse their own sins cry him up, saying that Gerald was powerful and rich, lived very well and yet is a saint.' Odo, however, did not want lay aristocrats to believe that simply renouncing your riches and station gives you direct access to paradise. In many ways the idea would be simony, the sin and crime of buying and selling privileges. Instead, Odo wished to present Gerald as a model for aristocracy where wealth and power could live alongside piety. In short, Gerald was a saint because he was a lord rather than in spite of it. This was the issue that had arisen since new ideas of sainthood when the Viking attacks merged sanctity and secularity – as seen with St Edmund the Martyr. Therefore, the idea of a 'holy king' was set forth with kings either being compared to saints or obtaining the sainthood themselves. As such, Odo jostled with the question of what sort of secularity could achieve and obtain sanctity? In order to answer this question, we must dive into the Carolingian aristocracy and their relationship with the church which, at this time in the tenth century, was confronting the notions of secularity head-on.

One of the first issues Odo had to contend with, since his saint was a lay aristocrat, was the topic of violence. War was an important aspect of early medieval hagiographies. Along with being categorised as a period of faith and devotion, the Middle Ages are equally as violent with wars, skirmishes and general violence plaguing kingdoms and duchies across the continent. In order for the newly formed feudal transformation to be successful, violence was a key tool to keep vassals and sub-vassals in their place. Venturing back to the eighth century is where war begins to emerge within hagiographical texts. This can be seen in The *Life of St Arnulf of Metz* which celebrated Arnulf's prowess as a warrior: 'Who can describe his outstanding qualities as a fighter … his crushing of the legions of the enemy with his sword?'

This, however, was before he became a bishop. As such, we never find saints fighting as saints – that is until the Merovingians. The *Life of St Gangulfus* written in the late ninth and early tenth century aims to draw together all the activities of Gangulfus within a picture of him as a saint. He is described as a holy warrior within Pippin's forces. Likewise, his sword and armour are relics that were venerated in the church dedicated to him. The problem, however, is that unlike Gangulfus or Edmund, Gerald was not a quasi-martyr. Nor does Gerald take orders and become a bishop like Arnulf of Metz. The answer Odo found to justify Gerald was to attribute taking up the sword to defend the poor. He thus wrote:

> It was legitimate for a layman in the order of warriors to carry the sword to defend people who are weaponless.
>
> […] men of war constituted an order, a functional social category with a place alongside the order of kings and that of orators.

Odo, however, makes a bizarre statement regarding Gerald's order of warriors as he writes that his triumphs were bloodless through the adoption of tactics whereby his troops were to only fight with the flat of their swords and blunt ends of spears. Still, Gerald's war is a war to defend the poor and not for personal gratification. The Gerald described by Odo does not want a warrior's fame and thus in order to be legitimised as a saint, he had to shed a degree of his fierce secular aura. A further problem arose from the fact that unlike Edmund, Gerald's wars were against fellow Christians and it was not under the command of a king. Thus, Odo could not present him as an aggressive soldier of Christ in a proto-crusade as Edmund would be. Rather, under the new banner of feudalism, Gerald was forced to fight fellow unruly aristocrats who were attempting to shake the political system.

Odo's vision of secular sanctity was therefore far from apolitical. If God was not to grant Gerald success, his tactics would have appeared absurd to the enemy and pointless to his own men. Thereby, in understanding the qualms of feudalism, Odo had to employ this bizarre idea of blunt swords to legitimise Gerald's backing by divine intervention. Odo clearly knows these tactics to be absurd as he mentions their oddity in the eyes of both allies and enemies, but he reiterates that despite this, only through God's intervention could Gerald triumph.

The reason for this is that Odo is attempting to circumvent the anticipated scepticism of the audience and present Gerald as a model for warrior aristocracy.

He states in his prologue, 'We believe that this man of God was given as an example to the powerful, let them see … how they may imitate him.'

Through absurdity, Odo is attempting to puncture the pride of aristocracy and chastise its attachments to the pleasures of the secular world. Odo thus specifies that the hagiography is not meant for monks, but rather the deeds listed within are aimed towards warriors and nobles. Gerald never stained his sword with blood and so Odo was able to circumvent the concerns raised by Hrabanus Maurus in the ninth century, who concluded that warriors, even when obeying royal orders, were subject to penance. But Gerald. under the banner of Christ. was neither able to wound nor be wounded and thus the concerns over penance were irrelevant.

Alongside warfare, marriage was equally as integral to aristocratic life. In 821, the Council of Thionville declared that if someone killed a bishop with intent, he was to lay down his sword-belt, refrain from drinking wine and travelling on horseback, and remain without hope of marriage forever. Other councils throughout the Middle Ages prescribed a similar punishment for the crime but the idea behind it was to strip the aristocracy of their primary attributes and hinder their ability to secure power, status and an heir. We can draw together an image of the feudal aristocracy of the tenth and eleventh century through such attributes and activities. A noble was to:

- Be born of noble descent
- Marry and have a family
- Hold office as a judge, count, etc.
- Wage war
- Hunt and feast

Such activities do not underpin aristocracy but do allow us to work with a definition that enables us to explore the life of Gerald as a feudal aristocrat and the overwhelming task Odo had to contend with in justifying his sanctity.

Churchmen certainly understood that lay aristocrats had special problems. Count Wido of the Breton March, for example, asked Alcuin to give him advice on his involvement in the affairs of war, hoping he would find solace in a middle ground which enabled him to keep his pursuit to heaven while also enjoying the pleasures of secular life. Alms-giving was highly recommended along with the avoidance of corruption and participation in chastity. Likewise, Count Matfrid of Orleans called for a guide who could lead him to a life of pleasing God while being 'tied to the bond of marriage'. Marriage was a particularly defining feature of aristocratic concerns and despite the unattached nature of ecclesiastical churchmen, they understood this to be a central institution of secular life. The question is, did the aristocracy take onboard this advice of moral behaviour? While difficult to say, we do see in the will of Eberhard of Friuli, for example, that he owned various 'moralising texts', one of which was Alcuin's book for Count Wido that was widely circulated. A great example comes in the form of the *Liber Manualis* which was written by the wife of Bernard of Septimania for their son William. While the book, written in 841, has little to discuss on the topics of war or marriage, it places a great emphasis on moral conduct and ancestry. She stresses to William to pray for his ancestors and uphold a high standard of duty to his father. In effect, this is the lay equivalent to St Benedict's Rule which provides a moral conduct for monks. Nevertheless, the point of the book here is to show that the lay aristocracy were concerned with moral conduct and the advice given to them by the church. Like Alcuin, the *Liber Manualis* recommends alms-giving and aims to demonstrate that a noble can be wealthy while also being saved. Odo was to be very conscious about the theme of family. Noble blood was by no means a guarantee to protect someone against corruption. In fact, having the status of noble blood could easily lead someone to corrupt behaviour, especially when concerning wealth and power. As such, Odo had to write and defend his saint in a way which would present Gerald's moral conduct and use of power and wealth in a good manner.

Odo confronts this head-on and tells us that his father and mother slept separately, apart from the night that he was instructed by a vision to have intercourse with his wife and thus produce Gerald. It is detailed that while pregnant, Gerald's mother and father were lying awake one evening when they heard her child cry three times while in the womb; an unnatural foreshadow of his later saintly career. Although a scene of domestic bliss, Gerald is not afforded any such intimacy. Gerald's sole encounter with women is his attempted seduction, under the influence of the Devil, by a daughter of one of his tenants. At the very last moment God makes the daughter appear hideous to deter Gerald. Nevertheless, even marriage is not undertaken by Gerald. Records show that William, Duke of Aquitaine offered his sister's hand in marriage to Gerald but his love for chastity led him to refuse. Odo then goes on to tell us Gerald's horrified attitude against wet dreams that were out of his control or to be seen naked – even in death.

While marriage or domestic bliss is not a necessary qualification for sainthood, marriage was a link that tied a man to the world and to the government. When Louis the Pious was deposed in 833, not only was he stripped of his weapon but also of his wife, Judith. As such, there was an important medieval emphasis on weapons and women that, for Odo's Gerald, he could not be linked to. As with the radical military tactics, Gerald being a lay aristocrat who was chaste was a rather odd model to propose. Even Odo states that it was bizarre that Gerald was to obsessively scrub himself clean after a wet dream. Nevertheless, for Odo, it was what had to be written in order to circumvent doubts about connecting the image of Gerald to that of a saint.

Hunting was yet another problem Odo ran into when constructing his saintly narrative. Hunting was a crucial activity in aristocratic life – even outranking war. Einhard, for example, tells us that Charlemagne was a mighty hunter. Likewise, Louis the Pious is said to have been a tireless huntsman. Hunting, however, was not well regarded in the church. Hagiographers deem hunting a legitimate activity for kings and nobles but not so much for saints. The *Life of St Trudo*, for example, details how the young saint was approached to join a hunt but then refuses on the basis that while it was a fitting activity for royal retinue, the saint's concentration on heaven meant he had to turn down their temptation. Returning to St Gangulfus, his hagiographer celebrates his saint's bouts of hunting by linking it to St Benedict's Rule against idle inactivity which can dull virtue. With such a complex phenomenon, how did Odo circumvent this? Quite simply, he ignored it as much as possible. As a youth, Gerald is said to have encountered hunts and knew how to handle falcons and hawks, but God struck Gerald down with illness for doing so. This was somewhat problematic as even the sickly Alfred of Wessex, whose concern for learning and deep piety as a comparative to Gerald, was a keen hunter whose hunting activities were integral to his Christian rulership. With that in mind, Odo never refers to hunting again and his silence speaks volumes in understanding the obstacles he faced when constructing the image of Gerald.

Gerald, in Odo's eyes, was therefore very odd in terms of his aristocratic life. For Odo, a lay saint brought with it a plethora of conflicting issues from bloodshed to sex – all of which were far from saintly. In order to provide solutions to these issues, validity was sacrificed and the narrative was altered in order to meet the demands of the audience and those commissioning the hagiography. The result is that even his own followers thought that his withdrawn asceticism was not a particularly desirable quality of an aristocratic lord and had he not won his battles his bizarre tactics would have been equally as undesirable and borderline lunacy. Despite this, Gerald's saintliness was hard-earned and Odo worked hard to ensure that no stone was left unturned about whether Gerald had chosen the right path. To achieve this, however, the truth was sacrificed. To circumvent the unruly warlords of the time who mocked the ecclesiastical efforts to restrain them, Gerald was used as a symbol for the perfect image to be attained. For the aristocracy to be morally controlled by the church, Gerald was key.

What is most fascinating and important about Odo's *Life of Gerald* is not so much the advice and image of perfection presented, but rather the gaps and silences as these tell us more about the attitudes of the church to this new warrior class. What this also shows is that the idea of sanctity was often questioned by both lay and ecclesiastical people. Later, through even more scepticism, Odo's work would be edited out to make a more moderate saint who could bridge the gap between the church and lay nobles. As such, this truly is a one-of-a-kind text that was created in a turbulent time of transformation.

Chapter Seven

Out with the Old, In with the New

Since the dawn of the medieval era, Christianity has gradually become more prominent in everyday life, society and, most importantly, the state. From the most recent chapter, we can see that by the ninth century saints were becoming an important source of control and power within the church. When we hark back to the age of Justinian, he too wielded Christianity within law to legitimise himself, yet for him the church was a weak asset to aid in consolidating his rule and the schisms during his reign show that his relationship with the church was often shaky. The previous chapter also revealed that in order to control the narrative of Christendom, one must control its focal points. For centuries, saints used to be mere icons to be worshipped, but if the era of iconoclasm showed us anything, it was that people were placing more devotion in these saints than the church itself. A rapid change was therefore occurring within Christianity, and the response to the various Viking attacks in England and the Continent showed that the life of a saint after their death was re-energised with a fervour of piety, power and control. This was just the beginning, as one of the greatest signifiers of this evolutionary change and adaptation was the introduction of the Normans into the Anglo-Saxon discourse; a major cultural change would occur following 1066 that would reshape England's faith and history forever.

The narrative of 1066 and William the Conqueror is one that has been told and retold a thousand times over and with good reason – the Norman Conquest of England in 1066 was a pivotal event in English history, marking the end of Anglo-Saxon rule and the beginning of Norman rule that would last for centuries. The story of the Norman Conquest is a tale of intrigue, betrayal and bloody warfare, and it all began with the death of the English king, Edward the Confessor. Edward had no children, and as his health declined in the mid-eleventh century, he began to consider who would succeed him as king of England. Edward's distant cousin, William, Duke of Normandy, was one of the leading candidates, but he faced stiff competition from Harold Godwinson, the powerful Earl of Wessex. In 1064, William visited England and claimed that Edward had promised him the throne. However, Harold, who was Edward's brother-in-law and one of the most powerful men in England, was also vying for the crown. In 1066, when Edward died, Harold quickly seized the throne, despite William's protests. William was outraged by Harold's actions and began to assemble an army to invade England. In September 1066, William and his troops landed on the English coast and defeated Harold's army at the Battle of Hastings. Harold was killed in the battle, and William was crowned king of England on Christmas Day that same year.

The question is, however, how was all of this legitimate? A lesser-known aspect of the Conquest is that, far from conquest, the Normans regarded this as a crusade for England. Shown twice in the Bayeux tapestry is a depiction of the Norman armies being led into battle under the cross of Christ. The reason for this is that in the spring of 1066, William sent Gilbert, the Archdeacon of Lisieux, to Rome as his messenger to enlist the support of the papacy. Gilbert presented Pope Alexander II with plans drawn up by William's advisor, Abbot Lanfranc, to dispute Harold's claim to the English throne. The main argument of this conquest was that it held that Harold had committed perjury and promoted a hybrid, old-fashioned faith that was not truly Christian. Alexander II, a close friend of Lanfranc, gave his blessing alongside a papal ring, banner and an edict to the autonomous Old English clergy guiding them to submit to the new Norman regime. As such, the Normans did not see themselves as invaders or aggressors, but rather as crusaders.

The Conquest, however, was not at all smooth sailing. William was crowned in 1066 and with it, an onslaught of new changes was imposed under the new regime. Lanfranc was made Archbishop of Canterbury in 1070 and would assist in reforming the Anglo-Saxon church into a new English church. At the time of the Conquest, only eight English cathedrals contained major shrines – most of which were those of early bishops: St Dunstan and Alphege at Canterbury; Ithamar and Paulinus at Rochester; Erkenwald in London; Chad at Lichfield; Swithun at Winchester; Oswald at Worcester; and Cuthbert at Durham. Other great abbeys such as St Albans and Bury St Edmunds also contained ancient shrines. With the arrival of the Normans, however, competition for theological domination was widespread and we see, for instance at Rochester, that Anglo-Saxon shrines of saints were quickly superseded by more fashionable newcomers in the post-Conquest period. Nevertheless, although the major saints of England were supported in an attempt to hybridise culture and create an affiliation between the old and new regime, they had to be up to the new code.

The Normans not only brought over new cultural and technological advancements, they also transferred the Continental style of saintly worship to their English counterparts. As such, in order for a saint to be legitimate in the new Norman regime a hagiography and translation ceremony would have to be undertaken to absolve them from their old-fashioned Anglo-Saxon ways. Given the limited literacy of the general population, hagiographies were less accessible to the general public. As such, translation ceremonies offered the chance for pilgrims to embrace their faith, witness the prowess of their saints, and offer donations for divine aid. Simply put, a translation was the ritual movement of a saint's body from one place to another and was almost always accompanied by extravagant ceremony and pageantry. The earliest account of a translation occurred in 1091 at Canterbury where a ceremony was held for St Augustine, the saint who, under Gregory the Great, brought Christianity to the native heretics – no doubt to symbolise a parallel with the new reformed faith William had brought over.

Nevertheless, why bother moving the saint? Sainthood was a title never to be enjoyed while alive – in other words it was only obtainable after death. As such, in medieval England the burial of a saint was no different to any non-saint. Even Thomas Becket was not instantly enshrined despite immediately being lined up to become a saint after his martyrdom. As a result, an extravagant burial could be undertaken, but this was not enshrinement until a recognition of canonisation had taken place. Prior to the Conquest, canonisation and translation were one and the same as a local bishop or abbot could enshrine a local hero that had a cult. Following the Conquest, however, the pope had a monopoly on canonisation and thus it became a lot more difficult for English saints to be recognised. While the translation was the result of local veneration, ultimately the papacy had control over canonisation and could (and did) refuse it. But once canonisation was achieved, the body had to be moved to a shrine. It was believed that saintly relics should not remain below ground like ordinary corpses, and many even believed it was shameful to do so. Of St Erkenwald it was said that, 'Someone who shines forth so gloriously in the heavens should surely not be buried in such a foul garment as the earth,' As such, the body would be raised and placed in a casket on an elevated base. It would then be moved eastward to a more holy and convenient part of the building to be laid within a magnificent shrine. This was no easy task; many accounts describe a terror and hesitation towards moving such a holy relic. When they came to unearth Cuthbert in 1104, the Durham monks, trembling and tearful, prostrated themselves before his tomb. It was for good reason that extreme care was to be undertaken as when the monks at Bury translated St Edmund in 1095, the fate of Abbot Leofstan was ever present in their minds. Back in the mid-tenth century, Leofstan wished to inspect the body of the saint to see if it was truly uncorrupted. Given that Edmund was decapitated, Leofstan wished to test how well the head was divinely reattached. With one monk yanking on his feet while the other pulled at his head, Leofstan was struck blind and dumb by St Edmund for his irreverence.

For the crowds, however, a translation ceremony was filled with spectacle and wonder. The clergy wore their best vestments, nobles and high ecclesiasts joined the crowds in a sort of red-carpet celebrity appearance. Music was ever present with hymns, minstrels and choirs echoing throughout the cathedral. Celebrations lasted for days – even weeks – as banquets endured long into the night. This was especially seen with the festivities surrounding Thomas Becket's translation as a banquet was given four days before, reportedly for 33,000 persons. Tuns of wine were placed at strategic locations about the city, distributed free to all. On the actual day of Becket's translation, wine is said to have run in the gutters. Likewise, St Swithun's 1093 translation claimed to have been 'in the presence of almost all the bishops and abbots of England'. By the 1110s, Augustine, Alphege, Cuthbert, Oswald and Edmund had been translated, and a further twelve saints were translated by the end of the century. As such, in order to legitimise their saints, all of the major cathedrals successively commissioned hagiographies and put on translation ceremonies to keep up-to-date with the new Norman rules. Equally, in time, the Normans added new saints to their post-Conquest roster – many of whom were bishops who had lived a saintly and exemplary life. The aim was to highlight that although things had changed with the new regime, community and sanctity remained.

This was not entirely plain sailing, as while saints became a tool for Norman clergy to culturally merge with the local population and uphold public order, many communities resisted the Conquest invasion and change of regime. The 'Harrying of the North' was a brutal and devastating campaign launched by William the Conqueror in 1069–1070 to suppress the rebellious north of England. The rebellion was sparked by the refusal of English nobles to accept Norman rule and was particularly intense in the counties of Northumbria, Durham and Yorkshire. William responded with extreme force, unleashing a campaign of terror and destruction. The offensive lasted for more than a year and involved the systematic destruction of farms, villages and towns, as well as the killing of thousands of people. The reasons for William's brutal tactics are still a matter of debate among historians. Some argue that he was simply trying to crush the rebellion and establish his authority over the north of England, while others suggest that he was driven by a desire for revenge against those who had resisted his rule. Whatever the motivation, the consequences of the Harrying of the North were devastating. William's army burnt crops, slaughtered livestock and destroyed entire communities. Many of the people who survived the initial onslaught were forced to flee into the forests, where they were hunted down and killed by Norman soldiers. The scale of the destruction was unprecedented in English history. Estimates suggest that up to a third of the population of the north of England died as a result of the campaign, either through direct violence or through starvation and disease in the aftermath.

What is so integral to this narrative, however, is the active role played by St Cuthbert on behalf of the community at Durham in the form of resistance and opposition. St Cuthbert of Durham, also known as St Cuthbert of Lindisfarne, was a seventh-century Anglo-Saxon saint who became one of the most revered figures in the Christian church of England. His life and legacy have been the subject of numerous hagiographies and legends. Cuthbert was born in Northumbria around the year 635. As a young man, he worked as a shepherd before joining a monastery at Melrose Abbey in Scotland. There he became known for his piety and his asceticism, living a simple life of prayer and fasting. In 664, Cuthbert was appointed prior of Lindisfarne, a monastery on an island off the coast of Northumbria. He quickly became known for his miracles and his ability to heal the sick, and soon gained a reputation as a saintly figure. Cuthbert's life was not without its challenges, however. In 678, he retired to a hermitage on Inner Farne, another small island off Northumbria. There he lived as a hermit for several years, spending his time in prayer and meditation. In 685, Cuthbert was appointed bishop of Lindisfarne. He continued to perform miracles and to be revered by the people of Northumbria, but his health began to fail. In 687, he retired once again to his hermitage on Inner Farne, where he died later that year. After Cuthbert's death, he was buried at Lindisfarne. However, his body was later moved to various locations to protect it from Viking raiders. Eventually, his body was taken to Durham, where a cathedral was built in his honour. The cathedral became one of the most important pilgrimage sites in medieval England, and Cuthbert's cult became a major force in English Christianity.

Move forward to the eleventh century and his sainthood was now reinvigorated with an immense power to defend the north against these foreign aggressors. Symeon of Durham's *Libellus De Exordio Atque Procurso Istius, Hoc Est Dunhelmensis Ecclesie* (or, *Tract on the Origins and Progress of this the Church of Durham*) provides a comprehensive and detailed chronology of the tensions and clashes between the Durham community and King William.

Written around 1104–1115, Symeon was a northern French, possibly Norman, post-Conquest monk of Durham, which is particularly interesting given the narrative he was constructing regarding the foreign oppressors he was culturally affiliated with. Still, his career as a monk is particularly notable as he was tasked with copying historical and hagiographical texts at Durham. He is even known to have copied the oldest version of Bede's *Vita S. Cuthberti* as well as the *Historia Ecclesiastica* and *De Miraculis*. All these were used by Symeon to construct the *Libellus de exordio* which once again highlights the relationship between the pre- and post-Conquest world.

Turning to the text, therefore, Symeon wastes no time in diving into the Northern rebellion and the role of St Cuthbert:

> In the year of Our Lord's Incarnation 1066, the most pious King Edward died on 5 January in the twenty-fourth year of his reign, and Harold ascended the throne of the kingdom in his place, but he ruled it for only a short time [...] When William had obtained the kingdom of the English, however, he still had to suffer for a long while the rebelliousness of the Northumbrian people.
>
> He [Earl Robert Cumin] entered Durham with seven hundred men, and they acted towards all the homes in a hostile manner. At first light, the Northumbrians who had assembled burst together through all the gates, and rushed through the whole town killing the earl's companions. So great was the multitude slain, that all the streets were full of blood and corpses [...] As balls of fire flew high to a great height, it seemed that the west tower which stood nearby was about to be burned. So the people knelt down and beseeched St Cuthbert that he should preserve his church unharmed from the flames, and at once a wind sprang up from the east and diverted the blaze.

Cuthbert's divine intervention does not stop there; in a scene that could have been from the Old Testament, when the Durham community were fleeing from the Norman armies with the body of St Cuthbert, they were hindered from reaching the island of Lindisfarne due to high tides. Nevertheless, the saint came to the rescue:

> They groaned, 'What shall we do? We are prevented from reaching the island by the height of the tide, nor is there any place where we can stay that's protected from the harshness of the cold.' As they were thus bewailing their plight, the sea suddenly drew back from just that one place and allowed them dry passage to safety. The sea-tide followed hard on their heels as they made their way.

While in flight, an issue arises when the party is obstructed by a certain lord named Gillo Michael who Symeon regards as 'the servant of the devil'. Gillo, an abettor of the Harrying of the North, is attributed with afflicting the fugitives with harm, obstructing them, robbing them, and doing whatever mischief he could. Under the veil of nightfall, however, Cuthbert would strike:

> He [the bishop of Durham] lay down to rest for a while in the middle of a field where he fell asleep and saw a clear vision of the death of the aforesaid man [Gillo].

The vision of the bishop is detailed as such:

> I was taken to Durham and there it seemed to me that I was standing in the church when I saw two men of the highest authority who stood before the altar and looked towards the east. One of them was a middle-aged man whose vestments had the dignified features of a very reverend bishop. The other, who stood on his right and was clad in a robe of reddish colour, a noble stature, and the appearance of a very handsome young man.
>
> [...] While I was yearning to approach them but in no way dared to do so, the young man pointed to me, asking if I knew the identity of that episcopal personage. When I replied I did not know, he said, 'He is your Lord, that is the Holy Bishop Cuthbert.' At once I threw myself to his feet, begging him to come to the aid of his church. Shortly afterwards they bowed their heads to the altar and together set off. Looking round Cuthbert called to me as I was following at a distance. 'Tell me, Ernan, do you know who that young man is?' 'I do not know, my lord,' I replied. 'This,' he said, 'is St Oswald.'
>
> Then they went on together a short distance on the southern side of the city and there they stopped. The bishop called me to come and when I looked down as I was ordered to, I saw a valley of infinite depth full of the souls of men. There Gillo Michael was being tormented with appalling sufferings, for he lay stretched out in the fullest of places and, run through from one side of his body to the other with a sharp scythe, he suffered intolerable tortures.
>
> St Cuthbert asked me if I knew anyone there, I replied I recognised Gillo. 'That is indeed he,' the saint said, 'For he has died and been consigned to these miseries and sufferings.' 'But, lord, he is not dead. This evening he dined safe and sound in his home.' 'And I say,' said he, 'that he is indeed now dead. For he and the others whom you see with him are compelled to suffer these agonies because they have infringed my peace and have done harm to me through my people.'

The bishop awoke the next day and rushed to tell his companions of the news – of which they were in disbelief and shrugged it off. Nevertheless, soon townspeople reported to the bishop that certain members of Gillo's household had arrived and announced their lord had died that very night. This vision is symbolic as a product of this new age of medieval sainthood whereby saints were actively interacting with the world around them. The story above is also reminiscent of a proto-Inferno from the Divine Comedy whereby the bishop and Cuthbert briefly take on the role of Dante and Virgil as they travel amongst the damned. Here we are seeing a development and evolution in the understanding of good vs evil, heaven vs hell, and ultimately the image of the afterlife. One of the major reasons for this is a contemporary apocalyptic fascination with the year 1000 whereby it was understood that judgement would occur. As such, in England during the Conquest and subsequent rebellion, this idea of good vs evil and end of a former world takes its form in the jostle between Anglo-Saxon and Norman culture. A saint was, therefore, no longer a mere idol to be worshipped but rather took on a new role as an active leader, protector, healer and warrior who could evoke powers harking back to the Old Testament. This vision is one of the best examples of the medieval psyche and the emphasis people placed on saints in this time.

Saints and their divine power were taken very seriously and this is further seen when Symeon writes in St Cuthbert's hagiography that the angered King William sent an army to avenge his losses:

> When they [the army] reached Allerton, with the intention of going to Durham as soon as morning had broken, such a dense fog covered everything that those who were there could hardly see one another, and they were quite unable to find the way. While they were wondering why this was and discussing amongst themselves what to do, someone came to them and told them that those men had in their town a certain saint, who was always their protector in adversity, and that with him as their avenger no one was ever able to harm their immunity.

The response of the army shows the true power saints could hold as, while nowadays we may have a degree of suspicion and scepticism, this caused the army to flee south. In fact, even the king himself is seen to have feared Cuthbert's power:

> Some time later King William entered Durham on his way back from Scotland and where he had been with his army. He diligently enquired whether the body of St Cuthbert rested there, but although everyone cried aloud and swore he was there, he refused to believe it. So he decided to investigate the matter by a visual inspection, having with him bishops and abbots who were to perform this task on his orders. For he had resolved that if the holy body were not found there, he would give orders for all the most noble and senior to be executed.

While everyone was in fear and was imploring the mercy of God [...] William suddenly began to burn with a terrible heat and to be so wearied by it, that he could hardly bear such a high temperature. Hastening to leave the church, he left behind a great feast which had been lavishly prepared for him, and he at once mounted his horse, ceaselessly urging it to gallop until he reached the river Tees. By this sign he acknowledged that the great confessor of God Cuthbert rests there, and he was not permitted to harm the people because God prohibited him from doing so.

It is no coincidence that following this, William held Cuthbert and Durham in great veneration and honoured it with royal gifts and landed possessions. He restored to the community Billingham which had been founded for Cuthbert by Bishop Ecgred but which had been seized during the rebellion. William also confirmed by his authority and consent the laws and customs of the saint, as they had been established by the authority of former kings, and ordered that they should be kept by all without infringement.

The power of a saint was thus truly great and at the forefront of the minds and hearts of both the aggressor and defender. William, however, was ultimately successful in his campaign of subduing the north. As a result, the destruction of farms and communities led to widespread famine and vast economic loss, and the north of England remained a marginal and neglected part of the country for centuries, with many of its people living in poverty and squalor. Yet, despite the horrific nature of the campaign, Cuthbert would remain as the 'Saint of the North' for centuries and stand as a protector of its people.

The year 1066 represents a time in England between the old-fashioned and modern whereby reform and new styles of worship were being implemented that would force a multitude of monastic communities to adapt or otherwise fall into disrepair. As the Normans continued to expand throughout modern-day France and Italy, the imposition of their culture would set forth a new era, regarded by historians as the High Middle Ages, that would hold saints within their central doctrine as a tool of control, power and piety.

Chapter Eight
The Age of Intellect

If I were to say that Guibert of Nogent was crucial in understanding medieval Europe in the twelfth century, many would wonder who he even was let alone the impact he had. This is a fair estimation as Guibert himself led a fairly quiet and solitary life. Yet, the twelfth century is marked by a bustling melting pot of intellect, especially in France, with powerful minds like Suger of Saint-Denis; the infamous Ivo of Chartres; Heloise and Abelard; and Galbert of Bruges, to name a few. For us, however, Guibert of Nogent has done perhaps more than any of these other characters of the twelfth century in shaping our understanding of power, belief and saints.

On the Relics of Saints, written in 1119, was not a widely publicised book. In fact, it is only found in one edition in the twelfth century that was written with Guibert's own hand and most probably never ventured further than the church it was written in. Nevertheless, the words within the pages unveil one of the most striking and original narratives of the twelfth century. He does not state to know all the answers and he is deeply emotive in his writing, but this aids us in understanding how this century, known as the Age of Intellect, saw people question good and evil, the theories about the workings of the world, and above all, the nature of saints and their relics. Relics were a particular point of discussion, as by the twelfth century there were thousands of them that featured heavily across the continent in worshipping traditions and pilgrimages.

Relics were believed to possess spiritual power and were venerated as a means of connecting with the divine. They were seen as tangible links to the holy and were thought to have the ability to perform miracles, offer protection and grant divine favour. They were categorised into three types:

First-Class Relics

These were the physical remains or body parts of a saint or martyr. For example, bones, teeth, hair, or preserved flesh were considered first-class relics. These were highly valued and considered the most potent in terms of spiritual power.

Second-Class Relics

Second-class relics were objects that had direct contact with a holy person or were associated with significant religious events. This could include clothing, personal belongings, or items used in religious ceremonies. These relics were considered to hold a lesser degree of power than first-class relics.

Third-Class Relics

Third-class relics were objects that had been in contact with first- or second-class relics or had been connected to a holy shrine. These could be small items such as pieces of cloth or tiny fragments believed to carry the spiritual essence of the original relic.

The authenticity and provenance of relics were of utmost importance. Relics with documented histories tracing back to the apostolic era or early saints were highly sought-after and revered. Pilgrimages to shrines and churches housing relics were common, as people sought spiritual blessings and hoped for miraculous cures. The veneration of relics also served as a unifying force within the Christian community. Relics were often enshrined in churches, cathedrals and monastic communities, becoming focal points for worship and sources of inspiration.

The Siege of Antioch during the First Crusade in 1097 and 1098 (only twenty years prior to Guibert's book) stands as one of the most remarkable and pivotal episodes in medieval history because of such relics. It was a test of endurance, faith and strategic prowess that ultimately reshaped the destiny of the Crusader states in the Holy Land. Moreover, the tale of the siege intertwines with the legend of the Spear of Destiny, a relic of immense significance said to possess mystical powers.

Antioch, a formidable city situated in modern-day Turkey, was a crucial target for the Crusaders as they sought to secure their foothold in the East. The siege began in October 1097, with the Crusader forces led by Bohemond of Taranto, Raymond IV of Toulouse, and other prominent leaders. Despite the city's imposing defences, the Crusaders were determined to capture it. Months turned into a year, and the Crusaders found themselves facing extensive hardships. The defenders of Antioch, led by Yaghi-Siyan, skilfully repelled numerous assaults, leaving the Crusaders disheartened and weary. Their situation seemed dire, with supplies running low, disease spreading through the camps, and morale plummeting. However, it was during this darkest hour that a spark of hope emerged in the form of a sacred relic, the Spear of Destiny. According to legend, this spear was the same lance that pierced the side of Jesus Christ during his crucifixion. It was believed to possess extraordinary powers and grant invincibility to its wielder.

In the winter of 1097, a humble monk named Peter Bartholomew claimed to have received a divine revelation. He announced that the spear was buried within the city walls, hidden away for centuries. Excitement spread among the Crusaders, who saw this as a sign from God and a potential turning point in the siege. Under the guidance of Peter Bartholomew, the Crusaders launched a feverish search within the city. After weeks of digging, to the astonishment of all, the Spear of Destiny was indeed uncovered. The news spread like wildfire, rekindling the spirits of the beleaguered Crusaders. Emboldened by the discovery, the Crusaders launched a final assault on 3 June 1098. The spear, now wielded by Bohemond himself, was carried into battle as a symbol of divine favour. Its presence seemed to inspire the Crusaders, who fought with renewed fervour. After a long and gruelling battle, the Crusaders fought off the invading Arab armies and established the Principality of Antioch, securing a crucial stronghold in the region. The Spear of Destiny, enshrined as a treasured relic, played a significant role in the subsequent history of the Crusader states. It passed through the hands of various rulers and conquerors over the centuries, each believing in its extraordinary abilities.

While the historical accounts of the Siege of Antioch are well documented, the true nature and authenticity of the Spear of Destiny remain shrouded in mystery and controversy. Whether it possessed genuine mystical powers or merely served as a psychological catalyst for the Crusaders' morale, its impact on the outcome of the siege cannot be denied.

Still, the siege of Antioch and the intertwined legend of the Spear of Destiny remain enduring symbols of the extraordinary events that unfolded during the First Crusade. They remind us of the lengths to which individuals will go in the pursuit of their faith, and the profound influence that relics and beliefs can wield in shaping the course of history.

All that said, however, it is important to note that throughout history, and especially in the twelfth century, the authenticity of some relics and heroic stories was questioned and debated. As such, in this chapter, we shall explore Guibert's perspective on relics within *On the Relics of Saints* to understand the almost-scientific pushback within the church against the new divine powers being attributed to relics and saints alike, as well as why this pushback was occurring.

On the Relics of Saints came about for Guibert because a monastery in Soissons, Saint-Médard, about 10 miles from his home, claimed to have an ancient relic that was the baby tooth of Christ. Founded in the sixth century, the ancient church of Saint-Médard had played a pivotal role in some of history's great events. It was, for example, the place where Louis the Pious, the son of Charlemagne, was imprisoned when he was being deposed. With this in mind, it seemed strange to Guibert that a site which was wealthier and more powerful than that of Nogent would claim to have something so absurd. As such, there is scepticism within Guibert's tone. He writes:

> There exist, on the other hand, certain practices that we hold and that are preached in churches, although they do not figure among the things that we must do for our salvation and without which we cannot live rightly, many might live out their lives well without receiving any help from these practices, and in fact, many do live out their lives well without them. Such as the case with saints' bodies and their relics. We ought to revere and honour the Relics, both because of the Saints' examples and the protection they provide, but we must have truly sound evidence as to the authenticity of these relics, such that someone is called a saint only if there is a sure tradition of antiquity about his saintliness or else if true writings, not mere opinion, confirms it.

In other words, he is pondering here the utility of saints and relics if Mass and more so the Eucharist already exist. If the wine and bread representing Christ's body bridge the gap between human and eternal, then what is the need for an intermediary in the form of a relic or saint? He then moves on to criticise the potentially blind worship afforded to some saints:

> What then can I say about men who have become illustrious elsewhere through the support of no evidence but who, because some believed them to, have been celebrated in some type of writing, prove especially elusive? What am I to make of one whose birth and whose life are known to none, and whose Death is entirely obscure, though because of that death, his praises are sung? And what person would pray to those Saints for help, when he does not know if they are merited anything from God? Doesn't a man's conscience cause grave offence if it calls as an intercessor before God someone who in fact offers no great hope? Surely the keenness of your prayer – more truly, of your intention – grows dull when you do not know whether the one you pray to shares anything with God.

The above is a very blunt and somewhat damaging statement to the thousands who place so much hope and faith in their idols, but without getting too theological, that in itself is the problem at hand. Guibert retains the belief that the former Byzantine Iconoclasts had centuries before: faith and worship should be directed towards Christ and Christ alone, or at least to those who we know lived with piety such as his apostles. As we will come to see in a later chapter when sainthood gets out of control and twisted by fraud, there are a plethora of saints and relics, such as the tooth of Christ, that are just simply too good to be true and quite simply distract the worshipper from the main goal of salvation.

Here we find a hint of modernity in Guibert's voice as if he were a proto-scientist dispelling the work of God. It should be said, though, that his scepticism towards relics does not mean a rejection of Christianity and faith. Many contemporaries and predecessors analyse and criticise aspects of the Bible. Bede, for example, in the eighth century, wrote an exegesis, an analysis/critique, on the story of Noah's ark where he attempted to rationalise the claims made within it – even rejecting some of the more far-fetched ones. As such, Guibert was not an unbeliever, rather he is concerned about these so-called 'pointless wonderworks' that were seemingly so widespread and distracting people from the true rewards of faith.

Within miracle stories of saints, often readers will find very similar stories about deafness being cured, sailors being saved at sea, or the crippled being healed miraculously. Historians have said that either this could be a literary genre whereby when writing the hagiographies of saints, churchmen would sprinkle such stories to play into the image of what a saint was believed to be capable of. Alternatively, it could have been a chicken-and-egg scenario whereby these common stories occur because that is what people sought from saints and thus the more that these stories occurred, the more people went to saints with such afflictions. Nevertheless, Guibert also notices this and comments the following:

> That ever so wise Abbot of Brittany and his religious monk saw it all and encouraged the contrived miracles, seduced by the piles of Pilgrim gifts. Faint cases of deafness, pretended bounce of Madness, fingers cunningly bent back to the palm, or feet contorted underneath the buttocks can capture the avaricious hearts of the common mob, but why would a discrete and wise man, under the appearance of sanctity, make himself the promoter of such events? We have heard how such things are bandied about in repeated whispers and have witnessed ridiculous deeds performed during the translation of reliquaries, and so we have seen the depths of another's purse daily emptied by the lies of whom Jerome calls 'enraged by the rage of their Oratory'. We are stirred by their adulteration of the Divine, such that according to the aforesaid Father Jerome, they Triumph on preying on fools, spendthrifts, and plate-lickers.

In some ways, I am not sure who Guibert is criticising more, the so-called 'stupidity' of pilgrims in falling for the false miracles of the saints, or the clergymen themselves. Nevertheless, it is an insightful take on why we find so many common miracle stories within hagiographies. The introspection of

Guibert leads to an incredibly insightful discussion whereby he then attacks the heart of sainthood – who exactly is a 'saint'?

Although we hold the apostles to be Saints, as well as those whom the church has convincingly demonstrated to be Martyrs, in the case of the confessors we must take greater care in reaching a verdict. By their blood alone is the exaltation of martyrs justified, even if we lack sufficient written evidence about them, and we do not enquire in the case of martyrs what sort of life they had earlier led, since blood is enough to purge the oldest sins. Sweet Jesus!

This harks back to the chapter on St Edmund. Here we have a martyr who died for his kingdom and in a wider sense for Christianity but did not ultimately live a pious life. Likewise, with Gerald of Aurillac, the author jostles throughout as to whether the laity can or should be saints. In Guibert's opinion, only those who lived a full life of piety should have the opportunity to become a saint and in order to become one, there has to be vast amounts of evidence about their virtues. He even goes on to say that people become envious of other patron saints and thus attempt to invent their own. We know, for instance, that in the case of St Gerald the author did twist the truth to avoid certain questions about sanctity and we shall come to find with the blood libel of St William of Norwich that this is definitely true and did happen.

What is particularly interesting about *On the Relics of Saints* is that Guibert uses figures from the past to elaborate on his perceptions. Not only does he discuss Suetonius, a Roman historian who was incredibly popular in the medieval era, but also Gregory the Great who was the focus of Chapter 2 and still relevant to our narrative centuries later. He states:

> As a rule, according to Gregory the Great, when a person in disfavour is sent to intercede, the mind of the person who was angry only becomes angrier still, but all deny that they have chosen patrons who might be in this favour. Just let them explain to me how they believed their patron might protect them when they don't know anything about him! The only thing you can learn about him is his name, but if the clergy keeps silent, then old women and flocks of vile little ladies will chatter together, telling fictitious stories about their patrons, discussing them over their treadles and weaving rods.

Guibert is extremely emotive in his critique but it hints at a wider understanding of how miracle stories and the popularity of saints occurred. Gossip is key to popularising and maintaining a saint. Although hagiographies existed, we must remember that the general public simply could not read them as they were produced in Latin, and often a convoluted form that even historians today might struggle with. As such, gossip about healing or cures would travel along the pilgrim routes from village to town and capture the hearts of those who were desperate to be healed and cured. What Guibert fears, however, is those who seek to poison this (such as Soissons) and popularise stories about relics and saints that simply are not true; it is also extremely insightful to understand what source material was available in the twelfth century for Guibert to reference Gregory the Great.

He then references one such example of this fraud:

> There was a bishop of Bayeux named Odo, the illegitimate son of Count Robert of Normandy and patrilineal brother of William the Elder, king of the English, who fervently searched for his saintly predecessor to the bishopric, Exuperius, a man greatly honoured, especially at the local town. Odo paid £100 in coins to the Guardian of the church where the Saint had been taken, intending to remove the body from it, but instead that wickedly clever guardian found a tomb of the peasant named Exuperius, dug him up, and offered him to the bishop. The bishop asked whether these remains brought to him really did belong to Saint Exuperius and even demanded that the Guardian give him an oath. 'I swear to you as a solemn oath that this is the body of Exuperius, about his sanctity, however, I will not swear, since that forename has been given to many men judged to have wandered far from sanctity.'

Tricked by this rogue, the bishop felt more at ease. The townspeople, however, learnt about the profits that this custodian had made off their patron. Just think how much shame this fraudulent episcopal double-dealing brought to all religion!

Even Abbot Suger of Saint-Denis was guilty of fraud and forgery to boost his own power as well as that of his abbey.

Suger built an enterprise of forging documents and traditions to link Saint-Denis to the Carolingian and Merovingian legends. In 1109, Suger commissioned and created a solemn liturgical ceremony to commemorate the memory of Dagobert, the first Frankish king who was buried at Saint-Denis. Furthermore, Suger emphasises and writes about an ancient custom to sit on Dagobert's throne when receiving the first homages from the great lords of the realm which reiterates the concept that the king was the apex of feudal kingship. Such emphasis on Dagobert provided longevity in the fidelity owed to Saint-Denis by kings.

Longevity in the history of kingship and fidelity legitimised Suger's claims of Saint-Denis's primacy above all other Frankish churches. Suger also fabricated documents and charters to strengthen the image of the king and Saint-Denis through the Carolingian legend. The *Descriptio qualiter Karolus Magnus*, fabricated at Saint-Denis by a monk, sought to authenticate the relics of Saint-Denis, namely the nail and crown of Christ brought back from Constantinople by Charlemagne, and later donated by Charles the Bald. Another fabricated charter, said to have been given by Charlemagne, explicitly emphasised Saint-Denis's status and superiority over all other churches, and stated that the consecration of the king can only happen at Saint-Denis. In the same way Suger claimed that Louis owed fidelity to no one but served his kingdom through Saint-Denis, this charter by Charlemagne declares that he holds his realm from God and through Saint-Denis.

The impact and influence of such charters and documents is difficult to prove, but one particular custom from this charter by Charlemagne can suggest that Suger's campaign of forgery was, to an extent, successful. According to the charter, a chevage of four gold bezants was granted to Saint-Denis and Charlemagne requested that his nobles do the same. Unfortunately, by the end of Louis VII's reign, and long after Suger had died, Queen Adele had reduced Saint-Denis's role in royal affairs and Louis VII would be buried at Barbeau. Suger's legacy and concepts of kingship, however, would endure as Louis VII's son, Philip Augustus, placed four coins on the altar at Saint-Denis and declared the protection of the abbey – the same custom recorded in Suger's false charter.

Ultimately, the point that Guibert makes within *On the Relics of Saints* is that Christ has no need for physical memorials as the Eucharist already fulfils this with the wine and bread representing body and blood. The supposed tooth, umbilical cord, or even foreskin of Christ were therefore useless and offered nothing to the pilgrim worshipper and only signified a growing corruption within the church that needed to be extinguished. As such, Guibert sought to limit the seemingly infinite power afforded to relics and saints in the tenth and eleventh centuries – a reform that was part of a wider movement against the nature of power.

Despite his fraudulent efforts, however, we also see such movement in the *Vita Ludovici Regis* written by Abbot Suger. Much of the book we explored in the former chapter about the feudal transformation, but there is another aspect of kingship that many who watched the Coronation of King Charles III in May of 2023 would have witnessed. That is, the king as a sacral figure.

Even to those unfamiliar with medieval history, the concept of a 'Divine right of rule' is a well-known one as it has endured and reoccurred through centuries of royal history. The so-called thaumaturgic power (or Royal Touch) of the monarchy was popular in the Early Modern era, but there is an absence of divinity in perceptions of kingship in the intellectual current of the twelfth century. *The Deeds* contains very few examples of Capetian divinity. One such example Suger describes is that Louis, at his coronation, cast away 'the sword of secular knighthood' and, 'girded him with the ecclesiastical sword for the punishment of evildoers'. In a later passage, regarding the conflict with Hugh of Le Puiset, Suger writes that the church 'pleaded that the king, as the representative of God, renders free the part that belonged to God, whose image he maintained and kept alive in his own person'. While these examples would suggest Suger's perception of kingship complements that of a 'divine-king', Suger does not portray Louis as a sacral figure and places little emphasis on royal consecration. In Louis's coronation, Suger says very little about the coronation ceremony, only that the archbishop:

> Took from him the sword of secular knighthood, girded him with the ecclesiastical sword for the punishment of evildoers, and joyfully crowned him with the diadem of the kingdom. With the approval of the clergy and the people, he devoutly handed him, along with the other royal insignia, the sceptre and the rod that symbolize the defence of the churches and the poor.

Nowhere in this chapter does Suger describe a *consecratio*, instead he deploys secular expressions: 'anointment' and 'crowning'. Suger extends this concept to state that becoming king has no effect on Louis's nature, character, or religious association. Suger states in the following chapter that:

> Louis, king of the French by the grace of God, could not put aside what he had grown accustomed to do in his youth, namely safeguarding the churches, protecting the poor and the needy, and working for the peace and defence of the kingdom.

This suggests a continuity between Louis before being anointed king and after, thereby showing no attainment of divinity when crowned. In *The Deeds*, there is no record of a divine inspiration, thaumaturgic power, or royal touch, which is bestowed on to Louis once he becomes king. Any divine aid given by God is also received in battles before his coronation. This lack of divine inspiration among contemporaries (along with Guibert's opinions on relics) all plays into a unified support for the papal reforms of the eleventh century under Pope Gregory VII.

Pope Gregory VII emerged as one of the most influential figures in the history of the papacy during his reign from 1073 to 1085. His tenure marked a pivotal moment in the struggle for power between the papacy and secular rulers, as he sought to limit the authority of monarchs and establish the primacy of the church. Gregory VII's reforms, known collectively as the Gregorian Reforms, had a profound and lasting impact on the political, social and religious landscape of medieval Europe.

Born in a town in central Italy, around the year 1020, Hildebrand of Sovana (as he was named) entered the Benedictine monastery of St Mary on the Aventine Hill in Rome. There he received an exceptional education and developed a deep understanding of canon law and theology. His talents and intellect did not go unnoticed, and he soon caught the attention of Pope Gregory VI, who recognised his potential and appointed him as a papal advisor. Hildebrand's ascent continued under Pope Gregory VI's successors, and he became a trusted advisor to several popes. His influence expanded as he served as papal legate, travelling across Europe to resolve disputes and enforce the church's authority. Throughout his travels, Hildebrand witnessed first-hand the corruption, simony (the buying and selling of church offices), and moral decay that plagued the church. These experiences shaped his worldview and inspired his determination to bring about reform.

In 1073, after a period of turmoil and controversy surrounding the papal elections, Hildebrand was elected pope and took the name Gregory VII. From the moment he assumed the papal throne, he embarked on a mission to reassert the spiritual and temporal authority of the church. Gregory VII firmly believed that the pope, as the Vicar of Christ on Earth, held ultimate authority over all secular rulers. This conviction laid the groundwork for his reign that would see the papacy expand its territory in Italy and intervene in secular politics to assert its own authority over kings and emperors.

One of Gregory VII's most significant reforms was his campaign against simony and the practice of lay investiture. Simony had become pervasive, with church offices being bought and sold like commodities, often falling into the hands of unworthy and corrupt individuals. Lay investiture, on the other hand, involved secular rulers appointing bishops and abbots, essentially asserting control over the church's leadership. Gregory VII saw these practices as detrimental to the spiritual integrity and independence of the church and aimed to eradicate them. In 1075, Gregory VII issued the *Dictatus Papae*, a collection of twenty-seven propositions that asserted the supreme authority of the pope over secular rulers. It included the claim that the pope could depose emperors and kings, and that the Roman pontiff should be obeyed by all bishops. This bold statement of papal power ignited a fierce struggle between the papacy and secular rulers, particularly the Holy Roman Emperor Henry IV.

The conflict between Gregory VII and Henry IV reached its climax during the Investiture Controversy. In 1076, Gregory excommunicated Henry IV, effectively releasing his subjects from their oaths of loyalty. Henry, realising the threat to his power, travelled to Italy in 1077 and made a dramatic penitential journey to Canossa, where he sought the pope's forgiveness. Gregory, displaying his unwavering resolve, initially refused to grant absolution, forcing the emperor to endure three days of humiliation in the snow before relenting. The episode at Canossa, though a temporary victory for Gregory VII, highlighted the struggle between the papacy and secular authority. The conflict would persist, with Henry IV launching military campaigns against the pope and his supporters. Gregory VII, on the other hand, rallied the support of other European rulers who shared his vision for church reform and opposed the encroachment of secular power.

In 1080, Gregory VII formally deposed Henry IV and excommunicated him once again, declaring him unworthy of the imperial crown. In response, Henry IV gathered his allies and appointed an anti-pope, Clement III, in an attempt to undermine Gregory's authority. This led to a schism in the church, with competing popes and rival factions vying for legitimacy. The struggle between Gregory VII and Henry IV continued for several years, with shifting alliances and military confrontations. Gregory sought alliances with powerful rulers such as William the Conqueror of England and Matilda of Tuscany, who provided him with military and financial support. These alliances helped to bolster the papal cause and weaken Henry IV's position.

Despite the challenges he faced, Gregory VII made significant strides in his reform agenda. He convened church councils that condemned simony, enforced celibacy for priests, and reasserted papal authority over the selection and appointment of bishops. He promoted the idea of the church as a separate and independent institution from secular powers, with the pope as its spiritual and moral leader. It was these reforms that had broader implications for the concept of medieval kingship and the relationship between church and state. By challenging the authority of secular rulers and asserting the supremacy of the papacy, he laid the groundwork for the later development of the doctrine of the separation of powers. His reforms challenged the notion of absolute monarchy and contributed to the evolving concept of limited government, where both secular and ecclesiastical authorities had distinct spheres of influence.

As such, Guibert's critique of relics and Suger's *Deeds* are part of the collective intellectual reform movement in the twelfth century that was focused on one thing: power. There was a Gregorian war cry for freedom within the church to separate itself as it used to be in the Age of Justinian and return to a more primitive church. They sought to reshuffle the resources of wealth within Europe and attack the idea of simony and heresy that was being upheld by power. Underpinned by paranoia, contemporaries sought to limit spiritual power from the perceptions of kingship as they believed it allowed kings to enslave the papacy and clergy. As the church and papacy were forever growing in power and domination within Europe, there was continuous tension within itself as well as with secular powers over the nature of primacy. Quite simply, the later Middle Ages was a free-for-all, but it was this mobility in power that would lead the church to flourish, and then later fall.

Chapter Nine

A Unified Faith

By the 1080s, society was divided into two distinct orders – the clerical and the lay. This is a concept which underpinned feudalism and upheld the powers that be. Nevertheless, the definition of the lay order was a particular concern of the papacy. This gave birth to one of the most iconic phrases in medieval history concerning feudal society: *Oratores, Agricultores, Pugnatores.*

These were the words of Bishop Gerard of Cambrai who, in 1036, stated that 'the human race was divided into three: those who pray (*oratores*), those who till the land (*agricultores*), and those who fight (*pugnatores*)'. Some decades later, in 1090, Bishop Bonizo of Sutri would expand this to place kings, judges, knights, craftsmen, businessmen and farmers within the lay order. On the topic of Christians, however, many writers harked back to that of St Jerome to state that there were 'two kinds of Christians'. The first were those who prayed, lived in monastic communities, and dedicated themselves to God. The others were 'Laymen' who were allowed to possess wealth and goods but only for immediate use. They were also allowed to marry, pay tithes, etc. Nevertheless, although the gap between these orders was sometimes crossed with nobles like Gerald of Aurillac becoming a saint, it was seen that the lay life was to be separate and distinct from the spiritual sphere. In no way could the 'human weakness' of the laity infiltrate the work of those who sought a life through God. That was not to say that their role was unworthy, as many theorists understood the positive and necessary role of secular politics.

Despite this pursuit to separate and reform the church, by the end of the century, the lines between laity and spirituality would become blurred with the rise of the 'Warrior of Christ' in the Crusades. A decade prior to Pope Urban II's call to arms in Christendom is where we can see the seeds of this blend of social orders. The pamphlet of Wenrich of Trier in 1081 states the following:

> They declare that ... you incite to bloodshed secular men seeking pardon for their sins; that murder, for whatever reason it is committed, is of small account; that the property of St Peter must be defended by force; and to whomsoever dies in this defence you promise freedom from all his sins, and you will render account for any man who does not fear to kill in Christ's name.

The so-called 'Vassals of St Peter' here have been recruited through the promise of absolution from sins in return for military service – a notion that underpins the legitimacy of the violence incurred during the Crusades over the next two centuries. In fact this notion, which has for so long been regarded as a novelty of the crusade, was in practice for over a century. Pope Leo IX, for example, led papal armies against the Norman expansion into Southern Italy in 1053 under the promise of absolution. Likewise, Gregory VII appealed to the Norman prince Robert Guiscard as a 'Vassal of St Peter', to defend the rights of the papacy against Henry IV. The promise of absolution was thus a deeply ingrained concept within the church and even harks back to the ninth-century popes Leo IV and John VIII who died defending the church against Arab and Viking attacks. Such a concept was also used to defend the martyrdom of secular saints such as St Edmund. The difference, however, between these examples and those of the late tenth century is that lay warriors had a duty to St Peter and his vicar as much as they did to a feudal lord:

> If a knight ... or any man performing any office which cannot be exercised without sin ... comes to do penance, let him recognize that he cannot achieve true penitence ... unless he lays down his arms and bears them no more; save according to the counsel of holy bishops, in defence of righteousness.

While prior to 1080 absolutions were to be granted so long as they were contingent upon the performance of penance, now that was no longer evident. Gregory instead 'offered the guilty impunity for past sins and freedom to commit others in the future, without confession and penance'. The predominant reason for this was the need for military support against both internal and external aggressors. Earlier in the tenth century, the Byzantine Orthodox Church moved to become independent from Christendom and parts of the empire were even invaded by the Normans from 1081 to 1085 (all of which damaged relations with the papacy). Likewise, the papacy was having great conflicts and schisms with the Holy Roman Empire and Emperor Henry IV. All of this was occurring while conflict was brewing in the Middle East as Asia Minor fell to the Seljuks, and Christians fell to Muslims. The papacy was thus quickly losing its grasp on power as rulers opposed its influence. As such, for the papacy to survive, it depended on its promises of absolution for military service. The fate of Christendom, therefore, rested on the Christian laity and the lines between sanctity and secularity, that were upheld for so long, merged.

After Gregory VII's death, whereby it seemed that the flame of papal power was to be extinguished, Urban II succeeded with a primary aim to improve relations with the biggest looming threat to Europe – the Byzantine Empire under Alexius Comnenus. Harking back to Gregory the Great, Urban wanted to overturn the failures and schisms witnessed in Gregory VII's reign and attempt to promote a union after the breakdown of relations between the Eastern and Western Churches.

In the late eleventh century, the opportunity arose when the Byzantine Empire was facing increasing pressure from the Seljuk Turks in Anatolia (modern-day Turkey). The Turks had been steadily encroaching on Byzantine territory and posing a significant threat to the empire's stability and security. Alexius I Comnenus, as the Byzantine emperor, recognised the need for military assistance to combat the Seljuk Turks and protect his realm. Aware of the martial capabilities of the Western Christian knights and the growing tensions between the Catholic and Orthodox Churches, Alexius sent envoys to Pope Urban II in 1095 to request military aid. The envoys conveyed the dire situation in Byzantium and the threat posed by the Seljuk Turks. Alexius hoped to secure Western support, particularly from the powerful European nobility, to help defend his empire.

During the Council of Piacenza and later Council of Clermont, Pope Urban II addressed the assembly of bishops, nobles and clergy, and he responded to Alexius' plea for assistance. The pope saw an opportunity to consolidate his authority and influence in Western Christendom while also addressing the East–West schism that had divided the Catholic and Orthodox Churches. Pope Urban II used the council as a platform to rally support and motivate the faithful to take up arms in defence of their Christian brethren in the East. He highlighted the plight of the Byzantine Empire and the need to reclaim the Holy Land from the Muslims, appealing to religious sentiments and the concept of pilgrimage. The pope's call to arms, known as the First Crusade, aimed to unite the fragmented European nobility, channelling their martial energy towards a common cause.

Though this gave opportunities for gaining wealth, power and territory in the Middle East, for half a century people put aside their differences and united under the banner of Christendom against all odds to achieve a common goal. Since its conception, this would be the first, and only time, that Christianity would truly unite in such a way – and even then, its union would be brief.

Nevertheless, this concept of a unified faith is particularly significant, and one we should linger on for a moment. Imagine for a second how news of the deteriorating situation in the Holy Land spread like wildfire throughout Christendom. Tales of oppression, desecration of sacred sites, and persecution of Christian pilgrims reached the ears of thousands as the faithful were commanded to take up arms and embark on a sacred crusade. The pope's words were electrifying, fuelling a collective sense of righteous indignation. Men from all walks of life were inspired to answer the call, driven by a potent mix of religious devotion, the promise of salvation, and the allure of adventure. The response was overwhelming, as waves of enthusiasm rippled across Europe, setting in motion a grand mobilisation of armies.

Amidst the nobility, a charismatic figure emerged: Godfrey of Bouillon. Renowned for his military prowess and undying piety, he quickly became a focal point of the burgeoning movement. His noble lineage, combined with his zealous devotion, made him an ideal candidate to lead the crusading forces. Others, such as Raymond IV of Toulouse and Bohemond of Taranto, were equally eager to take up the cross and joined the ranks of the crusading commanders. But it was not only the nobility who answered the pope's call. Peasants, inspired by religious fervour and seeking redemption, swelled the ranks of the crusade. These common folk, often ill-equipped and untrained for war, displayed an unwavering determination, fuelled by a belief that their faith would carry them through the trials ahead. Their participation brought a sense of unity and purpose to the crusading armies, as they marched alongside the nobles and knights.

The logistics of mobilising such a massive force were daunting. The challenge of provisioning, organising and leading an army spanning different regions and cultures tested the mettle of the crusading leaders. Supplies were stockpiled, weapons forged and contingents assembled. Throughout the summer of 1096, armies began to set forth on their arduous journey eastward. The crusading forces embarked on different routes, converging from various points in Europe towards Constantinople, the gateway to the East. Along the way, they faced a myriad of challenges, including treacherous terrains, bandit raids and internal strife. Yet, their unwavering determination propelled them forward, driven by the common goal of reclaiming Jerusalem. By the time the crusading armies arrived at Constantinople, their numbers had swelled to unprecedented proportions. The combined force now stood as a formidable tide, eager to unleash its righteous fury upon the infidel lands. Picture Alexius, standing at the gates to the eternal city with thousands of troops before him, a mixing pot of culture, social class and languages – all of which were united by Christianity.

Over the following century, a successive wave of armies under the banner of Christianity ventured forth towards the enemy. These can be condensed as such:

Second Crusade (1147–1149)

The Second Crusade was called to defend the Christian territories in the Levant, particularly the County of Edessa, which fell to Muslim forces in 1144. Led by European monarchs Louis VII of France and Conrad III of Germany, the crusade aimed to retake Edessa but ended in failure. The Crusaders faced setbacks and suffered significant losses, achieving little territorial gain.

Third Crusade (1189–1192)

The Third Crusade was launched to recapture Jerusalem after it fell to Muslim leader Saladin in 1187. Led by notable European leaders such as Richard the Lionheart of England, Philip II of France, and Holy Roman Emperor Frederick I Barbarossa (who reformed the code of law in the Holy Roman Empire after rediscovering the *Corpus Civilis* law codex of Justinian), the crusade aimed to regain control of the Holy City. Although the Crusaders achieved some victories and negotiated a limited access agreement to Jerusalem, they ultimately fell short of their objective.

Fourth Crusade (1202–1204)

The Fourth Crusade initially aimed to support the Byzantine Empire against Muslim threats but took a dramatic turn. Due to financial difficulties, the Crusaders diverted their efforts and attacked the Christian city of Constantinople in 1204, leading to its sack and the establishment of a Latin Empire. The Fourth Crusade is widely regarded as deviating from its original purpose and causing significant political and religious upheaval.

After the Fourth Crusade, the fervour that had once sung in the hearts and minds of those a century earlier had faded. In some ways, Urban's attempt at a union with the East was achieved through the imposition of Latin ways in Constantinople. Following this, the iconic and infamous Fourth Lateran Council, held in 1215, was called. Appearing to have periodically united Christendom through force, the moment for widespread and unanimous reform seemed to be ripe. Held at the Lateran Palace at the Vatican, the council sought to address various issues within the church that would set precedence and framework for the Fifth Crusade and Francis of Assisi's theology. With the differences between the East and Western Church, the first (and main) aim of the council was to affirm several doctrinal beliefs of the church, including the nature of the Trinity, the Eucharist and the sacraments. It reaffirmed the doctrine of transubstantiation, which states that during the Eucharist, the bread and wine truly become the body and blood of Jesus Christ. Equally, measures were introduced to strengthen discipline and moral standards among the clergy. It addressed issues such as simony, the celibacy of the clergy, and the conduct of bishops. It emphasised the importance of regular confession and the imposition of penalties for those who violated their clerical duties.

It is perhaps no surprise that as the council emerged from the Crusade, the topic of war would also be at the forefront of discussions. The council called for the organisation of a new Crusade to retake the Holy Land from Muslim control via Egypt rather than Jerusalem. It also addressed the rising threat of heresy, particularly the Cathars (a dualist sect of Christianity that believed in two gods; one good, and one evil) and Waldensians (a pacifist sect that rejected clergy holding religious office). To combat them, various reforms were implemented with the most recognisable being the establishment of the Inquisition. Alongside this, the council issued decrees aimed at restricting the rights and activities of Jews and Muslims. It mandated that Jews and Muslims wear distinctive clothing to distinguish themselves from Christians and prohibited them from holding public office.

Despite creating a standardisation for Christian practice, it was on the terms of the Latins as opposed to the Greeks. As such, this only left a bitter taste that would cause later issues when the Greeks fought back in 1261. Nevertheless, the Fourth Crusade and Fourth Lateran Council left the church and papacy strong. Monasteries continued to attract benefactions, the prestige of monastic communities grew, and the arts flourished. The access to Greek texts enabled a small golden age in important works of Greek Theology with a vitality in painting and mosaics. As per the council's request, the call for war endured and in 1217, the Fifth Crusade, where our noble saint resides, was called to arms.

The Fifth Crusade in 1218 sought to launch an attack on the fortress stronghold of Damietta in Egypt rather than Jerusalem. There were several reasons for the aggressors to divert from recapturing the Holy City. Firstly, Damietta, situated at the mouth of the River Nile, held great importance due to its strategic position. Controlling Damietta would provide the Crusaders with a strong foothold in Egypt, allowing them to access the interior of the country and potentially threaten Cairo, the capital. The city's location also made it a crucial transportation hub for goods and military reinforcements, facilitating further advances in the region. Egypt was also one of the wealthiest and most populous regions within the Islamic world at the time. By targeting Damietta, the Crusaders sought to gain access to its rich resources, including agricultural lands, trade routes and potential ransom from captured prisoners. Additionally, the conquest of Egypt was viewed as a means to weaken the Muslim forces and disrupt their political and economic stability which would provide the perfect foundation to retain a foothold in the Middle East. This was especially the case given the idea that it was believed that Egypt, ruled by the Ayyubid Sultanate at the time, was relatively weak and more vulnerable compared with other Muslim territories. They saw an opportunity to strike at the heart of the Ayyubid dynasty and potentially destabilise the entire region.

As the Vassals of St Peter set off on their perilous journey, so too did a certain man who had been preaching the Gospel throughout Europe. Saint Francis of Assisi, born Giovanni di Pietro di Bernardone, was an Italian Catholic friar, preacher and mystic who is widely regarded as one of the most beloved and influential figures in Christian history. As a young man, he enjoyed a comfortable and indulgent lifestyle. He received a good education and was expected to follow in his father's footsteps as a successful businessman. However, Francis displayed a growing discontent with the materialistic pursuits of his time and an increasing longing for spiritual fulfilment. Yet, in his early twenties, Francis embarked on a series of military campaigns, but such experiences in the war left him deeply disillusioned. One of the most profound events of his life was during his captivity after the Battle of Collestrada. At this time, Francis had a vision from God that called him to renounce his worldly ways and embrace a life of poverty, humility and service to God. This encounter marked a turning point in his life and set him on a transformative spiritual journey. Following his spiritual awakening, Francis publicly renounced his family's wealth and possessions, even returning his costly garments to his father. He donned a humble brown tunic and devoted himself to a life of radical simplicity and austerity. As Francis continued to deepen his relationship with God, his way of life and his preaching attracted followers who were inspired by his unwavering commitment to poverty and humility. In 1209, he established the Order of Friars Minor (commonly known as the Franciscans) with the approval of Pope Innocent III. The order, initially consisting of a small band of devoted followers, was characterised by its emphasis on poverty, preaching and service to the poor and marginalised.

In 1219, however, he saw that his calling was in Egypt – but not in the same way that others were taking up the call. No doubt through his experiences of the turmoil and discontent after the former Crusades (especially the third and fourth), Francis saw his calling as that of a peacemaker. Ridiculed for his pursuit by fellow Crusaders who were deeply ingrained with Urban's message to 'destroy that vile race', Francis took it upon himself to visit the Muslim camps where he met Melek al-Kamil, the Sultan of Egypt. In a sense this was a meeting of monumental value – it was a meeting of East and West, of Europe and Asia, of Islam and Christianity.

Time has altered the details of the meeting in more ways than one, however. Twentieth-century historians, for example, contested the idea that Francis could transcend the political and religious narrative of Europe and the church he grew up in. Alternatively, Franciscan scholars have tended to adapt and emphasise the spirituality of Francis to suit certain needs, especially in a modern world where religion plays a controversial role. As such, let us travel back to the thirteenth century to the roots of the facts and fiction that have since emerged to decode the true understanding of this meeting and highlight its incredible importance in medieval history. Prior to Francis's arrival, the Crusaders in 1218 had conquered the gates of Damietta which had hindered their travel from the north. Here, they wintered and awaited reinforcements. Such forces never came and, on top of this, sources describe an incredibly hot summer that pushed the European armies to their limits. The result was an uprising which forced the hand of commanders to take the city. This would prove to be disastrous. The Sultan, in return, proposed a generous offer: if the armies left Egypt and ceased their attacks, they could have the city of Jerusalem with funds to rebuild their walls and defences. At this time, Francis visited the Sultan and most probably preached the Gospel. He stayed in the region for nine months and then returned to his Franciscan Order in Italy. Meanwhile, the papacy refused the offer of a truce and two months later captured Damietta.

Considering that sources for the past are generally scarce, the story of Francis has survived fairly well in hagiographies, chronicles and letters. By piecing together these details we shall be able to understand the full picture of what went down between the saint and the Sultan. There are four hagiographical accounts of the meeting, two of which were by Thomas of Celano in 1228 and *c.*1250. The oldest account, however, is in a letter by Jacques de Vitry, the bishop of Acre. In his letter from Acre only six months after the encounter, he wrote:

> The master of these brothers, who also founded the Order, came into our camp. He was so inflamed with zeal for the faith that he did not fear to cross the lines to the army of our enemy. For several days, he preached the Word of God to the Saracens and made little progress. The Sultan, Egypt's king, privately asked him to pray to the Lord for him, so that he might be inspired by God to adhere to that religion which most pleased to God.

It is interesting to see that the bishop is not aware of who Francis is as this was before Francis and the Franciscan Order truly became popular. What is interesting, is that Jacques's letter would not indicate an 'interreligious dialogue' but rather an attempt at conversion which still somewhat aligned with the crusading values of the time. Jacques in his letter is also partly sympathetic to the Sultan, calling him 'Egypt's King' which is more positive than the 'Wild Beast' the Sultan was described as in a retelling of the story in the *Historia Occidentalis* a few years later. All that said, however, one cannot help but see an element of martyrdom in this letter. In a general sense, being 'inflamed with zeal for the faith that he did not fear to cross the lines to the army of our enemy' would hint that Francis is prepared for death. Some fifty years later, Bonaventure, who wrote the final and officially approved *Vita of St Francis*, would play upon this sense of martyrdom:

> Who would be competent to describe the burning charity with which Francis, the friend of the Bridegroom, was aflame? Like a thoroughly burning coal, he seemed totally absorbed in the flame of divine love. For as soon as he heard 'the love of the Lord', he was excited, moved, and on fire [...]

Here Francis's love is the central element of the story, but what is most notable about this retelling is how Bonaventure's story introduces an ordeal by fire. He goes on to suggest that Francis and the 'Muslim priests' walked through the fire before the Sultan, and whoever came out unharmed would represent the best religion. The Muslim 'priest' refused, but Francis suggested he would then do it alone to show off the prowess of Christendom. The Sultan, however, refused as he feared a rebellion if Francis survived unscathed. There is no doubt that Bonaventure made this story up to evoke a former story whereby Francis receives a vision of a seraph, an angel which represented burning love. Still, it shows that Bonaventure aimed to represent Francis as a model of burning love and religious zeal, and someone who fully experienced God.

The final tale consists of two stories which come from Illuminato, a companion of St Francis in Egypt. The stories come from a collection that was to be used in sermons by the end of the thirteenth century, which is something to bear in mind. The first story tells of Francis visiting the Sultan and having to walk across a carpet adorned with crosses to disrespect the Christian faith. Francis declared:

> Together with Jesus two robbers were crucified. As we have the true cross, these images must represent the brigands' crosses that have nothing to do with the holy cross of our Saviour.

In the second story, Francis is asked by the Sultan:

> Your God teaches that you should not render evil for evil, and that you should not refuse anyone who wants to take your cloak, and so on. How can you then invade our lands?

Without a moment's pause, St Francis answered:

> Our Gospel also tells us, 'If your eye hinders you, take it out and cast it away when it separates you from your God.' Because you are doing just that [namely, hindering us], we are justified in fighting you.

It is important to know that these two stories are historically inaccurate. It is known, for example, that Melek al-Kamil actually held the True Cross, not the Christians. As such, although not providing a great deal of information on the historical events of the meeting, this is a remarkable insight into perceptions of the Crusades that are somewhat contemporary to them. It also showed that Illuminato sought to present Francis as a keen debater and brilliant mind who did not hesitate to criticise and condemn others. Yet, this would also show Francis to be approving of the Crusades and not so much the peacemaker that others may believe him to be.

So what was Francis asking of the Sultan? Many historians have drawn a diverse range of answers to this question. To some, these stories show that Francis was a fierce opponent of Islam and did not seek diplomacy but rather to scorn the Sultan. Others have used contemporary chronicles to hypothesise that perhaps Francis was bargaining for permission for free access to holy places. Well-known French Islamologist, Louis Massignon, connected the stories of the encounter to similar stories of the Prophet Mohammed. Events describe an instance whereby the Prophet debated with Christians over religion and offered to walk through fire to prove Islam's truth. The Christians, however, were scared and thus refused the offer. As such, was Francis seeking compensation for the failure of these early Christians? Perhaps he was attempting to mock the Sultan? This is what is particularly interesting about this saint. Two schools of thought underpin this meeting. One side praises the pacifism of St Francis and his condemnation of the Crusades, while the other, more sceptical, side suggests that Francis was a great supporter of the Crusade and condemned Islam.

Unfortunately, Muslim sources offer no reprieve as the only possible reference was a chance remark by a fifteenth-century chronicle that references the Sultan 'who had a memorable adventure with a monk'. Whether this even refers to Francis is a whole other question. Christian sources, however, are ignorant of the Muslim side of things. They forget, for example, that there were thousands of Christians living in the Middle East and North Africa, many of whom the Sultan would have ruled over (most probably Coptics and Melkites). Francis would have been one among many who would have consulted the Sultan over the relationship between Christianity and Islam.

Perhaps by turning to Francis's own writings we can piece together a better understanding of this encounter. As with St Benedict and his Rule, Francis constructed his own Rule for the Friars Minor. Within this text, we can find a chapter which specifically details 'going among the Saracens':

> The Lord says: Behold, I am sending you like sheep in the midst of wolves. Therefore, be prudent as serpents and simple as doves. Let any brother,

> then, who desires by divine inspiration to go among the Saracens and other nonbelievers, go with the permission of his minister and servant. If he sees they are fit to be sent, the minister may give them permission and not oppose them, for he will be bound to render an accounting to the Lord if he has proceeded without discernment in this or other matters. As for the brothers who go, they can live spiritually among the Saracens and nonbelievers in two ways. One way is not to engage in arguments or disputes but to be subject to every human creature for God's sake and to acknowledge that they are Christians. The other way is to announce the Word of God, when they see it pleases God, in order that [unbelievers] may believe in almighty God, the Father, the Son and the Holy Spirit, the Creator of all, the Son, the Redeemer and Saviour, and be baptized and become Christians because no one can enter into the kingdom of God without being reborn of water and the Holy Spirit.

It is believed that this dates to around 1221, only two years after the meeting and only one year after five friars were martyred in Morocco after attempting to convert Muslims. As such, the Rule states that there are two ways to live amongst Muslims: either humbly, avoiding dispute, or boldly in hopes to convert them. The latter here evokes that former idea of martyrdom without fear. It is interesting to note too that the Rule instructs conversion in relation to Saracens rather than a general populous of people. If Francis produced this for his followers to subscribe to then it hints at which sort of Christian he sought to be.

After traversing all this contradicting mess of sources, the question is: What does this all mean and lead us to? Two main points stand out about Francis and his encounter: Francis holds a great amount of courage and the Sultan holds an equal amount of gentleness, and that ultimately Francis made little physical gain from his encounter. In terms of his motives, many of the sources point towards martyrdom. Harking back to Jacques de Vitry's letter, Francis was burning with a 'zeal for the faith' as well as love and spiritual fervour. His method can be seen in his Rule, but does this make him a facilitator of interreligious dialogue? In a sense perhaps. Ultimately, he engaged with a non-violent approach within circles of bloodthirsty warriors. It is understandable then that this story with so much death, failure and unrest, would shine as a model for peaceful encounters. To Francis, his weapon was his words and despite potentially searching for condemnation, conversion, or martyrdom, he did so in peace. We cannot discredit him for being trapped by his medieval mind, which had been influenced by two centuries worth of anti-Islamic propaganda. Paradoxically, it is his strangeness within these times that make him a popular saint for centuries to come. In fact, the non-violent encounter in the middle of one of the most blood-ridden wars in humankind (at this point in time) was an inspiration. Francis in a sense traversed the dogmatism and authority of religion and reached a freedom in spirituality. This message would endure when Pope John Paul II organised an interreligious meeting at Assisi in 1986. At the meeting, Catholics, Orthodox Christians, Protestants, Jews, Muslims, Buddhists, and other religious representatives, prayed for peace. It is known that the pope specifically chose Assisi for the site of this monumental event because of the saint who was a prophet of peace.

Returning to our Crusaders, after Damietta they marched on in 1221 to Cairo and camped along the Nile floodplain. Al-Kamil saw this as a prime opportunity and ordered the floodgates to be opened, while also sinking four ships behind the Crusader army to trap them. Thousands drowned as they were stuck in the silt and mud of the river banks. Surrounded, the Crusaders were met with certain death and surrendered. Damietta and the Muslim prisoners were returned to Al-Kamil and the Crusader army returned home in another spectacular flop. In the years after the Fifth Crusade, there was a great deal of debate over who was to blame. Nevertheless, one small success was that the decision to divert the focus of attack on Egypt as opposed to Jerusalem did leave lasting anxiety in the minds of the Ayyubid Sultans about the possibility of a much larger attack. This may well have contributed to the negotiations being made within the Sixth Crusade that would be led by Holy Roman Emperor Frederick II in 1228 who, within a year, gained Jerusalem through diplomacy rather than warfare. Perhaps the acts of St Francis did make a difference in the end.

Chapter Ten

The Golden Age of Saints

In his *Liber Miraculorum Sancte Fidis,* eleventh-century churchman and sceptic, Bernard of Angers reported hearing of strange miracles, and an even stranger saint located in the Duchy of Languedoc. As such, in *c.*1013, Bernard decided to undertake an investigation and pilgrimage to the shrine of Sainte Foi, also known as St Faith, to find the truth behind certain miracles and those who worshipped the saint. Bernard's scepticism for saints is demonstrated when he passes through Aurillac and comes upon the shrine and statue of St Gerald, resplendent in gold. Unimpressed by the shrine, Bernard believes the practice of saint worship is 'perverse and most contrary to Christian law' and that the holy cross was the only true image of Christian worship. Despite this idolatry, he continued to the shrine of St Faith at Conque, where he discovered the golden girl. The reliquary, which still survives to the present day, shows a gilded St Faith, enthroned and encrusted with jewels and gems which reportedly glistened in the sunlight. Bernard mocked the false idol and compared it to the golden bull featured in the Hebrew Bible.

Bernard would soon become enthralled in the shrine, however, and captivated by its cult as he began to encounter and familiarise himself with St Faith's pilgrims, and those who had experienced her miracles. He provides us with a remarkable description which encapsulates the incredible importance and connection between saint and pilgrim. He learnt that far from idolatry, the relic and remains of the young girl connected heaven to earth; that the beauty of the statue reflected the glory of heaven and allowed the everyday person to focus their prayer and access divinity. Bernard even goes as far as to state that the shrine and saint were more precious to the local region than the Ark of the Covenant was to the Israelites. This story, and the description of saint worship provided by Bernard, perfectly encapsulate the focal point of this chapter.

Through the use of various pieces of hagiographical literature, shrine account records, and legal documents amongst other general sources, this chapter aims to decode pilgrimage to understand pilgrims; the culture and traditions underpinning pilgrimage and worship; and the interconnectivity of shrines, monastic communities and regions as a result of pilgrimage.

Unlike typical historical narratives that aim to follow a specific individual, reign, or war, this chapter captures a topic which encompassed everyone, from every part and sect of society. As such, there is a multitude of issues and limitations that come with researching such a widespread topic, namely that because pilgrimage was such an ingrained aspect of society, rarely is it solely written about in detail. Thus, the historian must interweave multiple sources that only provide pieces of insight in order to create the full image as accurately as possible. By doing so, this also reduces the respective limitations of each type of source, once again aiding in building a complete and accurate narrative of pilgrimage in the period in question.

Hagiographical literature, more specifically the *Miracula*, of some of England and Northern France's most prolific saints, provides a helpful insight into constructing an analysis of pilgrims. Rather than general figures, the multitude of miracles in any given hagiography provides a highly detailed sample and representation of the wider pilgrim population. Miracles can provide us with the sex and social class of the pilgrim, as well as the type of miracle experienced, and even sometimes detailing where the pilgrim had come from. Individual miracles, however, are limited in providing details on worshipping culture. While chroniclers, such as Thomas of Monmouth, discuss a variety of pilgrim traditions, combining non-monetary donation records with written sources can construct an understanding of pilgrim traditions and worship culture, of which all levels of society partook. It is important to note that such traditions within pilgrimage were governed by oral tradition and systems of belief, rather than lay or ecclesiastical laws. This concept will be emphasised when understanding the jostling relationship between tradition and monastic communities as certain sites sought to endorse certain practices while discouraging others.

The term 'pilgrim' encapsulates far more than simply someone who wanted to express their piety and faith. The wide range of motives behind undertaking a pilgrimage were highly varied. Some people visited shrines in anti-royalist protest and opposition to kings by honouring their enemies. Especially when the saint was killed through royal command, a cult with a rebellious undertone and focus would emerge. This is particularly witnessed within the cults of Thomas of Lancaster and Simon De Montfort, especially since royal authority sought to prohibit and control these cults to reduce anti-royalist sentiment and protest. Another, rather amoral, motive for pilgrimage was to rob the shrine of its donations. Shrines were, without a doubt, fairly rich in nature and thus were a target for those seeking to make some money. The miracles of St Cuthbert provide a multitude of examples of thieves stealing books, coins and other offerings. One such instance is of a certain man, who sought to steal from the shrine by deceptively kissing the tomb and swallowing four or five coins while doing so. The idea of stealing coins through this manner is seemingly common and is written in many other miracle collections.

These motivations for pilgrimage, however, were a small proportion of the wider scope. Ultimately, pilgrimage was undertaken for one of two predominant reasons. The first was to undertake penance and absolution for sins or crimes committed. Pilgrimage as a form of penance could be undertaken as a voluntary act of devotion, but more often it was imposed by an ecclesiastical authority, particularly in the Celtic church, where there was a set of penalties which detailed conditions of pilgrimage to match certain crimes or sins. The Penitential of Columbanus, for example, prescribed a seven-year pilgrimage for a clerk who begot a child, while theft, on the other hand, only entailed a pilgrimage of three years. Penitential letters collected in the eleventh century provide an incredible insight into individuals who undertook such penance pilgrimages. One such example is a letter to Lupus, bishop of London, in the early eleventh century, whereby a certain man 'deceived by diabolical fraud' begged for mercy and requested penance as punishment. What is particularly notable about this letter is that certain conditions are outlined for his penance to ensure suffering is endured, and absolution is achieved. The idea of an ecclesiastical authority outlining conditions was common amongst criminals, and the conditions for this fraudulent man included:

> On the second, fourth and sixth days [of the week] he shall fast on bread and water, he shall enter the church on the Nativity of the Lord and Easter, he shall eat flesh on Sundays and major feast-days. On the three days on which he abstains from flesh, he is to wear woollen clothing and go barefoot, he shall not give peace, he shall not cut his hair except three times in the year, he shall not communicate unless he comes to the point of death.

There are also instances of self-imposed penance pilgrimages. Typically, these were undertaken by clergy and priests who sought to cleanse themselves of their sins. Furthermore, following the self-imposed nature of the pilgrimage, the itinerary of the journey was equally self-determined. Wills and other agreements made by departing pilgrims provide a notable insight into those who sought to undertake a journey by their own accord. The following is taken from an Iberian cartulary and involves Remundo, an eleventh century priest, who declares the following:

> I acknowledge that I am weak and a sinner and because of the horrible sins which I have committed, I fear the pains of eternal judgement; however, not despairing of the mercy of Christ, I desire to attain the joys of Paradise. I want therefore to go to the shrine of the blessed apostle James.

Nevertheless, aside from penance, opportunistic theft and protest, most pilgrims undertook pilgrimage to express their faith and ask for healing or special favours. Furthermore, as witnessed in the variety of contemporary sources on undertaking such a journey, it can be understood that pilgrimage had a degree of fluidity and flexibility, as while there were ecclesiastical guidelines, self-determination was a highly prominent aspect of this topic. Some pilgrims had a specific destination, be it local, regional or international; others simply wandered from shrine to shrine seeking divine assistance. Yet, all pilgrims understood saints as being vessels of God and a connection between heaven and earth. Thus, a statistical analysis of the numerous miracle collections across England and Northern France can provide the greatest insight into who pilgrims were, what social class they attached to, and why they engaged in pilgrimage.

Quite simply, without the belief in the power of saints, the concept of pilgrimage would not exist, or at the very least it would be mere tourism. Hence, to understand pilgrimage, we must understand those who experienced and witnessed the miracles performed by local, regional, or even international saints. Miracles are also important if we understand shrine worship in terms of modern virality because, quite often, patterns and influxes of pilgrim migration were influenced by the reputation and popularity of the shrine spurred on by oral tradition. An extraordinary example of virality is the twelfth century case of Eilward of Westoning, a man who was blinded and castrated for petty thievery. Upon asking the newly established St Thomas Becket for help, he quickly regained sight. Eilward's story, as understood by Benedict of Peterborough, went viral and 'word of this went out among the vicinity, and the new thing attracted no small multitude of people'. As Eilward travelled to the shrine at Canterbury to pay homage, he told his story along the pilgrim routes and created a large buzz, so much so that the story reached Canterbury before he did. Yet, Eilward is not unique, as multiple hagiographical texts reveal surprising amounts of information about the oral tellings of these legends in their own contexts.

Some historians have dubbed this oral tradition as a 'chattering atmosphere' and thus the telling of miracles can become a game of whispers. Benedict of Peterborough, narrating St Thomas Becket, remarks how he was told about a miracle from a 'truthful man', who had heard it 'from a certain Gilbert', who had heard it from a blind man. Likewise, the author of the *Liber Eliensis* at Ely received a letter from Osbert of Clare about a miracle he was told about by Prior Osbert of Daventry, who had heard said miracle by the friends of a woman. Though seemingly comical, Caesarius of Heisterbach's *Dialogus Miraculorum*, shows that 95 per cent of miracle stories arose from oral sources. The miracle collections of Thomas Becket have comparatively similar statistics as 94 per cent of miracles were from oral tradition.

Did stories become distorted as they were passed on? It is difficult to answer for certain, but we should treat the majority of miracle stories as the end-product of genuine attempts to formulate explanations of real experiences. Therefore, we must rely on the scrutiny and critique of miracle collectors for reassurance.

Such a notion is not overly far-fetched if we understand how miracle collections were constructed, and how certain miracles were omitted or grouped. What becomes clear from the introductions of some miracle collections is that collectors did take time to process miracles and decide how the collection should be curated. A modern and comparative example is that of sociologist Candace Slater who sought to record the miracles witnessed at Brazilian and Spanish shrines. Her fifteen years of research yielded over 47,079 miracles, and thus to keep her research manageable she based her collection on quality rather than quantity, and thereby deconstructed the personal experiences to group the miracles together. In essence, contemporary sources show that medieval miracle collectors undertook a similar methodology. The anonymous Beverley collector noted, 'The passage of time would detain me for a very long time if I wished to write down every single release of prisoners through the merits of St John.' Likewise, another anonymous miracle collector at Reading wrote that, 'In a similar way and by a similar remedy another knight named Ralph Gilbuin was cured of a similar disease, as also were so many others, both men and women, that I cannot cover them all in this account.' Therefore, considering this methodology, miracle collectors did seek to minimise any anomalies, half-truths, or distortions, so much so that miracle stories are known to be highly repetitive, all containing similar themes. We can, with a fair degree of reassurance then, understand these collections to be a qualitative sample of the wider pilgrim population. Statistical analysis can be conducted on such data to understand shrines and their pilgrims.

Arguably, the most impactful study on medieval pilgrimage, Finucane's *Miracles and Pilgrims* sought to examine the miracles of each of the major medieval saint cults and place their pilgrims within a system of classification to identify trends and social profiles in shrine devotees. Miracles provide stories on all types of medieval people: bakers, bishops, millers, peasants, knights, artisans, merchants, and more. Thus, Finucane aimed to divide pilgrims into six general social groups: the nobility; upper ecclesiasts; knights; lower ecclesiasts; gentry, merchants and artisans; and the unskilled, the peasantry, the poor and the unspecified. Finucane does note that these categories, as with any division, are highly contentious. While it is simple to identify nobility and upper ecclesiasts as these are usually named and eagerly mentioned by scribes, it can become difficult and less well defined when venturing further down the social ladder. This is especially true for women, who were often of unspecified social class unless they were from nobility or in an upper ecclesiastical position. Equally, Finucane also classified miracles by thirteen different categories: Unqualified Illness; Cripples; Non-Healing Miracle; Blindness; Accident; Mental; Abscess/Leprosy; Specific Infirmity; Deaf/Dumb; Gutta/Dropsy; Wounding; Visions; and Childbirth Problems. Again, this is a contentious categorisation. Most prominent is the fact that all non-healing miracles (such as sailors rescued at sea, or prisoners escaping from capture) are grouped together, which discourages any attempts to understand the non-healing function of certain shrines and to examine the relationship, for example, between coastal shrines and rescued sailors. Still, this methodology is sufficient in classifying pilgrims, and the results of such classifications provide insightful trends, analysis, and understanding.

Finucane was strict on which shrines to include; they had to follow all three rules that he outlined: at least 100 miracles were registered at each cult; the cults developed into the twelfth and thirteenth centuries; and all new cults. It is no surprise that the most prolific shrine for Finucane to analyse would be that of Thomas Becket. In *c.*1172, the Archbishop of Sens wrote to John of Salisbury stating that the numbers of miracles occurring in France were so numerous that they could scarcely all be counted. As such, there is plenty of evidence on the popularity of Thomas Becket's shrine within England, but also internationally on the continent. In fact, within the first decade of Thomas Becket's cult becoming established, Benedict of Peterborough had assembled the greatest miracle collection of the Middle Ages with over 703 miracles. William, another Canterbury monk, also amassed over 438 miracles for his collection which ends about *c.*1179. Finucane's analysis provides some incredible insight into where these pilgrims predominantly came from. Subtracting the pilgrims listed by Benedict and William where no origin is given, 531 individual pilgrims can be pinpointed. Of these, 360 pilgrims were from England, and over half of these (56 per cent) came from south-east England. The localisation to the cult, however, is striking as a quarter of all English pilgrims originated in Kent or Canterbury. Then, great numbers of pilgrims came from London, followed by Berkshire and Oxfordshire, Sussex, Essex and Suffolk. There were relatively fewer pilgrims from more distant counties such as Devon, Somerset, Cornwall, Hereford, Shropshire, Durham and Northumberland. Interestingly, of the northern, Midland, and western regions, York contributed the most pilgrims, most probably due to its prominence as an English monastic site.

Of the aforesaid 531 pilgrims, over a third of these pilgrims (171) came from Northern France. Abbot Peter de Celle describes vast numbers of Northern French pilgrims visiting Canterbury in the late *c.*1170s, and one such pilgrim was Louis VII of France who, in *c.*1179, visited the tomb of St Thomas Becket seeking a cure for his son Philip Augustus. Louis is recorded as placing a gold coin on the altar and granting the priory an annual income of 1,600 gallons of wine. The associations between Northern France and Becket are perhaps encouraged through his interactions as chancellor and exiled archbishop, but the proximity of the shrine to Dover, and by extension Northern France, meant that pilgrims from France, specifically Claremont, Eu, Liseux, Poitiers, Pontigny and Rouen all visited and worshipped at the shrine with ease. In terms of hagiographical literature, the popularity of the shrine can also be represented by mapping monastic communities whereby the manuscripts of Benedict of Peterborough established provenance. Once again, we witness a degree of proximity with the shrine as the manuscript is found at Lyre, Signy, Aulne, Clairvaux and Pontigny. Yet its prominence does not end there as the miracle collection reached as far as San Mames de Lorvao and Santa Cruz de Coimbra in modern Portugal, Salem and Boddeken in modern Germany, and Heiligenkruez and Lilienfeld in Lower Austria in modern Germany. Once again, this promotes the idea that although many monastic communities competed for influence and prominence, there was a vast interconnected network whereby pilgrims and miracle collections were vibrantly exchanged. In terms of wider Europe, Canterbury was included amongst the 'greater pilgrimages' that a pilgrim could undertake (others being Compostela, Cologne, Jerusalem and Rome). Returning once more to penance, Flemish cities also utilised pilgrimage to English shrines, mainly that of St Thomas Becket, for absolution. The city of Ghent, for example, sent pilgrims to shrines at Canterbury, St Andrew's, Salisbury, Walsingham, Yarmouth, Beverley, Peterborough, Bury St Edmunds and Louth. Other cities, such as Antwerp, ordered their pilgrims to visit not only those aforesaid shrines, but also Oxford, and St Patrick's Purgatory. As such, similar to those regions of northern France, there was a vast interconnected network of pilgrims travelling from Ghent, Aalst, Dendermonde, Oudenaarde, Leuven, Antwerp, Tournai, Lier, Courtrai and Bruges, to shrines along the eastern side of England.

We cannot disregard the fact that there were as many pilgrims leaving England as there were being received. This period, quite clearly, saw a huge influx in pilgrims as a result of the Crusades. These departing pilgrims are frequently registered in Patent Rolls, especially after the mid-thirteenth century. It is for this reason that so much of international pilgrimage is recorded, as alongside those who are registered to visit the Holy Land are those who registered and asked to visit other European shrines, namely Santiago de Compostela, Cologne and Rome. The following is an example of such a document from *c.*1223:

> The Abbot of St Augustine's of Canterbury, who by the royal licence has gone on pilgrimage to Cologne, has letters patent of protection, to last

> until the feast of St Michael [29 September], in the seventh year of the king's reign.

There are, however, plenty of other shrines that English pilgrims visited abroad. In the mid-thirteenth century, the canonisation of Edmund Abingdon, Archbishop of Canterbury (also known as Edmund Rich), at Pontigny provided a huge influx in English pilgrims. Patent Rolls record pilgrims venturing to Pontigny far into the fourteenth century, and even Henry III had vowed to undertake pilgrimage to Edmund's shrine in *c.*1252 during a bout of illness. These shrines also contained their own spheres of influence on the local French region and area. In his analysis of over 150 French miracle collections from the eleventh and twelfth centuries, Pierre-Andre Sigal discovered notable figures involving French shrines and pilgrims. All the miracles attributed to women concerned healing, and 90 per cent of these miracles were in relation to their bodies. Comparatively, only 70 per cent of men from the higher classes involved healing, notably less than women of the same status. Of this 70 per cent, only a mere 22 per cent were about their bodies; instead these men were concerned with their dreams, as over 44.6 per cent of male miracles involved visions. Furthermore, Finucane's analysis of the 209 miracles recorded for the shrine of Edmund showed that most of these pilgrims were men, and half of those were of the lower class. Unlike England, there were relatively few male pilgrims from the upper classes or clergy; a notable difference.

Upon setting off on a journey, certain routes could be taken to reach the destination. Much has been written about the Via Francigena, the multitude of complex routes connecting north-western Europe to Rome, and likewise the Via Tolosana, which connected France to the Compostela via Grenoble and the Rhone Valley. The sea, however, often provided direct pilgrim travel to certain shrines, particularly those in Spain or Italy. In the twelfth century, Icelandic Abbot Niklas of Munkathvera described a junction at Luni whereby pilgrims who travelled by road and by sea would converge on their way to Rome. Nevertheless, pilgrims had to adapt to the ever-changing political climates of Europe, and chronicler Ralph Glaber describes how a usual route to Jerusalem for French and Italian pilgrims by sea changed when Hungary converted to Christianity and opened its land borders. Likewise, fluctuations of pilgrims to Jerusalem notably declined in *c.*1009 when the Holy Sepulchre was destroyed by Caliph Al-Hakim. Only when it was later restored, did pilgrims, firstly of lower social classes, begin to return to this region. Hence, pilgrimage was well defined yet also highly flexible, and could adapt and change according to political climates, both positive and negative – perhaps because it truly was so ingrained within societies and cultures across Europe.

Miracle collections can also provide an understanding of domestic spheres of influence within a localised region and the true impact of oral tradition. The miracles of William of Norwich deliver great detail on the origins of local pilgrims, so much so that we can even visualise the growth of the cult over time. Thomas of Monmouth's extraordinarily detailed miracle collections on the saintly boy enable us to locate 94 per cent of pilgrims which can then be placed in the periods between the several translation ceremonies. Within the first few years of the cult's establishment, more than half (57 per cent) of pilgrims lived less than 10 miles from the shrine, many of whom were from Norwich itself. There is a notable decline in the recording of miracles outside of this margin. In 1150/51, the average distance rose to 23 miles; from 1151 to 1154 it rose to 32 miles; then from 1154 to 1172 it rose to 45 miles, double the original sphere of influence.

It is debatable and unlikely that it would take twenty years for the cult to grow as little as 40 miles, even by Norfolk standards. Yet, being able to map the organic growth of a shrine in this way allows us to visualise the impact of oral tradition and word of mouth. Particularly interesting is that the cult growth encapsulated the local community, to almost perfectly fit and resemble the regional borders of medieval East Anglia, reaching its peak growth at around 50 miles. After this boundary there is a sharp decline in the belief of Norwich's saint, and a reason for this is that from around 40–50 miles, Norwich's cult sphere intersects with the sphere of influence established by Bury St Edmunds, which was far more popular and influential, and contained a more powerful oral tradition.

In fact, upon analysing the social class composition of Bury St Edmunds, it becomes clear that the cult was far more established than St William's in Norwich, containing numerous high-profile pilgrims. The miracles collected at Bury St Edmunds are limited, only fifty-two being accounted for across the *Miraculas* written by Archdeacon Herman (*c.*1070), Goscelin (*c.*1100), Osbert (*c.*1130s), and Abbot Samson (*c.*1200). Nevertheless, the results are still relevant in understanding the composition of pilgrim devotees. Of the fifty-two pilgrims recorded, the sex of the pilgrims at Bury St Edmunds closely follows the overall national average outlined by Finucane. While the national average is 61 per cent male and 39 per cent female, Bury St Edmunds consists of 65 per cent male, 35 per cent female – nothing overly unique. The distinctiveness of the cult comes in the form of social class representation.

As we can see, in both male and female shrine visitors, there is a notable number of nobility, knights and upper ecclesiasts. A probable cause for such a function is perhaps due to the nature of St Edmund being an Anglo-Saxon king who was martyred at the hands of foreign invaders. Thus, when Edward I prayed before St Edmund, and was bestowed his blessed banner before fighting the Scots, it makes sense that Bury functions as a primarily royal and monastic patron. It is no surprise then that Herman, in his *De Miraculis*, was motivated to portray Edmund as a symbol of foreign resistance and military strength. In the aftermath of the Conquest, Edmund played a key role in bridging the gap between the foreign Norman culture and Anglo-Saxon tradition. Furthermore, with so many nobles having land disputes, levied taxes, and succession conflicts as a result of the Conquest, it is understandable why there is such a heightened interaction between the saint and high nobles, aristocracy and nobility. It should be noted, however, that St Edmund healed as much as he punished, and there are positive experiences of Norman knights being healed by the saint. Ranulf, a Norman knight who arrived with William I in *c.*1066, was cured of madness by St Edmund, while William fitz Asketill, a knight from Herefordshire, was cured of a fever after making an offering. Overall, healing a specific illness was the most asked for miracle amongst men, while being crippled was oddly popular amongst women, something seemingly unique to Bury. The *Miracula* constructed by Abbot Samson, however, describes how widespread the call for healing was:

> Those who are afflicted with sickness join together; the streets are congested with a multitude of invalids. They call out Edmund's name, 'praise Edmund' resounds through the mouths of the crowd.

Aside from specific infirmity, non-healing miracles were highly popular. These predominantly consisted of visitors to the shrine who had been saved at sea, escaped from prison, or required assistance in conflict. Nevertheless, Edmund was a patron who protected and healed his worshippers.

Apart from spheres of influence, analysing miracles can also provide an understanding of the sex of pilgrims which is particularly important in understanding the role of women in pilgrimage. Finucane analysed two local shrines in England, of which there is a unique number of female pilgrims. The first is Godric of Finchale, situated outside of Durham. Of the 244 miracles analysed, two-thirds of these are women, higher than any other shrine analysed by me or Finucane. No other saint also accounted for so many lower-class people but considering that the social class of women were typically unspecified, this is no surprise. The other shrine with predominantly female devotees was Frideswide of Oxford. Of the 108 miracles, again, two-thirds of these were women.

Miracles provide a special insight into how women were able to express their faith in this period, but other contemporary sources involving pilgrimage can also enable an exploration into understanding the degree of freedom women had. The following source, a letter sent to Eleanor of Provence, the queen of

England, from Pope Innocent IV, is particularly notable as it demonstrates that royalty frequently undertook pilgrimage:

> Yielding to your devout prayers, we concede to you by the present authority that since from time to time it happens, by reason of devotion, that you come to many monasteries, of Cistercians and others, of the kingdom of England, you are permitted, with ten good and honest women, to enter their churches and cloisters for the purpose of prayer; any custom or statute confirmed by the Apostolic see or other authority notwithstanding.

More than this, it expresses certain complexities within gender and pilgrimage that are a prevalent undertone throughout this period, namely that women could only seemingly undertake pilgrimage through the approval of men and more specifically, only with the permission of ecclesiastical males. The most striking aspect of the passage is that the pope 'concedes' his approval and is 'yielding' after her multiple attempts at visiting monasteries. This great reluctance to allow women on pilgrimage is seemingly a microcosm for common opinion as St Cuthbert, patron of Durham Cathedral, was equally as reluctant to provide women with access to the cathedral priory and other areas. By using Finucane's methodology on the eighty-six miracles of St Cuthbert (based on the collections constructed by Symeon of Durham in the 1100s, and Reginald of Durham in the 1160s), I discovered that 89 per cent of pilgrim visitors were men, which is notably higher than the overall male average of 61 per cent. Such a result only corroborates the understanding that St Cuthbert was a misogynistic saint. The ban on women entering St Cuthbert's church was first recorded in Symeon of Durham's *Libellus de Exordio*, whereby Cuthbert 'severed his monks from all female company' so that through 'the indiscreet association of women with God's servants the monks should not endanger their resolve and so ruin them, thereby giving joy to the Enemy'. It is perhaps not surprising then that a quarter of male pilgrims were ecclesiastical, one of the largest proportions across English and French shrines. In correspondence to what Symeon describes, it seems to be that certain shrines and monastic communities were highly protective over who could and could not access the shrine, but it is noteworthy that this rule extends to include even the queen.

Comparing any given individual shrine will only provide vast generalisations and limitations. Alternatively, by understanding pilgrimage through all the miracles across all the shrines researched, we can draw together patterns and trends within English and Northern French pilgrimage. To begin with, as previously stated, across 2,000 pilgrims analysed, over 61 per cent were male, and 39 per cent were female. Of those women, the majority were obviously of unspecified social class aside from named examples from nobility and gentry. The most frequent male pilgrims were of the lower clergy, such as monks or priests. A comparison between the English and French cults provides some interesting, yet peculiar, outcomes. The same proportion of sexes were found in both England and France, and exactly the same proportion of female pilgrims were from the lower classes. The only prominent difference between French and English pilgrims was that English male pilgrims were typically a higher social class than male French pilgrims. Nevertheless, the similarities are striking, and the reasons for these parallels are uncertain, yet it is certain that pilgrimage and oral tradition was incredibly ingrained into all sects and classes of society, and the motivation to undertake a pilgrimage was felt by most, if not everyone.

As of now, statistical analysis has shown that shrines had a variety of devotees; some received vast amounts of lower-class women, while others frequently obtained patronage from royal and upper-class pilgrims. Nevertheless, what unites and underpins this worship and practise of pilgrimage is an underlying, yet prolific, culture based on oral tradition. Shrine donations, particularly non-monetary donations, provide historians with a highly in-depth understanding into how people worshipped and expressed their faith in ways not necessarily governed by lay or ecclesiastical laws.

In *c.*1307, about midway between Thomas de Cantilupe's death and canonisation, papal commissioners travelled to Hereford to conduct an examination on the shrine donations. The following is, according to the commissioners, a small fraction of the total offerings donated but nevertheless provides an insightful look into worship. These items included:

- 170 ships in silver and 41 in wax
- 129 images of men or their limbs in silver, 1,424 in wax
- 77 images of animals and birds of diverse species
- 108 crutches
- 3 vehicles in wood and 1 in wax, left by cured cripples
- 97 night-gowns
- 116 gold and silver rings and brooches
- 38 garments of gold thread and silk

This vibrant array of items reflects many of the motivations and reasons why people take up pilgrimage. The 108 crutches, for example, most probably signify those who either asked the saint to heal their crippled limbs or were symbols of those who had been healed and believed it was through the saint's power. Either way, these items each contain extremely personal stories of those who, arguably in a degree of desperation or hope, placed their faith in the divine.

There is, however, an overwhelming number of wax limbs found at Hereford as well as other English shrines, and as part of the papal investigation, a certain pilgrim provided a detailed account which explains why such donations were made. Hugh le Barber, who had been the barber to Thomas in his later life, began to lose his eyesight as he grew older and thus appealed to the saint by sending two wax eyes to Hereford. These eyes were to the exact measurements, proportion and likeness to his real eyes and were placed by the altar in the shrine upon his pilgrimage completion. His prayers were seemingly answered as his eyesight returned. What is particularly noteworthy about this tradition is that it seemingly transcends social class as Henry III, in *c.*1245, spent £51 13s 6d for fifteen candles 'of his size' which were to be placed at the shrine of Edward the Confessor. Whether fifteen life-sized candles were actually made is unlikely, but this tradition of 'measuring' an ailment and making a candle of it is frequently described in hagiographies. A more logical approach, described in the *Miracles of St Osmund*, was that a string would be measured to the length of the afflicted limb or body of the pilgrim and then 'the measuring thread (sometimes doubled back on itself) would form the wick of a candle of standard proportions'. Thomas of Monmouth corroborates this tradition in his description of a certain man who measured a length of string around his sick herd of oxen and used such thread to construct a candle as an offering. The shrine of St Cuthbert also housed one donation whereby the string folded back on itself sixty-six times to form an appropriate wick. Perhaps the most extraordinary example of this tradition is that of the taper donated by the city of Dover to Thomas Becket at Canterbury. This 'candela in rota', or rather a taper wound around a drum several times, 'contained in its length, the border of said city' and thus hoped for Thomas to aid all its inhabitants. This incredible tradition of representing the afflicted in wax thus symbolically equated the disappearance of ailment and disease. What is particularly clear is that this tradition, as with many others, transcends the strict boundaries of social class.

One possible reason that enables these traditions to surpass class is that worship is so closely related to belief, and by extension, oral tradition. Rather than a set of rules outlining worship, many of these traditions become popular on an 'If it works, I'll try it' basis in the same way many of us will attempt the new internet dieting fad nowadays. As we saw with the story of Eilward, pilgrim routes are highways of gossip and therefore when people catch wind of certain practices that seemingly work, word of mouth can make them 'go viral'. Other so-called 'viral trends' included kissing the base of a saint's altar, donating a single coin, and even entering the 'Holy Hole' which enabled pilgrims to crawl beneath the tomb and absorb divine radiation. Yet, it is the practices which failed to take off that prove how worshipping traditions are based on gossip.

One such practice is that of bending a coin over an ill person when donating to the shrine of Thomas Becket. The *Miracula* discusses this practice as if it were commonplace, and while it may have been in Canterbury, there is a lack of references in Osbern or other contemporary authors. Another tradition, created by a certain man from Exeter, saw him boil eggs, cut them into quarters, write Thomas Becket's name on them, and eat them. It is no surprise that, though inventive, it did not gain traction.

What is particularly interesting is how a monastic community may jostle over particular worshipping traditions and change their opinion over time. Benedict of Peterborough describes an odd practice known as 'Canterbury Water' whereby pilgrims would drink a concoction that contained water and Thomas Becket's blood. Benedict states that the monks were fearful to endorse such a practice as it was highly unusual, and almost perverse, to drink someone's blood. Yet, over time the practice was allowed as it seemingly began to work miracles and Benedict writes, 'O marvelous water … that not only quenches the thirst of drinkers, but also extinguishes pain!' In fact, in the miracle collection of *c.*1172 produced by William of Canterbury, drinking this water is written as casual practice. Thus, it can be argued that monastic communities conformed to the traditions developed and established by pilgrims which is fairly atypical when we consider that there is an abundance of contemporary material (such as the Rule of St Benedict) on the rulings of how certain people should pray and act in life.

Fundamentally, pilgrimage is far more in-depth than what may first appear. People did not merely travel to the local shrine to give offerings and ask for divine favours. Rather, pilgrims contained both the male and female, moral and amoral, the rich and the poor, and the lay and the ecclesiast. While on one hand, pilgrimage was strict in legalities as kings, archbishops and popes attempted to control and regulate aspects of worship and travel, it was also extremely fluid. Quite simply, pilgrimage was largely held in the palms of pilgrims themselves, and it was they who established and developed their journeys, traditions and networks, all of which were based around belief and oral tradition. And though each shrine functioned and varied slightly differently – be it a royal patron, protector, or healer – these systems of belief meant that worshippers could transcend national borders, social class, political rivalries and ethnic divisions. From the research largely conducted by Finucane, miracles are perhaps the most important source for understanding the composition and patterns of pilgrims across English and Northern French shrines. Through these vast collections, we can gain incredible statistics which can map the development of saint cults, understand the function of shrines through their devotees, and decode the complex topic of pilgrimage and gender disparity. In some ways, pilgrimage is one of the few areas whereby women had vast freedoms: they contributed a sizable proportion of total pilgrims; they had the ability to undertake pilgrimage at free will, both domestically and internationally; and they even dominated the worship of some shrines, such as Godric of Finchale and Frideswide of Oxford. Yet, as witnessed with the letter sent to the queen of England by the pope, there is a dark misogynistic undertone within pilgrimage that did limit women to access certain shrines such as that of St Cuthbert. Nevertheless, pilgrimage overturns the predisposed 'Dark Age' idea that medieval people did not travel or know much of the world around them. Instead, this documentation proves that the pathways and seas within Europe were bustling with travellers from all parts and that England saw vast numbers of pilgrims from Northern France as well as the Low Countries via an interconnected monastic network.

Chapter Eleven
From Saint to Sinner

During the period in which the silver shrine of St Erkenwald was completed, the 'generous hands of the poor' flocked to collecting stations to grant gifts and donations in adoration of the saintly figure. One woman, 'of devout heart', who had wished to join the celebrations was instead rebuked by her husband for offering gifts. The man, in his bitterness, was later struck by an intense pain and swelling in his abdomen the following night, which was deemed as untreatable. Yet, as 'the unfaithful husband will be saved by the faithful wife', the woman received instructions from St Erkenwald in a dream. It was commanded that the husband should be taken to the saint's sepulchre in order for him to be cured. Upon doing so, the husband was healed and returned home. This miracle, as Arcoid writes, was 'set up as an example of those who stand in the way of the works of holiness'.

The abovementioned story is Miracle 6 from the *Miracula Sancti Erkenwaldi*, completed by Arcoid in the 1140s. What is particularly notable about this miracle is its multidimensional and underlying tones of intimidation and coercion in conjunction with shrine donations. Arcoid begins the miracle by demonstrating the central role of the poor as the 'heroic financial support' of the shrine to emphasise that, 'although the wealthy citizens contributed little or nothing, the generous hand of the poor set up collecting stations.' According to Arcoid, if even the poorest of London can give financial support, then why can't you? Hence, when the poor but devoted woman is rebuked by her husband for attempting to provide financial support to the shrine, he is presented as immoral, stupid and unholy. The miracle thus promotes a cultural attitude whereby there is an expectation that a proportion of a household income should be donated to the local shrine. Miracle 6 is not necessarily unique in its coercive tone towards financial support. There is a multitude of miracles written by Arcoid that follow the formula whereby someone undermines the wealth or financial support of the shrine and is then struck by severe illness. Such intimidation by an ecclesiastical community regarding financial support is thus the genesis of this thesis: to what extent were saints, such as Erkenwald, largely exploited by their ecclesiastical communities to gain wealth?

In the immediate aftermath of the Conquest, ten English monastic sites contained a major shrine. Despite this, the abbey of St Augustine was the first to promote and undertake translation ceremonies. In 1091, the tombs of the first six archbishops of Canterbury were opened and their bodies translated to a shrine in a ceremony of great liturgical splendour. The translation of these six archbishops represented a new Norman trend in saint worship, that is, post-Conquest England saw the rise and prominence of bishops as newly canonised saints. Bishops arguably became popular saints because they embodied the religious lifestyle and virtuous qualities that a cathedral would want to promote. Secondly, considering a bishop was among the few people to be buried within a cathedral, there was an automatic possession of relics if sainthood occurred. Still, as the recognition and canonisation of a saint required an expensive investigation into the person's sanctity of life and posthumous miracles, another way to gain sainthood was through power and wealth. Such wealth and influence was sourced from living bishops who could expend funds to promote the prestige of their predecessor's shrine, as witnessed in the canonisation of William of York which was secured through the funds of Archbishop Walter de Grey and Archbishop Antony Bek. As such, from the establishment of post-Conquest cults, there were already instances of an underlying system of wealth that sought to exploit saints.

Following the translations at St Augustine's, both Winchester and Bury St Edmunds had also translated their respective saints and updated their accompanying *Miraculas* by 1095. As such, a case can strongly be made for suggesting that the translation of 1091 was so successful in its liturgical celebrations and promotion of pilgrimage that it set a precedent and model for such events in the future. Yet translation ceremonies themselves quickly became so extravagant that they required vast sums of money. In the translation of Thomas Becket, who had the quickest canonisation in medieval England at just twenty-six months, Stephen Langton's expenses were so large that they were still being paid by Archbishop Boniface, the fourth archbishop after Langton. Given that the translation of St Richard in 1276 cost Bishop Stephen more than £1,000, it has been hypothesised by historians that the celebrations at Canterbury may have cost a few thousand pounds, a figure which may have been a usual expense for translations at major monastic communities. The question is, quite simply, was this worth it? If we are to understand if saints were viable incomes, then there is a predisposed estimate that the output (donations rendered by pilgrims) is greater than the input (cost of translation). It is notable that translations were planned in order to gain high congregations of pilgrims. Becket was murdered on 29 December, a terrible period for pilgrim travel due to the winter months. Instead, the major feast and translation of St Thomas in 1220 was held in July during the best of the summer weather in order to fully gather as many pilgrims as possible. Moreover, just as a product is marketed by a retailer, Langton spent two years prior to the translation marketing the celebration throughout Europe to entice potential pilgrims. Considering crowds of pilgrims along with twenty-four bishops and archbishops came to witness the translation ceremony in what is regarded as the largest episcopal attendance of a translation, Langton's marketing strategies were clearly effective. Yet this was not the only example, as the translation of St Swithun in 1093 claimed to have been attended by 'almost all the bishops and abbots of England'. Equally, in the translation of St William of York, it is said that, 'on no other occasion has the cathedral received within its walls a more illustrious assemblage.' It is also evident that royalty attended such celebrations. The first known attendance of a translation is Henry II at Westminster in 1163. Nevertheless, Henry III and his son Edward each attended at least three within their respective reigns. Arguably, the attendance of these ceremonies by monarchs was opportunistic as when larger translation ceremonies become rarer, so does royal attendance.

With the mass migration of pilgrims, lay, nobility and knights, translations typically turned into larger festivals. Becket's translation, though an extreme example, lasted two weeks and saw hay and provender being provided to the thousands of travellers along the route from London to Canterbury. Equally, tuns of free wine were placed around the city and banquets, each multiple days' long, catering for tens of thousands. Yet, within these celebrations was a network of ecclesiastical vendors encouraging the purchasing of indulgences and other religious paraphernalia. We find, for instance, in the celebrations surrounding the translation of St Edmund at Bury in 1094 that sermons were preached to crowds offering indulgences for a select period of time. Thus, shrine accounts show that more donations were offered during translation celebrations and feasts than at any other time. The financial records of Canterbury during the translation prove this to be true, as the shrine proceeds in 1220 were extremely high at around £300. Furthermore, considering that in the same year of the translation the Martyrdom accumulated £27 and the Corona accounted for £40, St Thomas was the source of 75 per cent of the total average income from all offerings. This revenue, combined with the sales of indulgences and other dubious enterprises means that there is an argument for translation ceremonies generating a large amount of wealth. Although the initial investment input to conduct such ceremonies was high, the output of revenue and prestige which could span multiple decades presents the impression that saints provided a strong source of income for their respective cathedrals.

Translations, however, were not a common and frequent occurrence. Aside from saints, such as William of Norwich, who were translated multiple times, saints were typically only translated once or twice in the cult's history. As such, a closer analysis of the shrine incomes of prominent saint cults, as well as an understanding of how this revenue was directed, will allow for a more general insight into the extent to which saints were economically viable.

As a focus has already been made on the translation of St Thomas Becket at Canterbury, statistical analysis will begin here. Between 1198 and 1207, the offerings being donated to Canterbury in St Thomas's name were already high and, on average, paralleled the revenue of the translation ceremony. The highest recorded revenue from donations accumulated at Canterbury was 1200/01 as King John and his queen held their coronation there. Such an event rendered £620 4s from donations. As the personal memory of Becket faded in the late twelfth and early thirteenth century, donations fluctuated between the low of £65 and the high of £300. From 1257 onwards, almost nine decades after Becket's murder, donations had reached a steady decline and stagnation as a result of a moderation of pilgrim travellers to the shrine as the virality of the cult's establishment and translation had dwindled. Yet this income should not be disregarded as it still accounted for 28 per cent of Canterbury's total revenue – a considerable proportion. These revenues were redirected in a number of ways, but it is certain that a great percentage of offerings were distributed amongst officials and clergy, a factor which reiterates the impression that these ecclesiastical communities accumulated wealth in a self-serving manner by capitalising on saints and their cults. Two clerks at the tomb of St Thomas Becket received a well-paid wage of 1d per day alongside provisions of bread and ale. Equally, when those said monks carried holy water in processions, they received portions of food from the refectory. Moreover, in 1284, a clerk of exchange at Canterbury gave the clerk of the shrine, Andrew of Bregge, 50s as payment for maintaining two tapers. Thus, Canterbury provides an outstanding example of the incomes incurred from a saint, and clearly the churchmen of Canterbury profited from this. What is particularly noteworthy about the cult's success is the extent to which Becket influenced and divided monastic competition over saints among other churches. Some religious sites claimed association to the saint to cash-in on this enterprise. Carlisle Cathedral was one such site that appropriated the saint as they quickly claimed to hold the sword that martyred Becket. On the contrary, with the establishment of Becket's cult, monastic communities with major saints were keen to protect their own saints, miracles and relics. Reading Abbey, for example, reaffirmed and emphasised visions of St James the Great who informed the sick that they could only be cured at Reading, not anywhere else. St Frideswide of Oxford and St Cuthbert of Durham follow similar narratives of striking down a coercive message that only they could help the poor, so as to deter pilgrims from diverting attention to Becket. Thus, there is an affirmation and marketing of saint power occurring across England, because of Becket, in order to maintain the flow of pilgrims that are key to shrine revenue and prestige.

In conjunction with the statistical analysis of Becket's cult, his *Miracula* provides notable examples of miracles with underlying tones of exploitation. There are two prominent miracle collections that will be discussed. The first was written between 1171 and 1200 by Benedict of Peterborough, while the second was written by William of Canterbury in 1172–1176. William, in describing the death of Becket, explains that many townspeople came into the cathedral to view the corpse and dip their fingers in his blood. As such, 'there was no-one who did not carry away some portion of that precious treasure'. While this does not contain a coercive voice as with the *Miracula of St Erkenwald*, William of Canterbury's description of the blood as 'precious treasure' emphasises a potential insight into his views on the commercial value of Becket's relics. Such a notion is greatly supported if we understand that shrine keepers accumulated high margins of profit from selling ampullae of what was regarded as 'Becket's Blood'. Furthermore, around 20 per cent of the miracles collected by Benedict and William discuss the use of Becket's healing water. Even Henry II is recorded as drinking some of it on his visit to Canterbury. This is interesting, as typically healing occurs through the saint's direct intervention rather than a consumable vessel of power. Only when analysing these miracles through the scope of commercialising saints is it clear why Canterbury repeatedly emphasises the power of Becket's blood. It is also noteworthy that this exploitation of Becket's cult would soon become controversial and contribute to the cult's downfall. Suspicion of relic souvenirs and simony involving the blood of St Thomas provided Tudor critics with a foundation to begin a process of defaming the cult.

Emmanuel Walberg, in a highly regarded article, argued that Benedict began his miracle collection 'almost the day after the murder'. According to the *Miracula*, the first miracle of a woman in Sussex was experienced just three days after Becket's death. By April 1171, only four months after the martyr's death, Canterbury opened its crypt to visitors and distributed his healing blood. During this time, the monks of Canterbury also allowed free access to Becket's relics, and with this, miracles occurred 'every single day' as Benedict records. The rate at which these events occurred in conjunction with the speed of Becket's canonisation and production of multiple *miracula*, are phenomenal, yet peculiar. Some may regard this as a testament to devotion, and while this may be partly true, it could be suggested that given this evidence and the hindsight of the revenues generated, certain churchmen of Canterbury may have foreseen the potential commercial opportunities of Becket's veneration, especially in light of successes at other cathedrals and abbeys. Understandably, this is all speculative, but considering that the political rawness of Becket's death and speed of pilgrim worship led to a planned attack on Canterbury, clearly policies were implemented sooner than would have been respectful. In conjunction with this, the first appeal for Becket's canonisation, written in early autumn 1171, was rejected on the basis that it happened too quickly. Alexander II wrote to the monks that they should 'seek to know the truth of this more fully from bishops and other secular persons', then, 'write to us about the miracles and make known to us the certainty of the thing with all diligence'. Alexander's doubtfulness surrounding the quick appeal reiterates the suggestion that Canterbury was impulsive towards establishing a cult surrounding Becket, potentially in order to establish a highly successful stream of revenue and prestige.

Canterbury, however, was not the only prestigious monastic house to exploit its saint; Bury also provides an overwhelming amount of compelling evidence on how saints were exploited for the accumulation of wealth. Bury had translated St Edmund in 1095, and Archdeacon Herman had constructed a grand miracle collection in the previous year to accompany the ceremony. Spearheaded by Abbot Baldwin and Archdeacon Herman in the late eleventh century, this was one of the first post-Conquest examples of a business enterprise surrounding a saint that included a series of strategies to market and promote the saint to pilgrim populations. As stated previously, at the translation of Edmund, a sermon preached by Walkelin outside the precinct to a crowd enticed them to purchase indulgences from the shrine within a specific period of time. Once the translation was completed and Edmund's casket was installed within the new presbytery for pilgrims, Herman exploited this by preaching sermons at the altar to pilgrims at the apse and granting those with money and donations the opportunity to touch, handle and kiss the martyr's relics. Equally, Herman also orchestrated private handlings of the relics held within the crypt to wealthier patrons of the cathedral. Healing oils, according to one miracle, also exuded from the saint's body and were sold to pilgrims in small ampoules. Another example of such enterprise was St Nicholas at Bari whose monastic community established a highly profitable business off such oils. Lastly, Baldwin, in order to encourage higher numbers of pilgrims, capitalised on contact relics which were distributed throughout the continent to promote the cult. All of this served to develop an ecosystem revolving around the saint that encapsulated pilgrims in order to take advantage of their pockets.

A major piece of evidence to corroborate this point is the details of Herman's death. It states that Herman, to entice crowds and donations, sent for the chest containing St Edmund's relics in order for him to display them and allow paying pilgrims to handle them. Three weeks later, when a powerful magnate arrived to see those relics, he was led into the crypt and handled them. Such an event spurred pilgrim visitors to want to see the relics, an opportunity which Herman could not refuse. It is notable, in a slight diversion from the story, that the author regarded these relics as priceless. Yet Herman, on the other hand, regarded the saint's relics as being worth 'more than all the gold of Arabia'. In other words, Herman, unlike other monks, did place a value and price on these seemingly priceless holy objects. This emphasises Herman's business- and wealth-driven mindset towards the saint and relics. Herman, with the bustling crowd awaiting, held up the bloodied garment punctured with arrow holes and invited anyone to kiss it. Seitha, a recluse resident of the abbey, is recorded to have borrowed money in order to donate and kiss the saint. Soon after, Herman became ill and died three days later in what is described as a sickness that 'befalls transgressors', *morbo illicitorum*. It was believed that Herman's death was the result of divine retribution and charges of simony.

Beside the retribution, St Edmund became a prominent saint in England, being regarded as the saint of the East. In fact, Abbot Lambert of St Nicholas in Angers regarded Edmund as the '*totius Anglie patronum*'. Miracles involving the North Sea, the Channel, and regions as far as Italy proved the influence that Baldwin had sought to promote. This 'golden age' of the cult, however, soon passed with the deaths of Herman and Baldwin. Yet, the utilisation of the saint for the acquisition of wealth remained. From 1097, the diocesan Herbert de Losinga took over as abbot after Baldwin. In 1101, Herbert, who owned the estate of Hoxne, sought to transfer the cult centre to his property. Such a notion arose from the first miracle of St Edmund whereby a blind man was given sight. This was deemed controversial as it occurred outside of Bury at the chapel at Hoxne. Herbert thus aimed to promote a rival cult within his domain to increase his personal wealth and prestige – a pursuit which ultimately failed but highlights the wealth connected to saints and how greed persisted.

Bury also provides evidence which shows that aside from pilgrims, a saint could yield extremely high donations from monarchs. In 1296, the fines and forfeitures exacted whenever the king's ministers of the market passed through Bury were granted to St Edmund. These large sums went towards adorning the shrine in luxurious items and detail. In 1238, Henry III granted both Bury and Canterbury over 300 1lb candles to burn on feast days. Considering that wax at this time cost between 5d and 7d per lb when bought in bulk, this was a considerable and wealthy donation.

From the wealth of Bury, it is understandable why cathedrals would later catch on to this phenomenon and virality of saints to also gain wealth and increase their prestige. Hereford provides a perfect example of one such cathedral that established a cult to participate within the monastic competition over pilgrims. The financial aid that St Thomas Cantilupe provided the cathedral was enormous. The cult of Cantilupe, in the first thirty years of its establishment, funded significant building projects at the cathedral. The fabric roll of 1290/91 shows that revenues from donations amounted to £178 10s 7d, or rather 60 per cent of the cathedral's total income. In fact, Worcester also found its income increase by £10 simply by being on the pilgrim route to Hereford. Thus, as a source of income the shrine was very profitable, and these funds were reinvested into the clergy and cathedral to boost pilgrimage and, in turn, develop the prestige of Hereford. In 1291, Hereford accumulated more wax through donations than it burnt, reporting a wax revenue of £20. Of this amount, a third was given to the chapter as payment. What is notable is that the veneration and establishment of Cantilupe as a saint emerges from the backdrop of Bury's successes with the cult of St Edmund. It is known that a great number of pilgrims from Hereford travelled to St Edmund. Thus Hereford, in competition with Bury over territorial influence, wished to elevate its saint to regional prominence just as St Cuthbert, for example, was regarded as the saint of the north in the twelfth century. Ultimately, adorning the cathedral in wealth to elevate the prestige of both the clergy and cathedral, as a result of the saint, shows that there is a viable economic gain from capitalising on saints.

The establishment of cults, however, was not always as successful as Hereford, Canterbury or Bury. Norwich provides evidence for the repeated pursuit to capitalise on a saint for the gain of wealth. Between 1144 and 1172, the body of the young boy St William was translated four times: first from Thorpe Wood to the Monk's cemetery; then to the Chapter House; then to a place on the south side of the High Altar; and lastly to a chapel on the north side of the High Altar. The question is of course, why was he translated so many times? One suggestion could be made that this was conducted in order for building works to progress. The shrine of Edward the Confessor, for instance, was translated 2 feet to the west to accommodate Henry V's tombs. Yet typically in those examples, a translation ceremony is not present. Another reason for multiple translations is that they are undertaken in conjunction with the completion of building projects. There is evidence to suggest that one of the translations of William coincided with the completion of a rebuilt church. Yet this does not fully explain why St William had such frequent translations. Instead, each translation at Norwich could be regarded as an attempt to rejuvenate the cult. An example of this can be seen at Much Wenlock where, upon the decline of the Anglo-Saxon community, Cluniacs went to great lengths to discover and translate the relics of Milburga and rejuvenate her cult. Quite simply, the popularity of Bury combined with the dubious nature of William's martyrdom meant that Norwich could not establish and maintain a prominent cult.

Nevertheless, in the *Miracula of St William* is an unusually high demand for pilgrims to donate candles. For example, a well-known man in Norwich named Hildebrand was struck by severe illness. Believing that he seemed to be near his end, his friends who were present advised that 'a candle should at once be made and taken to the martyr's sepulchre' for the recovery of the sick man. When this was done without delay, he began to get well:

> According to the testimony of those who were with him when he was ill and when he got well, we have been informed that it was at that very instant when the candle was brought to the holy martyr that the anguish of his disease abated.

The above is not the only example of candles being donated. Another miracle details a woman cured twice of a cancer. The woman, like Hildebrand, donated a candle to the shrine and her cancer subsided, but 'day to day she put off presenting the wax to St William in accordance with her vow'. As such, 'the disease again attacked her breast more violently than before'. This punishment is reminiscent of the coerciveness detailed in the *Miracula of St Erkenwald* because again, there is an inherent moral culture that you must donate to the saint and honour your vows for the reason that if you do not, then you will suffer more. The woman in the miracle once again donates and offers wax whereby she is immediately cured. Equally, only when 'a certain Ida' with pain in all her limbs, 'a certain man with the dropsy', and a '10-year-old whose whole body was powerless' donated candles to the shrine were these people then relieved of their pain.

What is interesting about the *Miracula* of any saint is that they will all contain a set of similar stories, for instance the blind being cured, which emerged from a conflict between personal stories and the typological canon reminiscent of writers such as St Augustine, Sulpicius Severus, Bede, Gregory of Tours, and Gregory the Great. The process in which *Miracula* were constructed can provide an in-depth understanding into the context and motivations of the authors. Thomas Head, for example, has stated that there are two movements within the hagiographical writing process: 'from the folkloric culture of the layman to the clerical culture of the monk'. In other words, from reality to the topos. It is in this understanding that a strong argument can be made that most miracles contained inserted motifs, and that other miracles were even invented in their entirety. Thus, in the *Miracula of St William*, once we remove the topos, very little 'folkloric culture' remains. As such, consistent motifs that reinforce the need for financial support, especially regarding wax, are highly frequent within the countless inserted miracles.

Candles were central to cult worship, yet for cathedrals they were a highly expensive commodity. Norwich represents a clear picture of the costs a cathedral might incur from candles. The sacrist spent, on average, £30 out of a £50 budget which included 10–12 hundredweight of wax as well as its conversion into candle form. In order to attempt to avoid such costs, any candles left unused at altars and shrines were collected by cathedrals to be melted and reused elsewhere. The bellringer and chamberlains at St Paul's Cathedral, for example, would collect unused candles offered to the image of the Blessed Virgin Mary situated in the nave and take them to a room below the Chapter House where the candles would be melted down and the wax reused for general ceremonies by the dean and chapter. Pilgrims also recognised the hefty cost of wax by occasionally granting rents to support candles, which is why cathedrals such as Norwich exploit their saints to specifically alleviate those costs. What is particularly notable is that on the occasion that the demand for wax was reached through donations or even exceeded, this great cost could transform into a wealthy revenue. This was the case with Hereford where, according to taxation records, so much wax was donated in 1291 that a wax profit, rather than deficit, was reached. Though true that this scenario was a rare occurrence, this pursuit to alleviate wax costs and even profit from them, provides strong evidence for Norwich's candle obsession in St William's *Miracula*. Especially considering that, unlike the other cathedrals previously analysed, records show that St William's shrine never accumulated an income more than a few pence. In fact, throughout the majority of the shrine's history, donations were so small that any gift could drastically change the year's total revenue. As such, the statistical analysis of St William's shrine is largely futile. Thus, given the financial strain of candles on cathedral expenses in conjunction with the lack of offerings to alleviate such costs, it is fairly clear that Norwich undertook a series of translation ceremonies with a coercive *Miracula* to 'kick-start' its cult following and acquire wealth.

From the analysis and research of the abovementioned shrines, it can be theorised that there is a two-tiered categorisation of saints that is key in answering the question at hand. All saints in their origin relied on an initial rapid spread of popular enthusiasm and fervour. Yet within the following decade, a divergence occurs which is dependent upon official veneration, the outcome of which distinguishes the commercial longevity of the cult. Saints, like St William of Norwich, who were never officially canonised, tended to receive a burst of high income in the initial establishment of the cult which was then followed by an extremely rapid downfall. As such, in these cases, the cult relied predominantly on reputation of the acclaimed saint which lasted only as long as that reputation and memory remained. Sacrist rolls show, for example, that the cults of Wharton at Durham and Archbishop Winchelsey at Canterbury cease after only fifty years, at which point donations fall below 1s. Equally, the cult of St William of Norwich had struggled to entice crowds and donations by 1272/3 despite the production of the *Vita*. The second category, however, equally began with the initial burst of popularity, but was able to sustain such enthusiasm through official veneration, sponsorship and clergy involvement. This includes St Edmund and St Swithun, but ultimately St Thomas Becket was the most prominent saint of this category. The enterprise surrounding these saints was vast and included grand translation and jubilee celebrations, as well as numerous collections of miracles written within the accompanying *Vita*. Typically, it was these cathedrals that also had successful underlying enterprises which capitalised on those said saints through operations of relic handling, indulgences and simony. Yet, it was not completely smooth sailing for this category of saint as these cathedrals consistently saw ebbs and flows of pilgrims, leading to an irregular pattern of revenue. Understanding these categories is significant as it leads to the conclusion that saints, at best, only ever provided their cathedrals with a temporary and highly unstable revenue, rather than a consistent income.

A large reason for such an inconsistency of revenue originates in pilgrim donation culture. Evidence suggests that offerings presented to shrines were not entirely related to the wealth of the person. Rather, it seems that pilgrims typically donated a single coin, as if it were part of a symbolic discourse of dedication and faith. Illustrated in numerous *Miracula*, such as the *Vita Sancti Wulfstani* by William of Malmesbury, are references to such devotional ideas that pilgrims not only offered a coin, but also partook in a practice of bending pennies or hanging them around the neck to seal an oath or vow of pilgrimage. With fluctuating wage-rates and inflation, there would be an expectation that as the value of the coin changed, so would thc donation, yet this does not seem to be the case. Obviously, some pilgrims, such as monarchs, would donate notable amounts of rent, commodities, or money. But, for the majority of pilgrims, a single coin was the appropriate devotional token. What is notable, however, is that there is little evidence found to accuse clergy of encouraging pilgrims to increase their spending at altars. Commercialisation instead took hold in the surrounding enterprises, such as devotional stations, indulgences and relic handling, which hoped to attract additional spending. It is this pilgrim tradition that leads to the consideration that faith and wealth co-existed together.

Unlike the arguments for wealth in which statistical and literary analysis can build an understanding, faith is an intangible factor. Yet this chapter has narrowly focused on a case-by-case scenario of only a few monastic communities and, within that, an analysis of a particular period and monastic administration. In the example of Bury, though Archdeacon Herman ran a large and successful enterprise of saint commercialisation, his *Miracula* was later revised and edited by Goscelin of Saint-Bertin because of accusations of simony (as well as personal vendetta). And though there are *Miracula* whereby coercive tones of manipulation are present, there are equally as many genuine miracle collectors who aimed to express faith and devotion in their writing. Such authors include Eadmer of Canterbury who sought to write with 'the love of truth alone', and Osbert of Clare who believed 'It is splendid to fill the ears of the people with a series of miracles [...] and even more splendid to set them down in reliable writing.' Many miracle collectors follow a pattern whereby they condemn their predecessor's 'negligence' while stating that they will uphold and promote posterity. As such, saints gave writers and church administrators either a humility or arrogance dependent upon their own point of view. Some believed in a genuine expression of devotion and faith while others sought to exploit. Yet even when exploitation was rife, certain representations of devotion and faith persisted in traditions.

Fundamentally, although the shrine of St Thomas Becket at Canterbury consistently attracted hundreds of pounds per year which accounted for 88 per cent of all offerings and 28 per cent of Canterbury's total revenue, this was an exceptional example of a saint cult that was unlike any other. Yet, even still, 1220 to 1260 saw a smooth decline in shrine revenue at a rate of 5.2 per cent (a natural relaxation of pilgrims following the translation ceremony). In conjunction with other shrines, the majority of donation incomes were inconsistent and rarely surpassed £100 (only usually when notable events occurred). Across the period in question, these incomes only ever accounted for an averaged 10 per cent of cathedral revenue. Though these percentages should not be disregarded as this was still a substantial contribution to church revenue, the question remains – were saints economically viable? Given the hefty cost of translation and jubilee ceremonies combined with expenses of wax, shrine maintenance and pilgrim hospitality, it is open to debate the extent to which cathedrals made profits. In 1218/19, the cellarer's expenses at the shrine of St Thomas Becket amounted to £692 7s 11d, while donation income accumulated £872 7d, resulting in a considerable net profit. A reasonable argument, however, is that the years which saw a profit were those that contained special events, ceremonies, or royal visits. Profits are evident in cathedral records. But when profits did occur, these were reinvested predominantly into the clergy. Ninety per cent of the pyx income at Durham, along with rents and other incomes, was enriched firstly to the monks, and secondly to the priory administration. As such, a sensible conclusion is that shrines provided a supplementary income to their respective cathedrals which was predominantly paid to churchman.

Though it is difficult to be precise, it is reasonable to state that saints were exploited by certain monastic communities due to the fact that they were largely profitable throughout the eleventh to thirteenth centuries. It must be mentioned, of course, that in its core, saints, shrines and their accompanying *Miracula*, were all part of a grand ecosystem of monasticism, patronage and devotion within Christianity. As such, faith and wealth have a symbiotic relationship within the enterprise of saints that is highly difficult to distinguish between in the Middle Ages.

Part III

The Fall

Chapter Twelve

Out of the Frying Pan, Into the Fire

The year 1000, as previously described, was an apocalyptic turning point in Europe as it was seen that the damnation of Revelations was on the horizon. Yet the year 1000 came and went without issue and the world endured as it had for centuries. Perhaps theologians may have miscalculated their countdown to the apocalypse as the thirteenth and fourteenth centuries were summed up by one chronicler who stated that, 'Not until the end of time will a catastrophe of such magnitude be seen again.'

While Christians and Muslims battled it out in the Middle East, a dusty wind was collecting in the Steppe. On the Onon River in 1206, hordes of leaders, princes and nobility from the Turco-Mongol tribes gathered to elect Chinggis Khan, more commonly known today as Genghis Khan, as their new leader and overlord. What separated him from former Khans was a new and energised sense of world conquest. Where such a mission arose from is uncertain; some contemporary sources claim that he believed he was divinely inspired and thus had a mandate from God to go forth and spread his word. This message was reflected in the demands of submission he and his successors gave to his enemies. To crowds at Bokhara, he declared:

> O People, know that you have committed great sins, and that the great ones among you have committed these sins. If you ask me what proof I have for these words, I say it is because I am the punishment of God. If you had not committed great sins, God would not have sent a punishment like me upon you.

This is an interesting concept given the nature of the Mongol Empire. Known to some as the 'peoples of the nine tongues', the Mongols were a mishmash of various tribes such as Keraites, Naimans, Merkits, Onguds and Qara Khitais who spoke Middle Mongol, Turkic languages, forms of Chinese, Persian, and a vast array of others. What this also meant was that the Mongols were extremely diverse in their religious beliefs. While Genghis Khan was believed to be Mongolian Shamanist, he was tolerant of other faiths and his sons would even marry Christian princesses of the Keraites. In fact, under Genghis Khan's grandson, Möngke Khan, the primary religious influence was Christianity within the empire. Nevertheless, there were also Muslims, Buddhists and Nestorians. Despite this tolerance, it only aided in building an idea and tension that Ghengis truly was the wrath of God.

In the period following 1206, however, there is no evidence to suggest the soon-to-be world conqueror regarded himself as anything other than a skilled and tactical warrior-king. He was proficient in politics and intrigue as he battled his way to Khan through promises, alliances, plots and wars. This was a key aspect that would stick with him throughout his reign as he held loyalty at the apex of his leadership. As such, tribes flocked to his call with promises of rewards for their loyalty to him. Likewise, when reorganising his armies, he rewarded command positions to those who had been loyal to him during tough times as opposed to any ancestral birthrights or nobility taking precedence as found in Europe. Redistributing armies and forces also hindered tribes from forming powerful confederations that the Romans had witnessed in the Balkans with the Slavs and Goths. This, again, only aided in building a sense of discipline, order and loyalty. Despite being organised soldiers, they were still nomadic at heart and so a reliance on specialist skills in horseback riding was crucial. Mongols were infamous for their ability to fire arrows at full speed in any direction, just like the Huns a millennium before. Strapped to their backs would be quivers of sixty arrows which were fired from two composite bows made of bamboo and yak horn. They were simply unstoppable.

With such a vast land-based empire, a *yam* and *barid* system was introduced by Genghis to uphold his organisational tactics and communication networks. Marco Polo, the great traveller to the east, claimed that the Great Khan's courtiers could cover 200–250 miles a day, adding that, 'These strong, enduring messengers are highly prized men.' The crucial element was a network of fresh horses, supply stations 10 or so miles apart, escorts, and a general sense of cohesion that enabled messengers to bolt on horseback, switch to another horse or runner at a station, and continue on at full speed. As this was largely run by the army itself, it spanned across the whole of the Mongol-controlled territory from Eastern Europe to the Sea of Japan. Marco Polo claims that at any post-station, 200–400 ready mounts could be found, a number also supported by Rashid al-Din who claimed he saw up to 500. According to Marco Polo, these messengers also wore bells to alert runners in the next village to prepare for the relay. Without these forms of organisation, an empire of this size in the medieval period would not have survived long.

Far from a tribal mixing pot, this was an empire somewhat more organised and cohesive than most in Europe and the Middle East. A report from Franciscan friars who visited Mongolia in the 1240s offers insight into the practice elements of this discipline and organisation:

> Among themselves, however, they are peaceable. Fornication and adultery are very rare, and their women excel those of other nations in chastity, except that they often use shameless words when jesting. Theft is unusual among them, and therefore their dwellings and all their property are not put under lock and key. If horses or oxen or other animal stock are found straying, they are either allowed to go free or are led back to their own masters. Rebellion is rarely raised among them, and it is no wonder if such is their way, for, as I have said above, transgressors are punished without mercy.

Justice and punishment underpinned the Mongols which is why such order was upheld. Execution was carried out on those who committed treason, desertion, spying, theft, adultery, and even bankruptcy. One particular example of a punishment for a man who double-crossed a rash Kurdish warlord was recorded as such:

> He [the Kurdish Warlord] ordered that he, Malik Salih, be covered with sheep fat, trussed with felt and rope, and left in the summer sun. After a week, the fat got maggoty, and they started devouring the poor man. He died of that torture within a month. He had a three-year-old son who was sent to Mosul, where he was cut in two on the banks of the Tigris and hung as an example to the city until his remains rotted away.

It is no wonder, therefore, that news of their arrival was seen as apocalyptic: 'The news of the Tartars is a tale to devour all tales, an account that rolls into oblivion all accounts, a history to make one forget all histories.'

The above is from an Arab source as those in Central Asia were the first to witness the wrath of the Khan. Writing from Mosul in 1220, a scholar wrote to a patron in Aleppo:

> A calamity that whitens the hair of youth and rips out the guts of the brave, that blackens the heart and confounds to the core … I reached – but only just – the safety of Mosul after suffering many perils and trials, sorely tested, my sins atoned for. Often I beheld death and destruction, for my path took me between drawn swords, through the ranks of routed armies … wading through blood that cried for vengeance … In short, had not my appointed span still had time to run, I would have joined the thousand thousand thousand thousand thousand or more victims of the godless Tartars.

However many zeros it may have been, there is no denying that massacres took place under the expansion of the Golden Horde. In fact, the depopulation of Central Asia, especially in the countryside, resulted in a rural devastation that still ripples today. Following this invasion, there was a lull in the expansion of the Mongols till 1258 whereby Hulagu, the grandson of Genghis, swept into the old Abbasid capital with a mighty strike of oblivion.

Iraq by this point was already in a state of decay. Travellers would note the ruins of a former golden empire upon arrival in al-Kufah. Likewise, Baghdad was often caught in civil uprising and violent upheaval as quarters of the city battled one another like territorial gang wars. By now, the last caliph of Baghdad, Al-Musta'sim, was on borrowed time, living in a vegetative state that relied upon Turk and Iranian slave troops – a shadow of the former Al-Mansur who formed the city half a millennium before. It appeared, however, that the destruction of the city was foreseen as Arab philosopher and astrologer al-Kindi predicted the city would fall and be destroyed some time in the thirteenth century (seventh century in the Arab calendar) due to the already present qualms in power and morality. Nevertheless, the fall of Baghdad in 1258 was a huge psychological blow to Arabdom. Not only did Arab political power shift but also geographical power as it became ever more crammed into the Gulf. All that had been achieved by the city over 600 years had been reversed and as the Mongols pushed west they overwhelmed urban centres, religious communities, razed libraries and centres of learning – and with it, wiped history itself.

With the fall of the Arab Empire in Baghdad during the thirteenth century, many areas would return to their nomadic and tribal roots, embracing their desert prehistoric origins alongside Islam. Equally, the faith itself had lost something as with the death of al-Musta'sim, the last caliph, the line of Imams that traced back to Muhammad was severed. From hereafter there was no unity, no leader within Islam that could become the figurehead for the faith and empire. While there would be remnants in Egypt and the Middle East, it would never truly recover and hold together the Arab world as it had done centuries before. As such, the fall of Baghdad to the Mongols made it seem as though they would wipe Islam from the world entirely. Arabs would need a 'Saladin' hero that could save them from the unstoppable force the Mongols presented.

With Baghdad in ruins, Damascus quickly fell and the Mongols pressed on further south towards the Holy City and the remaining major political power of the region that was Egypt. Prior to the battle, the Khan sent the following threat to the Mamluk caliph:

> From the King of Kings of the East and West, the Great Khan. To Qutuz the Mamluk, who fled to escape our swords. You should think of what

> happened to other countries and submit to us. You have heard how we have conquered a vast empire and have purified the earth of the disorders that tainted it. We have conquered vast areas, massacring all the people. You cannot escape from the terror of our armies. Where can you flee? What road will you use to escape us? Our horses are swift, our arrows sharp, our swords like thunderbolts, our hearts as hard as the mountains, our soldiers as numerous as the sand. Fortresses will not detain us, nor armies stop us. Your prayers to God will not avail against us. We are not moved by tears nor touched by lamentations. Only those who beg our protection will be safe. Hasten your reply before the fire of war is kindled. Resist and you will suffer the most terrible catastrophes. We will shatter your mosques and reveal the weakness of your God and then will kill your children and your old men together. At present, you are the only enemy against whom we have to march.

In response, the Mongol messenger was beheaded and his head was displayed on the gates of Cairo. With the Mongols advancing into the Crusader states, an unlikely pact emerged that set aside centuries of bloodshed. The Franks were as much an enemy of the Mongols as the Mamluks and thus hatched a treaty whereby the Mamluks could freely pass with all their armies – even resupplying by Acre – in order to combat the invading Mongols. For the first time in history, Arab and European faced off an opponent as allies.

Meeting at the battlefield of Ayn Jalut in Palestine, the gates to Africa, the forces clashed in aggressive blows. The Mongols, however, made a fatal mistake in underestimating the tactics of the Turk caliph. Seeing the tide of battle in his favour, Qutuz threw off his helmet to instil morale in his fellow troops and he called out, 'O Islam! O Allah grant your servant Qutuz a victory against these Mongols,' as he charged into battle. After pushing back the forces, the Mamluks were able to gain a strong foothold and force the Mongols into a retreat. Despite, for centuries, Arab caliphs relying on Turkish military slaves, it would be these Turks who would save Islam in 1260. The Mamluks would endure in power until 1798 whereby they would be defeated at the hands of Napoleon and later finished off completely in 1812 by the Ottomans. In the meantime, the Mongols were halted in their advance and remained in a perpetual standoff with the Mamluks, eyeing each other from either side of the Fertile Crescent.

Elsewhere, the Great Khans also pushed north to the eastern and central Europeans. After routing over 50,000 Rus and Cuman troops at the Battle of the Kalka River in 1223, the Mongol forces pushed far into the Kievan Rus territory over two decades. By 1240, they had sacked Kiev and driven their way through Poland, Austria, Croatia and Bulgaria. By 1241, the majority of Mongol forces were settled on the Hungarian plain ready to pounce. Lined up along the fortified banks of the Sajo and Hernad rivers, the Hungarian army, which vastly outnumbered its Mongol opponents, was awaiting battle in a deathly silence. The Mongols, who fought a psychological war as much as a physical, galloped in circles kicking up dust and banging drums to make their presence appear far larger. The Mongol storm, with their unparalleled horsemanship and archery, pounced upon their Hungarian opponents and drove through their lines and decimated their numbers. Cities were sacked, crops burnt, livestock stolen, and thousands slaughtered – so much so that 25 per cent of the Hungarian population was wiped out. Upon witnessing this, the Hungarian king, Béla IV, fled to the Dalmatian coast by Croatia where he awaited retribution. To his luck, however, the Khan, Ogedei, died and so, in the same lull period witnessed by the Arabs, there was a slight reprieve from invasion as the Mongols retreated.

The unfinished invasion of the Mongols had a profound effect on its survivors. Frederick II, the Holy Roman Emperor wrote that, 'The entire precious kingdom of Hungary was depopulated, devastated, and turned into a barren wasteland.'

Many, in desperation, turned towards the papacy, just as Alexios had done in 1095, to create a united front and crusade against this ungodly storm. The pope, however, was deeply distracted by a successive wave of crusades from the Bosnian Crusade, to the Livonian Crusade, Barons Crusade, and a host of other minor crusades, all of which occurred within a three-year period. Equally, the papacy was in the midst of political conflicts with kingdoms such as the Kievan Rus because they refused to join the Bosnian Crusade in 1238 (which was eventually cut short because of the Mongol invasion). The papacy had also excommunicated the Holy Roman Emperor four times for attempting to unite the Holy Roman Empire with Sicily by seizing Italy. As such, Pope Gregory IX labelled Frederick as the Antichrist. With the focus of the papacy spread thinly across Europe and the Mediterranean, only one of these crusades would be aimed at the Mongols and was organised by the Hungarian king. Yet, even here the pope had ulterior motives and attempted to persuade King Béla to rethink his goal and instead assist in a crusade against the Holy Roman Emperor. Eventually, an agreement was met which saw a small crusade sanctioned in 1241 but with the pope's death a few months later it was short-lived. The successor would use the resources of the Crusade in an expedition against the Hohenstaufen dynasty after a rebellion in the Holy Roman Empire against the emperor's son Conrad.

Nevertheless, Europe was somewhat less impacted by the invasion than the Arabs. The death of the Khan led to a civil war within the ranks of the Mongols that saw them split off into various war clans that were mere fractions of the former united front. As such, a period regarded by historians as *Pax Mongolica* followed which saw a rehabilitation of eastern Europe emerge that was founded on international trade. Under Mongol supervision, the Silk Road was reignited and sustained contact with China was established and with it, an inpouring of glass, spices, rice and porcelain entered the West. This would also allow new technologies such as printmaking and gunpowder to enter the European sphere. Perhaps one of the greatest legacies of the Mongol invasion of eastern Europe was the role it played in creating a unified nation that would become Russia. Prior to the invasion, the territory that was Ukraine, Belarus and western Russia was a diverse confederation of weak city-states with Kiev being the most powerful of these. With their destruction in 1240, the Grand Duchy of Moscow emerged from the ashes which saw a new cultural, religious and military epicentre develop. It was this duchy that would eventually overthrow its Mongol rulers and establish the Tsardom of Russia. Likewise, in Hungary the threat of invasion led to a vast array of reforms to prepare for future attacks. The king, along with the Knights Hospitallers, built a large number of castles and fortifications along the Danube to create an impenetrable front in the weaker, depopulated regions of the country. The result – when Mongol hordes returned in 1285 after their Arabian defeat, they too fell to these newly built fortresses and had to abandon their war efforts.

All was safe and returned to peace ... or so they thought. Just when the world thought it was safe to walk the Silk Road once more, the Black Death struck.

The fourteenth century is divided into three distinct periods of crisis. The first was to occur from 1300 to 1346 which, although a prelude to the Black Death pandemic in Europe, saw a distinctive upheaval in the nature of power in Europe, namely France under the absolutism of Philip the Fair. Due to the Anglo-French conflicts of 1294–1298 and, more famously, the Hundred Years War that was to begin in 1337, Philip had to contend with a weak economy in order to maintain control and bring victory over his aggressors. The year 1289 was the climax of French economic deficit with the amalgamation of Saxony's silver production decline, as well as the wars with England and Flanders amounting to 1.73 million *livres tournois* (LT) (one of the numerous currencies used in France), combined with the inherited expenditure debt of 1.5 million LT from his father's Aragonese Crusade. It signified the beginning of a controversial era of tyrannical economic reforms to bolster Philip's personal wealth and absolutist monarchy. Easy pickings could be found in the revenues of the church which had far more fiscal resources than the government and thus greatly undermined Philip's secular absolutist rule. As such, in 1289 Philip approached Pope Nicholas IV to grant permission to collect tithe from church lands in France, yet this would make only a small dent in the extensive loans owed by Philip to such groups as the Lombard Merchants, Knights Templars, Florentine Franzesi, and Jewish communities.

With the king owing so much money to so many different groups, Philip attempted to fight this by asserting his absolutist control over these groups through tyrannical policies. Government agents seized Lombard Merchant assets and forced them to purchase French Nationality which amounted to 250,000 LT. In an even more controversial policy, in 1307, agents arrested hundreds of Templars in France to be tortured for heresy. While these arrests of the Lombard Merchants and Templars were extremely controversial in nature, the 'Great Exile of 1306' is perhaps far greater in exemplifying the extent to which Philip changed the landscape of European power. In 1306, the Jewish communities in France were banished with real and personal property being seized by the government to be sold at auction and all treasures being directly given to the king. The sole aim of this was to fill the gap in the treasury and once again stamp out a community which posed any level of power over him. The exile dried up one of the most fruitful sources of finance and industry in France, and with such a long Jewish history ending, Philip's control and power had increased considerably.

This led to a direct and aggressive clash with the pope. Three main factors ignited the feud between Philip and the pope: these were monetary gain, religious influence and strengthening monarchical power. Marxist theories suggest that every conflict in history can be rooted in the competition and control of industry and production, and this can be used as a strong explanation to understand the origin of this feud. Continuing his controversial economic policies, Philip implemented a 50 per cent tax on the annual income of French clergy. In terms of possession of power, the fact that he could exercise controversial policies without inhibitions of law or councils demonstrated the definitive power of the king. Nonetheless, the reception of this law by the church was so strong that it prompted Pope Boniface to issue the papal bull '*Clericis Laicos*' in 1296, which was an attempt to prevent secular states from taxing church revenues without permission of the pope. Philip refuted this by the removal of bullion from France which led to a compromise by Boniface in 1297. This contest of power, which saw Philip seeming to come out on top, showed that anyone who could overcome the pope's rule could have the ultimate influence over Christendom.

Boniface proceeded to call together a congregation of French bishops in 1301 to discuss the actions of Philip. In response to this, the *Unam Sanctam* was published in 1302 which declared papal supremacy and Philip was excommunicated. The climax of this power struggle came when Philip sent Guillaume de Nogaret (with some French troops) to arrest Boniface at Anagni. Clement V was then elected as pope and the papacy moved from Italy to Avignon which began the period regarded by historians as the 'Babylonian Captivity of the Papacy' (*c.*1309–1376) whereby the papacy was subject to French control. Power over the papacy had been achieved, but only the foundations were established in the reign of Philip as he died in 1314, just five years after Clement V became pope. Nevertheless, the Capetian monarchy claimed for itself the mystic foundations of the papal theocracy and thus, this was only the beginning of the end for Christendom.

As the flame of the papacy in Italy was temporarily extinguished, a somewhat symbolic event was to occur whereby Europe was plunged into a very cold and dark period. Until now, and in many ways one of the causes for such an energetic period, Europe and the Mediterranean had enjoyed three to four centuries of warm weather. This, as previously discussed, is one of the aspects that influenced the growth of the Vikings, but in the fourteenth century, this luxury ceased. Instead, cold winters endured from 1310 to 1330 alongside wet and rainy summers that drastically reduced crop yields. In fact, archaeology shows a 50 per cent decline in wheat which, when trying to sustain a European population of 80 million, is rather tricky. As a result, famine and disease became rampant, with anthrax and murrain decimating livestock populations. In northern Europe, where the crisis was largely confined, 5–10 per cent of the population starved or died through illness due to climate change. This was mainly due to a combination of factors, both social and economic. Populations in Europe from 1100 had drastically increased. In England and France, the population tripled in two centuries while in the Low Countries it doubled. In order to meet the demands of this growth, a concoction of cultivating sub-par land as well as overusing the already fertile areas meant that agriculture quickly became unsustainable. As such, wheat yields withered away and economic productivity began to slow from the 1280s onwards. Various wars also did not help as the land was destroyed, fields burnt, labour forces were pushed to their limits, and high taxes were levied on populations who already could barely afford to sustain themselves. Children born during this time were typically malnourished and lacked an effective immune system to fight off the Black Death which loomed on the horizon.

From here, the second crisis of the fourteenth century emerged like a rolling fog from the East. The first onslaught of the plague, known to us now as the zoonotic bacterium *Yersinia pestis*, hit Europe in the 1340s and 1350s, killing perhaps a third of humanity in one fell swoop as though it was another horde:

> Ah, woe to him on whom it calls! It found chinks in China's walls – they had no chance against its advance. It sashayed into Cathay, made hay in Hind and sundered souls in Sind. It put the Golden Horde to the sword, transfixed Transoxiana and pierced Persia. Crimea cringed and crumbled …

The above, left unfinished as the author himself was struck down by the plague, gives us insight that contemporaries understood this plague to have emerged from China and traversed along the Silk Road. All, however, understood its devastation as 'the all-consuming plague, rolling up Earth's carpet and everything upon it'.

In Europe, one of the first places for the plague to hit was the bustling city of Florence in around 1346. By this point, the population was well over 100,000 with banking, commerce and trade at the forefront of economic production – so much so that the Gold Florin, the currency of Florence, became the universal currency of international trade. Aside from finance, over a third of the population participated in the textiles trade and agriculture. Here, however, were the roots of a growing crisis as a structural contradiction emerged. From the 1320s to 1340s there was a succession of incredibly poor harvests in the city which saw a dramatic 200 per cent rise in inflation of primary raw resources. This led to an imbalance between the population and its supplies that resulted in an economic crash from 1343 to 1346, similar to the Great Depression. From this weakened state, the plague swept through the streets. Sources state that up to half the population of Florence perished, with some more rural areas seeing a mortality rate of up to 75 per cent.

Panic ensued as people turned to the church for an explanation for this devastating pandemic. The medical profession, ill-equipped to deal with the plague due to a lack of scientific understanding on microbes, instead turned towards balancing the temperaments of people – women, who had cool temperaments, were urged to eat hot, spiced food for instance. With little aid, anti-Semitic scapegoats quickly emerged whereby Jewish communities were blamed for poisoning wells. In Germany, Iberia and France, systematic surveys were conducted from 1348 to 1351 to find proof of the Jewish cause of the plague. Subsequently, in order to find an answer to God's Punishment, many Jewish populations were exiled, imprisoned and killed. Alongside this, other social groups such as beggars, disabled individuals and foreigners were also targeted in the rampant hysteria. Others, instead, opted for a self-cleansing through flagellation. Thousands gathered to do penitential repenting for their sins, whipping their backs raw in hopes that God would free them from this injustice.

The church, however, condemned all this as a promotion of hysteria. Instead, in a time of desperate need they turned towards their intercessors. The church urged people to stay close to God, care for one another, and place their worship and vocation in their saintly protectors. In many ways, patronage to the saint was offered for healing, perhaps even a cure for loved ones, but it was also far more than this. Saintly intercession represents a symbolic gesture that we possess a communion with others that surpassed death. As such, saints became protectors of the dead as much as they did for the living. Evoking the practices of ancient Egypt, saints were almost like Anubis, guiding souls and protecting the dead as they traversed through Purgatory, leading them to enlightenment and heaven. When disunion was becoming rampant and hysteria infecting the minds of populations quicker than the plague, saints offered the possibility for a communion that could make sense of death and sorrow alike while also enlightening the minds of those with the plague at death's door, giving them hope for peace in the afterlife. Thousands of 'plague-saints' emerged during this time, but for our focus we shall look towards Michael the Archangel, St Sebastian, and Mary, the Mother of God.

Our first saint, St Michael the Archangel, was the defender of Jewish people during the Old Testament narrative but also features predominantly in the Book of Revelations. One of the most infamous stories of the saint is that he defeats Satan, who appeared as a dragon before him, and threw him from the heavens to the pits of hell where he would reside. During the papacy of Gregory the Great, the plague of Justinian and subsequent pockets of outbreaks led the pope to process through the streets of Rome with the icon of Madonna and Child (the same used during the Coronavirus pandemic by Pope Francis). According to sources, St Michael miraculously appeared in the procession, putting his sword into its sheath to signal that the fight was over and the war had been won.

What is particularly important about the depiction of Satan as a dragon is that the dragon was also deeply interconnected to the Eucharist liturgy. As such, during the Black Death before Ascension, men and women would walk the boundaries of their parish in procession with a dragon figurehead. With each procession the dragon was moved further back to signal his defeat. In England, this was taken further whereby the dragon itself was then slain during the consecration of the Blessed Sacrament. As such, St Michael becomes intrinsic to the Eucharist during the Black Death and was often depicted slaying a dragon with dark rolling clouds behind him that represented his victory over Satan and the pandemic. What also emerged was the idea within the Eucharist liturgy that St Michael purged his worshippers of sin and chaos in defeating the dragon, thus providing them hope of salvation. And as the Eucharist was a vital ceremony of the city and always took place, people could be sure that the protection of St Michael was always renewed.

St Sebastian, like St Michael, was not always a plague-saint. The story of this third-century martyr almost parallels that of St Edmund in England as both intercessors were struck with a volley of arrows. Sebastian, however, did not die and was instead rescued by St Irene of Rome whereby he was able to regain his strength and venture to Rome where he petitioned Emperor Diocletian for his sins. Clearly not a fan of Sebastian, the emperor clubbed him to death. Despite this, Sebastian's veneration led to an incredibly popular cult of worship

– becoming the third patron of Rome. In a sense, he was just any old saint. This was until a plague broke out in Pavia in 680. Paul the Deacon writes a vivid description whereby angels battled in the sky above against one another and thus the plague would not surpass until an altar of St Sebastian was built in the Basilica of St Peter. At the precise moment the altar was completed, the plague disappeared. This, however, is not the only reason why he emerged as a plague-saint. Within saint-lore, a volley of arrows was frequently a sign of divine wrath being inflicted upon humankind. With St Edmund, this was the Vikings. Often Sebastian was depicted as being wounded by the arrow of divine wrath in the same spot that Christ was pierced with the spear while on the cross. As such, just as the church emerged from the wound of Christ, St Irene is often shown tending to St Sebastian's wound, which poured with the blood of Christian charity. Sebastian was also commonly shown as luminated in order to connect him to the Eucharist. As with the body and blood of Christ, St Sebastian in late medieval society was almost an offering to the Eucharist in itself. A great example of this occurs a century later when the Renaissance composer Guillaume Du Fay offers a sacred choral for Mass that invites worshippers to listen to the salvation offered by the body of St Sebastian as an image of Christ. As such, he represented a hope for those experiencing the plague that their death was almost representative of an offering of salvation and thus not in vain.

And so we now move towards our final saint. Late medieval society sees a renaissance in the veneration of the Virgin Mary, no doubt popularised in part due to the Black Death. Mary, like the former saints, was not a plague-saint until the fourteenth century. Yet, unlike Michael or Sebastian, Mary flourished through a psychological devotion of relief as opposed to inciting salvation. Faced with the wrath of God, it was rationalised by many that in order to circumvent this, the Mother of God should be pleaded to as she was the benefactor of relief from such sufferings. In many ways, worshippers who cried and pleaded to the Lord at the bedside of their fallen loved ones were evoking the iconography of Mary at the foot of Christ's cross. When Christ's body was brought down from the cross, we see Mary fainting at the sight of her dead son. As such, she was a symbol for mothers and fathers who lost their children and had their hearts pierced with sorrow at the hands of the plague. Yet her popularisation can also be attributed to the role of the church as it saw itself as the spiritual parent of its Christians. As such, rather than flee, the church was directed towards Mary and told to stand strong in the face of death and care for its children. Often, therefore, the iconography of Mary would be attached to Sebastian.

Despite these early saints being evoked by the church, new ones arose as intercessors who had risen above challenges of the period to dedicate themselves to Christ. St Catherine of Siena, for example, who lived from 1347 to 1390, was born during the plague in Siena and lost three of her siblings amongst other relatives. Due to the heavy losses in the city, many were urged to flee in attempt to save themselves. Opposed to this, Catherine stayed in order to nurse the victims to health. What is remarkable about Catherine for historians is how she writes a dialogue with God contemplating the idea of suffering during the most devastating event of human history to that point. Rather than God's wrath, she believes this suffering was an attempt to lead people to a deeper sense of charity and union with Christ:

> You asked me for a willingness to suffer. So I have shown you all this to teach you and my other servants how you should make this sacrifice of yourselves to me. I am speaking of sacrifice both in act and in spirit joined together as the vessel is joined with water offers to one's lord ... you must offer me the vessel of all your actual suffering, however I may send them to you – for the place and the time and the sort of suffering are not yours to choose, but mine. But this vessel of yours must be filled with the loving affection and true patience with which you carry all the burden of your neighbours' guilt even while you hate and reject the sin.

Catherine is one amongst so many others such as St Brigid of Sweden and St Charles Borromeo who all saw this sickness and suffering as an opportunity for sacrifice and charity. Brigid, for example, jostles with several questions about the nature of plagues themselves and the existence of suffering and unexpected death:

> I [God] answer: If man knew the time of his death, he would serve me out of fear and faint with sorrow. Therefore, in order that man might serve me out of charity and that might always be solicitous about himself and secure about me, the hour of his death is uncertain – and deservedly so. For, when man deserted that which was certain and true, it was necessary and right that he be afflicted with uncertainty.

All of these aforementioned saints worked together to rewrite the narrative of suffering and transpose it to become one of love, hope and salvation. There is no doubt that the church played a hand in this in order to suppress the hysteria that was rampant during the plague. Yet, the aftermath of the plague shows that this worked, as social ties disintegrated and a new world order was put forward by the survivors in a paradigm of change.

> Things temporal are all doomed to pass and perish – *The Decameron*

In Florence, a combination of wealth redistribution and a surplus of vacant roles led many who were formerly oppressed to rise above the ranks to positions of power. Social mobility following the plague was at an all-time high. Vast mortality opened new doors for young survivors who inherited huge amounts of wealth that could be reinvested into rebuilding cities from their ashes. Lando di Fortino, for example, was a young notary who had significant socio-economic potential following the Black Death. He was a writing professional (of which there were few left) and a law operator who could draft public and private documents. Prior to the plague, he was a mere countryside itinerant officer for a village in the Upper Valdarno, the lowest of the low within the notary career. Following the plague, a communal society developed in Florence which placed a greater emphasis than ever before on civil institutions, justice and order. As such, as the number of guild notaries had halved, he became indispensable to social order. Through diversification and affiliation with other organisations, he became a notary and scribe for the abbot of the monastic order of Vallombrosa and, after a second outbreak in 1363, he rose to become a scribe for the episcopal curia, a role that was the dream for any notary's career. All of this was because of the social mobility post-pandemic. As a result, his sons, Benedetto and Paolo Fortini, would access prestigious Florentine public offices including the role of Republic Chancellor.

This then feeds into our third and final crisis of the fourteenth century – that is, Popular Rebellion. From 1355 to 1400, the masses in Europe sought to create their new world order off the back of the hope, charity and social care instilled by the former saints that saved them. Ranging from minor to major rebellions, they sought to tear down the feudal social hierarchy and create a new system. In England, for example, there was the Peasants' Revolt in 1381 that sought to erode serfdom and create a more fluid hierarchy. It emerged as a response to a series of grievances among the peasant population, particularly the implementation of a poll tax, oppressive labour conditions, and the feudal system's injustices.

In 1380, King Richard II, who was only a teenager at the time, introduced a poll tax to fund his military campaigns and the ongoing war with France, despite the losses incurred during the plague. The tax imposed a fixed fee on every individual, regardless of their wealth, which disproportionately affected the lower classes and thus ignited revolution. The revolt began in Essex in May 1381, led by a local leader named Jack Straw. As news of the rebellion spread, it gained momentum and spread to other parts of England, including Kent, East Anglia and London. The rebels, consisting mainly of peasants but also including some artisans and disgruntled members of the lower gentry, were united in their opposition to the poll tax and sought broader social and economic reforms.

Under the leadership of Wat Tyler, a charismatic figure from Kent, the rebels marched towards London, gathering support along the way. They stormed various manor houses, destroying tax records and symbols of authority, as a sign of their discontent with the ruling classes. In June 1381, an estimated force of 50,000 rebels reached London. Upon their arrival, the rebels confronted the royal government and engaged in negotiations with King Richard II. The king initially met with the rebel leaders, including Wat Tyler, to hear their grievances. However, tensions escalated during the discussions, and a violent encounter occurred between Tyler and the Lord Mayor of London. In the chaos that followed, Tyler was fatally wounded. Despite Tyler's death, the rebels continued their demands for change. King Richard II, only 14 years old at the time, showed remarkable political skill and managed to calm the situation. He made a series of promises to address the rebels' concerns, including the abolition of serfdom and the reduction of oppressive laws. These promises, however, were not fully realised, and many were eventually broken.

After the revolt, the ruling classes enacted repressive measures to suppress any further uprisings. This included implementing stricter laws to control the movement and activities of peasants, as well as punishing those involved in the rebellion. Nevertheless, the Peasants' Revolt had a lasting impact on English society, as it challenged the authority of the ruling elite and highlighted the growing dissatisfaction among the lower classes. In the long term, the revolt contributed to the gradual erosion of serfdom and the feudal system, leading to changes in labour relationships and the emergence of a more fluid social structure. It also paved the way for future movements that sought to address social and economic inequalities in England.

Yet, people sought not only to determine their own secular rights, and thus the church was attacked too. The Great Schism of 1378, also known as the Western Schism, was a significant event in medieval Christian history that resulted in a split within the church that divided Europe. It lasted for nearly four decades and involved competing claims to the papacy by two rivals – the pope in Rome, and the pope in Avignon.

The origins of the Great Schism can be traced back to the papal election of 1378. Upon the death of Pope Gregory XI, the cardinals convened to choose his successor. Tensions were already high due to the relocation of the papacy from Rome to Avignon in France under Philip which compromised the independence and authority of the papacy. Nevertheless, during the election, the majority of the cardinals elected Pope Urban VI, an Italian who would reign in Rome. This would not be favourable to the Capetians, however, as soon after his election, Pope Urban VI's authoritarian and confrontational style of governance caused dissent among the French cardinals. In response, the dissenting cardinals held their own conclave and elected their candidate, Pope Clement VII. He established his papal court in Avignon, which had become a traditional seat of the popes since the relocation from Rome.

The competing papal claimants, Pope Urban VI and Pope Clement VII, each had their own loyal followers, creating a divided papacy and causing a rupture in the church. The split led to a state of confusion and uncertainty among the faithful, as well as political and religious ramifications. Various kingdoms and city-states aligned themselves with one pope or the other, often based on political or national interests. The divided loyalties and rival papal courts undermined the church's authority and caused deep divisions within Christian communities.

Efforts to resolve the schism were made through diplomatic negotiations and church councils. One such council, the Council of Pisa in 1409, sought to resolve the issue by deposing both Pope Urban VI and Pope Clement VII and electing a new pope, Alexander V. However, this only exacerbated the problem, as now there were three popes, each claiming legitimacy. The schism was finally resolved in 1417 at the Council of Constance. The council deposed all three claimants and elected Pope Martin V as the sole legitimate pope, effectively ending the divided papacy. Pope Martin V's election was widely accepted, and the Western Schism came to an end.

The Great Schism had a profound impact on the church as it exposed the political and worldly nature of the papacy and revealed deep divisions within the church hierarchy. It also led to calls for church reform and paved the way for the Protestant Reformation, which emerged a century later and further challenged the authority and unity of the Catholic Church.

Overall, the fourteenth century would be a transformative one where Europe was continuously battered. Although it may appear as though the worst had come to pass, this was only a sign of things to come as over the next two centuries, the paradigm of change instilled from the Mongols, Black Death and Popular Rebellions would shake Europe and instil a paranoia within the church, which feared for its survival.

Chapter Thirteen

A Rift with Rome

With crusade after crusade, the tale of successive attempts to win the hearts, minds and military aid of the papacy through promises of a union between the East and West churches had begun to run stale. Nevertheless, it was a common gesture to gather aid from Rome in the face of opposition from the Turks. Even the staunch Orthodox Emperor Andronicus II raised ideas of a union in the later years of his life when civil war ensued between him and his grandson over the encroachments of the Turks. Likewise, Emperors John VI Cantacuzene and John V Palaeologus also naively considered the idea of a church union as a solution to the problems they faced. John V even proposed submitting himself to the Western Church was it not for the potential revolt that would no doubt follow. Such ideas, however, were entirely opposed. John's interests were shared by the likes of Demetrius Cydones who, having learnt Latin from a Dominican, translated the works of Thomas Aquinas into Greek. Demetrius is said to have discovered a great sense of joy from his translations and urged fellow Byzantines to discard this old worldview that the world was split between Byzantines and barbarians:

> Previously, there was no one to persuade our people that there is any intelligence in the Latins, or that they are able to raise their minds to consideration of anything more exalted than shipping, trading and war.

These efforts, however, led nowhere. In fact, when Emperor John V Palaeologus embarked on an embassy mission in 1369 to St Peter's in Rome, anxious to bring about a Crusade against the Turks in Asia Minor, there was a notable lack of energy. This was so much so that not a single Byzantine churchman accompanied him to Rome. The prominent reason for such a loss of support on John's behalf arose from the fact he was limited in his ability to direct church policy because of the endured succession of Hesychast Patriarchs. The Hesychast controversy of the fourteenth century was a theological and spiritual dispute within the Byzantine Empire, centred around the practice of Hesychasm. Hesychasm was a method of contemplative prayer and meditation aimed at achieving union with God through inner stillness and the cultivation of the 'Jesus Prayer'. The controversy arose primarily between two groups: the Hesychasts, who promoted this contemplative tradition, and their opponents, who criticised and sought to suppress it.

The roots of the controversy can be traced back to the early Christian Desert Fathers and the Eastern Christian monastic tradition. The practice of Hesychasm gained prominence in the fourteenth century, particularly through the teachings of St Gregory Palamas, a monk and theologian who became the chief defender of Hesychasm. Palamas argued that through the disciplined practice of Hesychasm, it was possible for individuals to experience the divine energies of God and attain a direct and transformative union with the divine. Palamas's teachings encountered opposition from some quarters, particularly from Barlaam of Calabria, a Byzantine theologian and humanist who had studied in the West. Barlaam was critical of the Hesychast emphasis on experiential knowledge of God and argued that such practices were a form of heretical mysticism. He accused the Hesychasts of advocating an erroneous notion of God's essence and suggesting that humans could attain a direct vision of the divine. Barlaam believed that God's essence was unknowable and that the human mind could not directly perceive it. The controversy escalated when Barlaam travelled to Constantinople to engage in public debate with Palamas. The debates, which took place between 1340 and 1341, centred around the nature of God, the distinction between God's essence and energies, and the possibility of direct divine experience (all things which were debated in the sixth century and continuously ever since then). Palamas, drawing from the theological tradition of the Eastern Church, defended the Hesychast teachings, arguing that the divine energies were distinct from God's essence but still accessible to humans through the practice of Hesychasm.

In 1341, a synod convened in Constantinople to address the controversy. The synod, presided over by Emperor Andronikos III, sided with Palamas and officially condemned Barlaam's views as heretical. The synod affirmed that the Hesychasts were not advocating a pantheistic or visionary form of mysticism but rather a genuine experience of the divine. The synod also declared that those who rejected the possibility of direct experience of God's energies were in error. However, the controversy did not end with the synod's decision. Barlaam and his supporters continued to criticise Palamas and his followers. The dispute took on political dimensions, with various factions within the Byzantine court taking sides. In 1351, a second synod convened in Constantinople, known as the Synod of Blachernae, which reaffirmed the teachings of the earlier synod and reiterated the condemnation of Barlaam's views.

The controversy continued even after Palamas's death in 1359, with subsequent synods and theological writings further solidifying the Hesychast position. Over time, the Hesychast tradition became firmly established within Eastern

Orthodox theology and spirituality, with St Gregory Palamas eventually being recognised as a saint and his writings regarded as authoritative. The Hesychast controversy had far-reaching implications beyond the theological realm. It reflected broader tensions between the Eastern and Western Christian traditions, with the Hesychast emphasis on inner prayer and contemplation contrasting with the more scholastic and intellectual approach prevalent in the West. The controversy also highlighted the distinctive spiritual and mystical traditions of the Eastern Orthodox Church that the West would see as strange and bordering on heretical.

According to Demetrius Cydones, the imperial palace was full to the brim with these Hesychast monks whom he describes as wandering around with their 'beards, theology and ignorance'. This actually caused many churchmen, including Demetrius, to flee and join the Roman Church as Dominican Friars. This showed the true lack of power the emperor held over his church and, as such, a theological crisis would ensue as there appeared to be no middle ground between the orthodoxy of the East and Western thought. Over the following two centuries, each church would throw counterclaims and arguments over their practices and beliefs at the other. For the first time, it appeared that there truly was an unstoppable rift between the East and West that would lead to the decline of the Byzantine Empire.

While the theological scene of Byzantium was crumbling, so too was its economic and military situation. The Constantinople of the fourteenth and fifteenth centuries was no longer the once grand city that stood in the centre of the world – now, it was merely a city-state in the Bosphorus with Peloponnesian attachments. Escaping the Turkish invasion, many of the senior churchmen of the empire fled to the capital for refuge and were able to leverage discontent against the imperial palace. The final fall of Thessalonica in 1430 combined with the heavy tributes being collected by the Sultan from Constantinople instilled an atmosphere of desperation within the palace compound. The future was uncertain; to many, it was grim.

In the face of the Turkish threat, John VIII Palaeologus (1425–1448) was strongly encouraged to seek an unrealistic, but hopeful, union with the newly conciliatory Western Church. The conciliarist movement, which had divided the papacy at the time, advocated for the supreme authority of church councils above the pope in matters of doctrine, church governance and decision-making. The proponents of conciliarism argued that church councils, composed of bishops and other clergy, held the highest authority in the church, even above that of the pope. They believed that decisions made collectively by these councils were binding and should be obeyed by all members of the church. Conciliarists often cited historical examples, such as the early ecumenical councils, to support their arguments and believed that these councils, such as the Council of Nicaea and the Council of Chalcedon, demonstrated the importance of collective decision-making and represented a model of church governance. The conciliarist movement reached its peak during the Western Schism (1378–1417), a period of division within the Catholic Church when multiple claimants to the papacy emerged. The conciliarists saw this as an opportunity to address the issue of papal authority and promote the supremacy of church councils. They argued that a general council, representing the entire church, could depose illegitimate popes and reform the church. The culmination of this was the Council of Constance that further issued decrees asserting its own authority and the principle of conciliar supremacy. For John, this was seen as a prime opportunity as the conciliarists hoped to gain the Byzantines as supporters for their cause. Despite the Byzantines previously calling together ecumenical councils, now the pope himself was calling for an urgent council and even supplied a fleet to ensure the participation of the emperor.

Several years earlier, however, the saint of this chapter, Archbishop Symeon of Thessalonica, had advised against any such council as he warned it 'would become a cause of disturbance rather than peace' amongst other condemnations of the West. He believed instead that:

> True peace was not to be had through the acquiescence in the wishes of the unionists. We should be with the Fathers. We are both servants and disciples of our Fathers who were earnestly devoted to the true traditional faith of the Church, and we ever remain inseparably united to them.

Little is known about the life of Symeon. He had lived within a monastery his entire life and was elevated to the role of bishop fairly quickly. He had an excellent knowledge in theological writings and worship. As archbishop, humility was a primary feature of his reign, no doubt from his experiences during his life. One of the most prominent was the brief conquest of the Byzantine Empire by the Venetians in 1423. Despite this, he endured as a preacher and sought to teach through spoken and written word, as well as care for the poor and distressed. He was locally venerated and worshipped by many but would not be officially sanctified until 1981 for his recognition of Byzantine theological works and his unrelenting stance in the face of religious opposition – especially when so many others would fall. As such, to Symeon, a rift with Rome was preferable to a breach or compromise of the Orthodox faith that had survived since the church Fathers. In a contradictory way, Symeon's writings show that he recognised the primacy of Peter among the Apostles and thus, as Peter was the pope of Rome that Rome ranked first above Constantinople. This is actually quite a remarkable understanding given the sentiment of other Orthodox Byzantines at the time. But Symeon did have fierce opposition to Latin doctrinal and liturgical heresies – especially the unleavened bread for the Eucharist. This shows that Symeon's views were substantially more aligned with ecumenical-minded Orthodox theologians in today's world who also express a primacy that the pope holds. By no means is this a primacy in authority and jurisdiction, but rather a sense of honour.

John and his ambassadors reached the council in Ferrara and then moved on to Florence whereupon they decided unanimously that a union was favourable. All the delegates of the Byzantines, aside from Hesychast theologian Mark Eugenicus, signed this union which was proclaimed in Greek and Latin on 6 July 1439. At home, however, churchmen were not impressed. It seemed as though John had ignored the history of his forefathers and as such, upon return, hostility towards unionist bishops was so severe that many would flee to Italy. In 1451, Patriarch Gregory III Mammas himself even migrated because of threats, which resulted in a patriarchal throne being left empty. Nevertheless, John VIII's brother, Constantine XI (1449–1453) also pursued the same illusion of union while recognising that his influence over the Latin faith, citizens of Constantinople, and Orthodox Christians was outside of his power. In 1452, an effort was made by Constantine to reinvigorate support by hosting a ceremony at the Hagia Sophia whereby the decrees of the union were read out and declared by former Orthodox Cardinal Isidore. Alongside this, a Roman Mass was celebrated to reinforce the ties to the West. Despite such efforts, the reception was limited as many of the emperor's own officials stayed away. The question was, how could the emperor be celebrating a Rome and Latin faith that was in the wake of its own schism with the conciliar movement? It was understood by many that the divided papacy, with anti-popes popping up here and there, was incapable of the united crusade that was called for by Alexios in 1095. Even if they did gather some armies, it would be nowhere near the force that could take on the mighty Turks. The attitude of the Byzantines was best summed up by Constantine's own chief courtier: 'Better to see the Turk's turban reigning in the midst of the city than the Latin miter'.

A year later, these words would ring true.

In April 1453, Mehmed II laid siege to Constantinople with a massive army and a formidable navy. The city was well fortified with thick walls and defences, but the Byzantines were heavily outnumbered and lacked sufficient resources to withstand a prolonged siege. The Byzantine Emperor Constantine XI Palaiologos, along with a few thousand soldiers, defended the city. The siege lasted for approximately two months, during which the Ottomans bombarded the city walls with cannons and engaged in frequent skirmishes. Despite the valiant efforts of the Byzantines, the Ottomans gradually gained ground and breached the city's defences in May. The decisive moment came when the Ottomans successfully penetrated the walls near the Kerkoporta (St Romanus Gate) and overwhelmed the defenders. The Byzantines fought bravely, but they were outnumbered and outmatched. Emperor Constantine XI perished in the final assault, refusing to surrender and fighting until his death.

With the fall of Constantinople, the Byzantine Empire officially came to an end after more than a thousand years of existence. Mehmed II, now known as Mehmed the Conqueror, claimed the city as the new capital of the Ottoman Empire and renamed it Istanbul. The conquest of Constantinople by the Ottomans had far-reaching consequences, as it opened up new routes for Ottoman expansion into Europe and marked the beginning of the end of the medieval Byzantine Empire.

But, how true were the words of the courtier? An early fourteenth-century list of bishoprics seems to hint at a fairly healthy state of numbers, thanks mostly to the Lascarid and Palaeologan support for the church, where it showed 112 metropolitanates. This list, however, is somewhat obscure and unofficial and so a memorandum composed in 1437 may provide a more accurate picture: sixty-seven metropolitanates, many of which lacked suffragan bishoprics, but only fifteen were still within areas ruled by the emperor. Thirty-six were listed as being within Turkish territory. For many, it would appear as though there was an element of continuity and little change between the pre- and post-Turk rule over Christianity. Nevertheless, there is an abundance of evidence that while there were indeed some of these metropolitanates who saw continuity under their new landlords, many witnessed a decline in pastoral care and Christian life. For Muslims, life improved as tax burdens decreased and life was more secure. In fact, evidence suggests that western coastal regions in Asia Minor prospered in lucrative trade and agriculture from incoming Italian merchants. This would have led to a rapid investment in Islamicisation of former Christian regions which saw churches and palaces like the Hagia Sophia converted into mosques. For Christians, conditions became very bleak as attempts at conversion and high taxation ensued. As Patriarch Athanasius lamented 150 years earlier regarding Christians within Arab territory:

> Not only have certain people, in an excess of wickedness, repudiated piety of their own accord but also countless numbers – even more than the grains of sand – of unwilling people have been driven to this by irresistible necessity.

Such an apparent widespread exodus would make it surprising to see that there were enough Christians left in Asia Minor for Demetrius Cydones to write that, 'Every day floods of Christians are drawn off into unbelief.'

While this may be somewhat of an exaggeration, there was a distinct shrinkage of Christians in Asia Minor, and the connection between this factor and the decline of the empire is unmistakeable.

A similar plague of unbelief seemed to also spread through the European centres of Orthodoxy in the first half of the fifteenth century. Symeon of Thessalonica writes that despite a profusion of monasteries in the city, their position was precarious in the face of the Ottoman Turks' advance. As such, he doubles down on his opinions about the royal imperial policy. Nevertheless, his writings reveal that in Thessalonica many people favoured bowing to what they believed was the inevitable (in line with what the courtier states), and thus surrendering to the Turks with ease. In 1413, a delegation had even reached the point of handing the city over to Sultan Musa when suddenly St Demetrius appeared to intervene and kill the Sultan with divine powers. In 1422–23, Symeon himself had to come to terms with the fact that the majority of the city 'actually declared that they were bent on handing over to the infidel'. Symeon and other officials would even be slandered for supposedly not caring for their citizens when they received attacks and blockades from Turks. Everything seemed to be pointing towards favouring Turkish rule but Symeon denounced these traitors who wished to surrender, scorning their 'laziness', 'pusillanimity' and 'desire to be fed like farm animals and to lack none of those things which fatten the flesh and bloat it, and which bring in money and turn men into grandees'. His staunch position to not surrender to Turkish or Venetian occupation earned him a great amount of criticism:

> [the people] demonstrated publicly against me myself, continually gathering in a great crowd, rioting against me, threatening to pull down the churches, and me with them, if I refused to do as they wanted.

This does not necessarily mean that the mob of Thessalonica were hoping for a conversion to Islam – no doubt they needed to surrender to ease the hardships of food rations. Still, their indifference to their faith is evident and the hardships experienced shook the faith of many of the last Byzantines. Gregory Palamas, for example, while in captivity under the Turks, found that although many of the men and women were firm in their faith, 'the majority were demanding the reason for God's destruction of our race.' Perhaps the greatest setback to Symeon was his staunch position that many have argued aided in the fall of Thessalonica.

The fall of Constantinople had significant implications for not only the Byzantines, but also for the rest of Europe, one of which was a sense of urgency to find alternative trade routes to Asia – an Age of Exploration which will be examined in a later chapter. Additionally, many Byzantine scholars and intellectuals fled to western Europe, bringing with them valuable Greek and Arabic knowledge which contributed to the Renaissance. In terms of the Turks, or rather Ottomans, they would endure until the First World War almost five centuries later.

Chapter Fourteen

Heresy and Revolution

The post-pandemic world, which many at the time of this book are familiar with, is rife with dissent and disillusion. The same can be said about the post-plague medieval world which entered a phase of pandemonia, dissent and revolution against its papal overseers and thus a dramatic rise in diverse religious sects emerged. The Fourth Lateran Council sought to combat specifically the Cathar and Waldensian heresies. Yet, there is another group, the Hussites, who were a force of nature in the heretical Christian world and drew such attention that a Crusade would be called against them. And so, we traverse the lands, mountains and valleys of Europe to a religiously reforming Bohemia in the east to see the heresy and reform that gripped the Czech lands in a sort of proto-Bohemian Reformation that lasted from the mid-fourteenth century until the early seventeenth century.

It would be superficial to argue that the Hussite movement was solely either a religious reformation or a political revolution, as this neglects the transitional change that occurred between 1405 and 1431. Rather, unlike Cathars or Waldensians, the Hussite movement transformed from a localised religious movement into a wider political revolution founded on the emphasis of nationalism in Jan Hus's reforms, the inclusion of the lower classes which brought its own demands and trepidations and, lastly, the introduction of the political entity that was the National Diets.

The story of the Hussites begins in Husinec, a small town in Bohemia where a certain Jan Hus rose to prominence as a steadfast critic of the corruption within the church. He was born into a peasant family with a humble background that would shape his perspective and empathy for the common people. Gifted with a sharp intellect, he received his early education in a local school before joining Charles University in Prague, where he distinguished himself as a promising student. Hus embarked on a path of theological study, immersing himself in the works of prominent theologians and philosophers of his time. This rigorous academic training laid the foundation for his later theological and intellectual pursuits. During such time, a religious awakening occurred within Hus through the writings of John Wycliffe, an English theologian who had challenged the authority and practices of the church. Wycliffe's ideas resonated deeply with Hus, prompting him to question the church's wealth, political power and doctrinal deviations from biblical teachings. Hus's convictions led him to adopt a firm belief in the importance of scripture and the need for a reformation within the church.

With this in mind, he was ordained as a priest in 1401 and began preaching at Bethlehem Chapel in Prague, captivating audiences with his impassioned sermons delivered in the vernacular Czech language as opposed to Latin. His emphasis on moral integrity, simplicity in worship, and access to the Bible in the language of the people drew large crowds, resonating particularly with the lower classes who had long felt marginalised by the church. Hus's reputation as a vocal critic of church abuses grew, and he became a central figure in the Czech Reformation movement. He ardently denounced the sale of indulgences, simony, and excessive wealth and corruption among the clergy. Through his writings and sermons, he advocated for a return to the early Christian church's principles and the abolishment of practices that he deemed contrary to the teachings of Christ. These challenges to church authority did not go unnoticed. In 1410, his ideas were condemned by the church, and he was excommunicated. Notwithstanding this setback, he continued to preach and gained support from both the Czech nobility and common people, who admired his courage and commitment to reform.

In 1414, Jan Hus received a summons to the Council of Constance, with the promise of safe conduct to present his case to high officials within the church. Naively trusting in this guarantee, Hus left for Constance, hoping to defend his teachings and clarify any misunderstandings – as previous theologians had done since the time of Gregory the Great. Upon his arrival, however, he was arrested and imprisoned, stripped of his clerical garments, and subjected to a highly biased trial. Sources describe an eloquent defence and unwavering commitment to his beliefs, but he was condemned as a heretic and sentenced to death. On 6 July 1415, he was led to the stake and burnt as a martyr.

There is no doubt that before his death, the Hussites were purely a religious reform movement. In the original call for reform, Hus's primary concern was the religious life of both the individual and the church. He emphasised personal morality, to 'love thy neighbour', call for reform of the clergy by secular government, and create a community and life based on the law of God. However, while Hus believed prominence was rooted in reforming religious life, a separate detail would be extrapolated by the wider community to become the major motivation behind the political revolution, that being the call for all levels of Bohemian society to be identified by common faith and by the Czech language. This detail was extrapolated by prominent scholars of political thought which prompted ideas of national consciousness, identity and unity while also providing a legitimate cause of ethnic conflict between the Czechs and Germans.

This advocation began to gain momentum with the ethnic rivalry surrounding the university where the Hussites were based in 1403. On said date, a German university master, Johann Hübner, constructed a list of forty-five articles of religious reforms which was condemned by vote as heretical. The significance of this vote can be found in the inequity of the ethnicity of the university masters as the German masters had three votes while the Czech masters had only one. In 1409, Archbishop Zbynek refused to send a representative to the Council of Pisa during the great schism which prompted King Wenceslas to give control of the university's administration, through the Kutná Hora decree, to the Czech masters and students who swiftly authorised a delegation to go to Pisa. These two examples are key in understanding the origins of ethnic friction being interwoven with the Hussites and why emphasis was strongly placed on the Czech identity.

This gained further momentum when two of the most prominent followers of Hus also stressed national consciousness. Jerome of Prague was one of the chief followers of Jan Hus and in 1409 described his nation not by territory, but rather by a community based solely around the Czech language, essentially describing a political unit unified by its vernacular. Already we begin to see a political tone among the early religious calls of Hus. Another important follower of Hus was John of Jesenice who also placed great influence on Czech national consciousness by arguing that the king had the right to favour the employment of native citizens (Czechs) over foreigners to high positions in royal and ecclesiastical offices because natives would act on the behalf of the welfare of the kingdom while foreigners would not. This combination of literature with the ethnic conflicts of the 1410s is the beginning of this diverging pathway leading to a heretical political revolution. It seems apparent that as ethnicity was such a strong theme in the obstacles opposing the movement; this is perhaps why this minor detail in Hus's original theological beliefs became as prominent as it did. Hus's death in 1415 marked a point where the political revolution became equal to religious reform, as protests about his death were called in the name of the Czech crown, on behalf of the Czech languages, and all Czechs. In fact, the prominence of 'Czech' was so important that Czech churchmen who joined the opposition were accused of betraying national identity and community. From 1415 onwards, the political motivations of national consciousness, identity and language become one of the main pillars behind the Hussites.

While the death of Jan Hus begins this transitional period towards a political revolution, the establishment of the National Diets in 1419 signifies when the Hussites fully became a political entity. The first diet of the revolution recognised urban power and was determined to give Czechs a dominant position within Bohemia. It also excluded Germans from office where Czechs were able to govern, as well as demanding that Czech become the default and only language used in the government. Concerning religion, Latin was no longer to be the language of the church and instead, Czech should be used in singing, worship and reading.

The establishment of the National Diet represented a major victory for the Hussite movement. With its primary motivation of establishing degrees of independence where it could, it attempted to fulfil the calls of religious reform by Hus as well as respond to the ethnic friction between Czechs and Germans in the 1410s. It appears to be very modern in its form and function, appearing as though it would be found in the twentieth century rather than medieval because of this underlying tone of nationalism. Even when regarding the church, the opportunity for reform was presented through an understanding of nationalism whereby Czech was to be used to emphasise Czech identity, community and the idea of a nation unified by Czech. From the first diet alone, it can be seen that 1419 takes a political revolutionary tone and establishes the Hussites as a political unit as well as a religious one. Following this, in 1420 a manifesto was published to inspire and emphasise national identity which only aids in emulating the political revolutions of the twentieth century. Between 1419 and 1436 there were numerous diets, all of which had the primary concern of reforming the Czech church, forging national unity, establishing social order, and discussing the conditions to accept Sigismund as king. Particularly notable is that in this two-decade period, there is a transformation where political reform takes precedence over religious reform, showing the extent to which the Hussite movement had transformed since Hus's original call.

The question as to why the Hussites became a political unit can be answered with the argument that as different social classes became involved with the Hussites, they each brought with them their own trepidations and demands. In its origins, the Hussite movement began amongst scholars like Hus, Jerome of Prague, and John of Jesenice who were inspired by other scholars such as English philosopher and theologian John Wycliffe. Therefore, in its roots, there is a very philosophical and intellectual approach that was taken by the movement when concerning religion. This eventually adapted with the inclusion of the noble class and lower class. From 1394 to 1404, there had been a great power struggle between the nobility and the king over the centralisation of power. In the pact of 1394, the nobles claimed to seek the good of the country by taking control of the government. Therefore, it can be theorised that the nobility saw the Hussite movement as another chance to secure more power for themselves. At the National Diet of 1433, the nobility appointed Ales Vrestovsky as the country's regent which gave legitimacy to the nobles' move to restore social order and attain power. The nobility hence used the National Diets and, by extension, the Hussites, to secure and extend their own political power.

Meanwhile, in response to the growing influence and defiance of the Hussites, the church and its supporters launched the first Crusade against them from 1420 to 1421. Led by Sigismund, the Holy Roman Emperor, and supported by papal forces, the Crusaders aimed to suppress the Hussite movement. However, the Hussites, under the military leadership of Jan Žižka, displayed exceptional tactical prowess and successfully defended themselves, leading to a stalemate. Following this, negotiations took place between the Hussites and the church whereby the Hussites were granted certain concessions known as the Compacta, which recognised their right to Communion in both kinds and permitted the use of the Czech language during religious services. Unfortunately, these agreements were short-lived, as the Hussite movement following the Crusade fragmented into further political and religious entities.

The inclusion of the lower class also disrupted the original reforms called by Jan Hus as they brought with them the experience and distaste of being subjected to the church. Jan Hus and the original Hussites only wanted internal reform within the Christian Church, by no means did they wish to withdraw from the church, the international Christian community, or break from Rome itself – only an internal reform. The fact that Hus fought so much to be involved in the Papal Councils is evidence of this pursuit to remain included in the papal community. When the lower classes became involved with the Hussites, they brought with them a hatred for the church as both a corrupted, greedy institution, and also as a landowner. As the church was a major property owner in Bohemia, it meant that the peasant class was subject to taxes, and the church acted as if it was a feudal lord. Therefore, while the official Hussite doctrine led by Jakoubek of Stribro preached Hus's original ideas, there was great pressure from the lower classes who were energised to make greater changes. This is why, in the 1420s, there was an eventual split between the Taborites, who represented the lower class, with the upper-class Utraquists. While the nobility was more concerned with politics than religion, the lower class were more concerned with religion than politics as Christianity had a far larger impact on them. The Taborites, to an extent, fought for the closest version of Hus's original calls for reform as they attempted to apply ideas of personal morality and religious cleansing. As such, they would lead the charge against the further Crusades launched by the papacy.

Frustrated by the lack of progress and the continued defiance of the fragmented Hussites, the church and its allies once again launched a series of Crusades. These campaigns witnessed brutal clashes, sieges and devastating scorched-earth tactics. The Hussites, led by military commanders such as Prokop the Great, adapted their strategies and employed innovative weapons, including the famed Hussite war wagons, enabling them to withstand the attacks. The Hussites' military successes and the ongoing power struggles within the church prompted a repeal of the Compacta. In response, the Hussites united under the banner of the radical Taborite faction and launched a massive revolt against the church and its supporters. The conflict raged on until a series of peace agreements were reached in 1434, effectively ending the Crusade. Following the Crusades, Sigismund granted Tabor, the home of the Taborites, the status of a free royal town (until 1448 when it was integrated under the government) which allowed an expression of reformed religion as they worshipped in Czech and did attempt to implement a degree of Hus's original reforms. The Crusade on the Hussites left a profound impact on the religious and political landscape of Central Europe. The Hussite movement successfully challenged the authority of the church, paving the way for future religious reformations, including Martin Luther's Protestant Reformation in the sixteenth century. The Hussites' military successes demonstrated the effectiveness of innovative warfare tactics and inspired later military leaders. Furthermore, the Crusade fostered a sense of national identity among the Czech people, solidifying their cultural and linguistic distinctiveness. It also contributed to the decentralisation of power within the Holy Roman Empire and the rise of Bohemia as an influential political entity.

Returning once more to Hus's ideas of reform, the conflict resulted in various reforms being passed through the government. One such reform to emerge from this conflict was the Four Articles. The Four Articles sought to reform ideas about the Eucharist, free preaching of God, limits to priestly property, and the purgation of public sin, all of which attempted to reform the church in some way. However, this was published in 1420, and it was not until Sigismund's accession in 1436 that a revised, watered-down version was confirmed. Nevertheless, the impact of the revolution was most significant in the redistribution of church property where it is estimated 30–40 per cent of productive land changed ownership. The church was hence reduced to a minor landowner which strongly fulfilled an aspect of Hus's original claims for reform. However, Tabor and the Taborites were undoubtedly the strongest evidence for the legacy of Hus's ideals as they preached and fought for personal morality, church reform and a rejection of the social and political hierarchy. The limitation of this is that it was contained only to Tabor which while it did flourish as a peasant commune, only lasted from 1420 to 1448 and was essentially confined to just one town.

Thus, when considering the Hussite movement, we can see that while in its foundation Jan Hus preached and pursued religious reform, after his death his ideas emerged into a wider political thought concerning national identity. Over the four-decade period following his martyrdom, the original religious ideas faded under the new political revolutionary motivation commanded by the noble class who sought to extend their power – though credit must be given to the Taborites who presented the closest example to the original Hus ideals. While it makes sense that within Catholic jurisdictions Jan Hus is not considered a saint (rather noted as an enemy of the papacy), within the Orthodox Church and Bohemia, he is very much venerated as a martyr who represented a mix of Eastern and Proto-Protestant faith.

Chapter Fifteen

Apostle of the Americas

In the spheres of power, it appeared as though for the last few centuries Christendom was trapped within a recurring stagnation that saw each century cycle through crusades, schisms and attempted reform. Of course, there is no doubt that being enclosed on all sides by Mongols, Rus, Mamluks, Berbers and Ottomans formed an impenetrable and inescapable border that blocked Christians' access to the wider arena. Yet, with the final fall of Byzantium, the churning wheel of stagnation was broken and it appeared as though there would be an escapable route via a back door. For if the Silk Road and continental prospects were blocked, there was still an ocean opening out from the Philippines to Mozambique and beyond. With religious zeal, material exigency, scientific curiosity and commercial spirit, the Age of Exploration was set forth.

In a letter to the secretary of the Aragonese royal treasury, Lord Suis de Santangel, Christopher Columbus wrote the following in 1493:

> I have decided upon writing this letter to acquaint you with all the events which have occurred in my voyage, and that the discoveries which have resulted from it. Thirty-three days after my departure from Cadiz [October 1492], I reached the Indian Sea, where I discovered many islands, thickly peopled. Of which I took possession without resistance in the name of our most illustrious Monarchs, by public proclamation and with unfurled banners. To the first of these islands, which is called by the Indians Guanahani, I have given the name of the blessed saviour [San Salvador], relying upon whose protection I had reached this as well as other islands.

Believing he had reached islands off the coast of Asia, he described them as such:

> All these islands are very beautiful, and distinguished by a diversity of scenery; they are filled with a great variety of trees of immense height [...] There are very extensive fields and meadows, a variety of birds, different kinds of honey and many sorts of metals, but no iron.

Turning to the people, he commented:

> They are naturally timid and fearful. As soon as they see they are safe, however, they are very simple and honest, and exceedingly liberal with all they have [...] the women seem to work more than the men. I could not clearly understand whether the people possess any private property. I did not find, as some of us had expected, any cannibals among them, but on the contrary men of great deference and kindness.

Columbus's letter was the talk of the town. By the time he had reached the Spanish court, the letter had already reached the pope and had been translated and reprinted into several editions. By the end of the year, the letter had been circulated in Basel, Paris, Antwerp, Rome and Florence. After centuries of decline, Europe was re-energised with this impression of the 'New World' that was coined by Florentine explorer Amerigo Vespucci who would later lend his name to the continent of America.

What is particularly interesting about the aforementioned letter is that despite venturing to unknown oceans, Columbus had very firm ideas of what he might find. He had images of Amazonian warrior-women, cannibals and primitive people. These images, however, have been regarded by historians as laying the groundwork for the subsequent interactions and relations that would occur between Indigenous and European peoples. Expectations were based on notions of cultural difference and inferiority between the 'Old' and 'New World'. In these encounters, religion, ethnicity, race and language were more different than anything ever previously witnessed. Even North Africa and the Middle East, though culturally different, had been on the radar of Europe since the Ancient Greeks. For America, however, there was no ancient text within the renaissance of Greek learning that could inform the explorers. As such, the notion of 'the other' known as 'othering' quickly developed. The extent of these preconceptions is so powerful that many historians have said that European sources on Indigenous peoples are useless for the study of Indigenous cultures because they rather inform us more about the culture of Europe. This is not entirely true as there are still facts buried within the bias, but whenever possible, keep in mind that the Indigenous cultures did not have a voice.

Following this, the fifteenth-century world would become more interconnected than ever before as explorers sought adventure, with kings and merchants alike as patrons. What is interesting too is that, given the period, many of those who sought this adventure, such as Gadifer de la Salle, were former Crusaders. These Crusaders hoped to form their own kingdoms and become kings just as Baldwin and Bohemond had once done in the First Crusade. One such explorer was Amerigo Vespucci. His letter to Pier Soderini in 1497 appears to show him touching the mainland weeks before John Cabot, an explorer commissioned by

Henry VII of England to explore coastal North America, and fourteen months before Columbus. He writes about his motives for exploration as such:

> I resolved to abandon trade, and to fix my aim upon something more praiseworthy and stable: whence it was that I made preparation for going to see part of the world and its wonders.

Once again playing into these powerful ideas of preconception:

> We set out from the port of Cadiz on the 10th day of May 1497, and took our route through the great gulf of the Ocean-sea: in which voyage we were eighteen months [engaged]: and discovered much continental land and innumerable islands, and great part of them inhabited: whereas there is no mention made by the ancient writers of them: I believe, because they had no knowledge thereof: for, if I remember well, I have read in some one [of those writers] that he considered that this Ocean-sea was an unpeopled sea: and of this opinion was Dante our poet in the xxvi. chapter of the Inferno, where he feigns the death of Ulysses, in which voyage I beheld things of great wondrousness, as your Magnificence shall understand.

Many scholars have hinted that the mention of Dante here would suggest Amerigo was influenced by the new wave of Humanism, showing his journey not to have been made through a dedication to God, but in a pursuit to further his country. The reference to Canto 16 of the *Inferno* is also notable. Here, Dante sarcastically praises Florence for its widespread fame in hell as well as on Earth. Dante condemns Ulysses as ambitious and lacking a care for his people whereby he sails west to the end of the world to abandon everyone and seek forbidden knowledge. For Amerigo, he uses this reference to mock Dante's scorn. As he said previously, he wanted to undertake something that would be praiseworthy but the reference to Dante shows that this goes beyond personal ambition. Amerigo hopes to bring true fame to the Florentines through his discovery of the so-called forbidden knowledge and further interconnect his people.

Amerigo set sail for *la gran Canaria* which he said were situated in the Ocean-sea at the extremity of the inhabited west and 280 leagues from Lisbon. Here they stopped for eight days to gather more provisions, water and wood before heading further west for thirty-seven days after which 'we reached a land which we deemed to be a continent'. It is not long before we see this idea or Order vs Disorder in his preconceptions:

> We made towards the land, and before we reached it, had sight of a great number of people who were going along the shore: by which we were

> much rejoiced: and we observed that they were a naked race: they shewed themselves to stand in fear of us: I believe [it was] because they saw us clothed and of other appearance [than their own]: they all withdrew to a hill, and for whatsoever signals we made to them of peace and of friendliness, they would not come to parley with us: so that, as the night was now coming on, and as the ships were anchored in a dangerous place, being on a rough and shelterless coast, we decided to remove from there the next day, and to go in search of some harbour or bay, where we might place our ships in safety.

The clothed vs unclothed is a particularly notable focus of Amerigo's letter as he further elaborates that:

> For so much as we learned of their manner of life and customs, it was that they go entirely naked, as well the men as the women. They are of medium stature, very well proportioned: their flesh is of a colour that verges into red like a lion's mane: and I believe that if they went clothed, they would be as white as we.

It is here we see this ingrained racial difference. Amerigo attempts to present that the whiteness of the Christians through their clothes speaks of a wider order the Europeans have as opposed to the chaotic nature of the natives. If the natives, as Amerigo would suggest, had clothes and, by extension, Order and Civilisation, then they would be equal to the European – they would be white. Likewise, with both men and women being naked among each other this greatly contrasts the conservative nature of Christian virtues whereby open nudity is scorned upon. This is a very powerful idea that echoes the fundamental racism that underpins the slave trade. Very quickly we are venturing into the waters of Social Darwinism with skin colour being interwoven with ideas of civility and civilisation. This is further witnessed in the following:

> They are not accustomed to have any Captain, nor do they go in any ordered array, for every one is lord of himself: and the cause of their wars is not for lust of dominion, nor of extending their frontiers, nor for inordinate covetousness, but for some ancient enmity which in by-gone times arose amongst them: and when asked why they made war, they knew not any other reason to give than that they did so to avenge the death of their ancestors.

To Amerigo, it appears as though there is no social order, no feudalism, and no centralisation to uphold their civilisation. He seems puzzled at the idea that war is waged over revenge rather than for wealth, territory, or power. He continues in the comparisons:

> They have no judicial system, nor do they punish the ill-doer: nor does the father, nor the mother chastise the children [...] The manner of their living is very barbarous, for they do not eat at certain hours, and as oftentimes as they will.

Once again Amerigo is comparing all the hallmarks of what he believes is a civilised society and it appears as though the natives do not measure up against it. Harking back to Chapter 1, the hordes of tribes were regarded as barbarians by the Romans and we now see a similar situation occur whereby the Europeans are regarding the natives in their time as barbarians. In Europe law, government, order and hierarchy are the pillars of state-building and so it shows a huge inferiority between them and the natives which will, in the future, provide a justification for enslavement and colonialism. On religion, Amerigo writes:

> Amongst those people we did not learn that they had any law, nor can they be called Moors nor Jews, and [they are] worse than pagans: because we did not observe that they offered any sacrifice: nor even had they a house of prayer: their manner of living I judge to be Epicurean.

It is interesting that Amerigo denotes these people as worse than pagans, Muslims and Jews as they apparently pursue earthly pleasures of goods, food, drink and sex. In every shape and form, this way of living contradicts and opposes the way of life Amerigo is familiar with. Nevertheless, Amerigo and the crew eventually leave the Indigenous community and venture further along the shore whereby they find several other Indigenous communities – some of whom are hostile, while others were friendly:

> Many tribes came to see us, and wondered at our faces and our whiteness: and they asked us whence we came: and we gave them to understand that we had come from heaven, and that we were going to see the world, and they believed it. In this land we placed baptismal fonts, and an infinite [number of] people were baptised, and they called us in their language Carabi, which means men of great wisdom.

This is a key aspect of this Age as the new realms of possibilities and opportunities opened up new ways to expand religion. For too long was the known world locked by the constraints of Christianity and Islam and while civilisations like the Byzantines rose and fell, the religious map hardly changed over the former centuries. With a seemingly endless array of people in the New World, the opportunity for conversion and domination over the rapid popularity of Islam was rife. Yet Christianity was not the only one to see this opportunity, as in the meantime Islam had its own explorers who had been sailing and exploring eastward.

Known as one of the most well-travelled people before the age of steam, Ibn Battutah, a Moroccan explorer, had criss-crossed his way from Mecca to Niger, Tanzania, the Volga, and to the Grand Canal of China. Ibn Battutah, however, was a rather lousy father as he admitted after entrusting his son to a friend, 'I do not know what God has done to either of them.' Despite his rather lackadaisical approach to his children, he was a keen social climber and close companion to Ghiyath al-Din, the great-great-grandson of the penultimate Abbasid caliph of Baghdad (a tenuous connection but nevertheless one that held prominence). Both men, however, had been attracted to the lands of India, specifically Delhi, after a campaign by the Sultan to draw Arabs in to bolster his legitimacy.

While the fate of Ibn Battutah's son and close friend is unknown, we do know where Ghiyath's son, Abd Allah, ended up. Despite the two friends residing in Delhi, a tombstone in the royal cemetery in Northern Sumatra, Indonesia, was found with his name. Samudra-Pasai, where Abd Allah died, was the capital of the newly formed Islamic state in what is now the country with the largest Islamic population. The tombstone inscriptions place him in 1407 (809 in the Muslim calendar) which is some time before Columbus discovered the islands off the coast of America. Nevertheless, this shows what the post-Mongol Arab world appeared to look like, and it was very similar to the narrative we see in Christendom: stagnation at home, and opportunities abroad. What is particularly notable is that the headstone found in Sumatra was produced in the port city of Cambray in Northern India. Similar headstones with Islamic inscriptions from Cambray had been found along the south Tanzanian coast, Mogadishu, Aden, Southern Oman, Iran, Goa, Kerala, Sri Lanka, Maldives, Sumatra and Java. Why such a tombstone should be ordered from somewhere thousands of kilometres away is a question without answers, but it demonstrates that the New World of the fifteenth century was an arms race of religious expansion with Islam heading east while Christianity traversed west.

The adventure for Arab expansion may have been motivated by the words of Muhammad: 'Two hungers are never satisfied: the hunger for knowledge, and the hunger for worldly things.' In the aftermath of the Abbasid fall in 1258, it appears as though this hunger meant that Islam could endure and survive in a sort of mercantile empire that expanded across the width of the world. They had 250 years of uninterrupted opportunity to form firm foundations before the Europeans entered India and the effect on many of these eastern countries such as Afghanistan, Iran, Iraq, Bangladesh, Indonesia and Malaysia shows that this opportunity was not ignored. Even Ibn Battutah was surprised to see how far-reaching Islam had become. In 1346, after leaving Samudra-Pasai, he ventured on to see the Arab diaspora of Southern China at a place he regarded as Kaylukari. In a similar way to Amerigo's recorded expectations about the natives he met, Ibn Battutah writes a fascinating narrative about the native inhabitants. He describes that the people there worshipped idols, a conflicting ideology to his iconoclastic beliefs, but that they also owned elephants and were governed by a princess named Urduja who had a guard of female warriors. Perhaps this was the Amazonian-like warrior princess Columbus had hoped to find. Nevertheless, Ibn Battutah notes a particularly striking detail as the princess wrote: *Bismi 'llah al-rahman al-rahim.* That is, In the name of Allah, the Merciful, the Compassionate. Unbeknown to him, she could write and speak Arabic – specifically a sort of Turkish that, as he states, was of a pretty good level. Many places have claimed to be the elusive Kaylukari, including the Philippines, Vietnam and Borneo, but (and whether or not the story itself is true) it was most likely a colony of Indonesia or Malaysia. We know, for instance, that Arabic had begun to be used as the script of Old Malay and many coins bear the inscription of the Islamic declaration of faith. Yet, the Muslim world was not the only one to have its fair share of mythological kingdoms. Returning to Christendom, the opportunity to venture abroad gave rise to a chance to rediscover a place potentially lost to the ages.

Prince Henry of Portugal, otherwise known as Prince Henry the Navigator, supported Portuguese explorations down the west coast of Africa to circumvent military expeditions of Muslim forces in the Northern territories. When he was only 21, he succeeded in conquering the Muslim city of Ceuta in Morocco and became its governor, whereby he learnt about the trading routes from the city which led into central Africa. He saw that going via sea could provide more direct supplies of gold and slaves. In doing so, there was also a hope to reconnect with the ancient Christian kingdom of 'Prester John'. As previously touched upon in the chapter on Ethiopia, Prester John was thought to be a Christian ruler who had descended from one of the three kings who presented gifts at the birth of Christ. Around 1165, a supposed letter from Prester John was sent to the Byzantine emperor which stirred attention; hundreds of copies were made throughout the successive centuries as it played once again on the notion of these preconceptions and of the exotic. The letter described a vibrant and fabulous Christian kingdom in central Asia that was filled with 'Men with horns, one-eyed men, men with eyes before and behind, centaurs, fauns, satyrs, pygmies, [and] some people subject to us who feed on the flesh of men'.

In a similar sense to Ibn Battutah, the location of this alleged kingdom was unknown and the vagueness of central Asia was unclear to European geographers. Over the following centuries, several locations were thought to have housed the elusive priest, including Mongolia, Persia, India and Armenia. In 1507, a new map which included the New World with the first use of 'America' put Prester John in the Himalayas. Nevertheless, with European merchants and missionaries venturing across Central Africa and sailing around the Cape, for the first time in millennia, they were surprised to find a small, tucked-away Christian kingdom that had been lost. The kingdom of Ethiopia had become lost to Christendom as communications were cut off due to the ever-expanding Islam. Still, a number of Ethiopians remained Christian and so it seemed clear to the European explorers that these were the descendants of Prester John.

Henry and successive Portuguese kings would establish colonies on the Atlantic islands of Cape Verde, Madeira, Azores, Sao Tome and the Canaries. From here, investors from Portugal and Italy would grow, harvest and process sugar to be traded along the African coast as well as with their newly formed Ethiopian friends. Mali and Kongo in particular were trading partners as there were bustling gold mines within these kingdoms that brought riches. In order to meet the supply and demand of goods, the caravel was built which could withstand long and harsh voyages by carrying a variety of sail types and new navigation equipment such as the compass. Alongside reinforcing trade relations with Africa, the Portuguese were motivated to find routes to the Indian Ocean which would allow them to buy spices directly from the source and thus cut out the middlemen of Arab, Ottoman and Italian merchants charging extortionate prices. In 1497, King Manuel I of Portugal sponsored a fleet of four ships that were equipped with the best and newest technology to navigate the southern Cape of Africa and search for India. The captain, Vasco da Gama, hired an Indian pilot to navigate and successfully reach Calicut on the west coast of India by sailing across the Arabian Sea. For his success, Manuel bestowed the title 'Admiral of the Indian Ocean' on da Gama and sent him back and forth repeatedly to enforce trade relations. Da Gama returned three years later to Calicut with twenty warships whereby he attacked and seized the city and its riches. Over the century, missionaries and merchants would travel to India and China to seek their riches. This would provide the fuel to the fire that would be the Colonial Age.

The 1500s thus saw trading in Africa and Asia as incredibly profitable, but tropical diseases such as malaria, yellow fever and sleeping sickness would be a major obstacle to the missions. As such, Portuguese traders set up fortified trading posts and utilised existing trading networks to buy and sell goods. Equally, the kings of Portugal made commercial treaties with rulers in Benin,

Oyo and Kongo, supplying them with silk, tools, weapons and wool, in return for gold, cotton, ivory and slaves. Missionaries also ventured into the depths of Africa where they had the most success in the kingdom of Kongo, a powerful state ruled by the *manikongo* who had both religious and political power over six rich and powerful provinces that today encapsulate the Republic of Congo, the Democratic Republic of Congo, and Angola. Nzinga Nkuwu who ruled in 1506 was one of the many to convert to Christianity. His successor, Nzinga Mbemba adopted the Christian name Alfonso I and was raised specifically as a Christian – even sending his son to Europe to be acquainted with the young elite and the church. To the people of Kongo, ideas of the heavenly realm, saints, baptism, angels and demons paralleled many of the religious ideas already present and so a Kongolese version of Christianity would be formed. Churches and chapels were built in all Kongolese provinces, and Kongo became a base of operations for conversion missions to neighbouring kingdoms.

At the same time, operations in America were rising exponentially. In 1500, Bartolomeu Dias, a Portuguese explorer, commanded a fleet of ships to sail around the south coast of Africa whereby they were blown off course and landed in eastern South America which they named, 'Land of the Holy Cross'. Immediately, efforts of colonisation began as the Portuguese Crown leased territory to a Lisbon merchant group who began harvesting brazilwood to be used as a vibrant and rich red dye – said to be like the colour of burning coals. As such, the area would later become known as the 'Land of Brazil', eventually shortened to Brazil. Portugal's claim to this area was supported by a former treaty in 1493 whereby Pope Alexander VI, more famously known as Rodrigo Borgia, drew an imaginary line down what he thought was the Atlantic Ocean, giving Portugal everything to the east, and Spain everything to the west. What he was unaware of, is that this line cut directly through what would be the western border of Brazil which is why today Brazil speaks Portuguese and the rest of South America speaks Spanish.

What all these sources show is that Europeans were carving up the world around them as they liked – with no regard for the native inhabitants that they deemed primitive and inferior. As demand for these new goods rose, solutions had to be made to keep prices low. By 1600, Brazil was Europe's largest source of sugar which was now a highly prized luxury resource throughout the known world. In order to keep costs down, an idea that had been used in the Atlantic islands was brought in on a much larger scale: import enslaved Africans and natives to set up huge and vast plantations and keep the supply of sugar at an all-time high. Slave traders from the west and central Africa captured, bought and traded slaves to be brought to South America and the Caribbean for work. They instilled warfare and greed into the hearts and minds of those who sought a profit and as such, thousands and then tens of thousands were stolen from their homes to be brought to the New World. For 350 years after Columbus's voyage, more Africans crossed the Atlantic than Europeans, not as explorers but as slaves – 10 to 12 million by current estimates. The enslaved were marched from interior Africa to the coast to be locked in pens, dehumanised and crowded into extremely poor living conditions on vessels. Food and water were limited and frequent beatings occurred to render these people mere shells of their former selves. Many would die on the journey later called the 'middle passage'.

Though true that slavery had been a part of many societies in Europe, Africa and Asia for centuries, the plantation slavery of the Americas was far different to anything seen previously. One of the prominent reasons was this new racial undertone. Although the Renaissance gave birth to a new age of rediscovery, the Aristotelian texts also gave rise to new ideas of civility and order that were interwoven with racial differences and Darwinism. European Christians and Arabic Muslims saw Black Africans as inferior, barbaric and primitive. Slave traders linked whiteness to freedom and blackness with slavery – all of which were emphasised with the plantation system. By the time the enslaved arrived at the Americas, they were no longer humans – just mere machines made to work for around seven years before dying of exhaustion, disease or starvation. The church also attempted to rationalise slavery, stating that their suffering on earth would lead to paradise in heaven.

Nevertheless, not all supported the slave trade and the treatment of Indigenous peoples. Louis Bertrand was born to a relatively normal family in Valencia in 1526. Relatively normal as he was related via his father to St Vincent Ferrer, the patron saint of Valencia who was deemed a magician, or thaumaturgus, of the Dominican Order. Louis, from a young age, also sought to join the Order despite being dissuaded by his father. His hagiography describes him as a fairly stern chap who had little sense of humour, yet had a deep and loving heart and disposition. Unlike some of the previous saints mentioned, he had no intellectual or oratory gifts, he was merely a hard worker and someone dedicated to his Order. When the plague broke out in 1557 at Valencia, he devoted himself to caring for the sick and dying, preparing the latter for burial. When the plague subsided, Louis was filled with a warmth of zeal and sought to extend the scope of his Order through preaching despite sources claiming that, 'His voice was raucous, his memory treacherous, his carriage without grace.' Nevertheless, he did captivate audiences and many sought to visit and see his preaching. His fame was so extensive that cathedrals and churches could no longer hold his admirers and thus he had to opt for public squares in the city. At this time, he met another saint, Teresa of Avila, who was a Spanish Carmelite, mystic, missionary and reformer who sought Louis to assist her in reforming church practices. It was here that Louis's longing for missionary work would bring him to the Americas. He set sail in 1562 and landed in Cartagena.

His hagiography asserts that he developed a gift of miracles like his ancestor whereby despite preaching in native Spanish, potentially Catalan, he was understood by all. Tides would change, however, when he would become a close companion to Bartolome de las Casas, a man known to history as the 'Protector of the Indians'. Bartolome is known for his text *A Short Account of the Destruction of the Indies,* which was a chronicle of the first few decades of the West Indies whereby he described the atrocities of the colonisers against the Indigenous people. Bartolome had a profound effect on Louis who became compelled to oppose the abuses committed by the colonists. While Bartolome gave up his slaves and petitioned Holy Roman Emperor Charles V to uphold the rights of natives, Louis moved from Cartagena to Panama where he worked to convert 6,000 people. From here, he moved to Tobara in Colombia whereby sources in his own hand show that he worked to list all the inhabitants of native and African people (over 10,000) in the baptismal registers. He was also to do the same at Cipacoa and Santa Marta whereby 15,000 people were converted, baptised and registered, including 1,500 natives who travelled from Paluato to Santa Marta to meet the saint and convert. According to his *Miracula*, there was opposition to him by some tribes. One such story describes an attack by a tribe of Caribs in Colombia whereby one of the Indigenous held a rifle to him, Louis made the sign of a cross over the barrel and it turned into a crucifix.

Surviving such an encounter after years as a missionary in South America, Louis inspired and converted tens of thousands; in turn, he received inspiration from them. After learning about the atrocities committed under colonialism, he returned to Spain in 1569 to plead for the cause of the oppressed Indigenous communities. No doubt upon leaving, Louis yearned after his spiritual children whom he could no longer protect from the oppressors. Nevertheless, news of his return reached Valencia before he did. Upon arrival, Louis declared that he returned home to serve God earnestly and lobby for the rights of those he had converted. He is seen to have reached a contemplation that the true religion of Christianity was so often tainted by the immoral lives, avarice and unjust cruelties of many who were Christian in faith but not in spirit. He refers to a scene whereby a Spanish officer abused the natives at his church, calling them idle dogs and hitting them with his stick. The tyranny of the Spaniards, as Louis and many natives had seen, echoes a story whereby a native asked if any Spaniards would be found in heaven and expressed no desire to go to paradise if any of his oppressors were there. These experiences clearly had a profound influence on Louis who relayed these stories to listeners at home in Spain, preaching a doctrine whereby all those who ill-treated the natives were unworthy of the Sacraments of the Church.

In 1580, Louis fell ill and died a year later. For his work and charity towards Indigenous communities, he was venerated and given the title of 'Apostle of the Americas'. Despite his work, being one of the few to go against the grain, the mistreatment of Indigenous communities and Africans endures to this day.

Chapter Sixteen

Forbidden Friendships

Medieval history is like a jigsaw puzzle, one of those in which the majority of the pieces are missing and distorted. As such, it is full of paradoxes and contradictions – especially between the powers that rule and the 'boots on the ground' everyday citizen. The discovery of America was underpinned by the newly rediscovered texts of the Renaissance which set forth the precedence that would be a hierarchy of race with 'whiteness' at its apex. These texts not only fermented ideas of race but also gender and sexuality, and the disparities within them. Recent research into the history of gender and sexuality as a result of the progress made by the LGBTQ+ community (the most up-to-date abbreviation at the time of writing) has yielded pioneering work. But, before diving into this history, a word of caution, or disclaimer, surrounding the notions of such topics so far back in the past.

There has been a great debate over whether the disparities and terms we use for these could, or even should, be reflected on to the past. What will become clearer as we delve into medieval medicine is that the concepts of the body in the later Middle Ages border on the fictitious with concepts of climates, humours and biblical ancestry all playing pivotal roles. A prominent and well-regarded historian, Geraldine Heng, who has dedicated much of her career to medieval race and racism states that we should not see race as a category in the Middle Ages, and to do so is to underplay the significance of structural inequalities such as feudal hierarchies, inheritance laws, etc. Likewise, African American medievalist, William Chester Jordan, extends this argument to state that race is a modern category and that seeking a pre-history to the injustices of the colonial era only aids in legitimising its behaviour. With this in mind, when venturing into notions of feminism, gender and sexuality which are incredibly intimate and personal, we should be wary to reflect terms such as bisexual, gay, lesbian, trans, etc., as we cannot truly know how this person felt in their own bodies a millennium ago. This is further complicated when we look towards non-Christian communities. Written in the 920s by Muslim-Abbasid traveller Ahmad Ibn Fadlan, the following passage is taken from his *Risala* and is a first-hand account of his experiences along the Silk Road as a member of the Abbasid caliph embassy of Baghdad travelling to the king of the Volga Bolgars. While travelling, Fadlan encounters the Rus Vikings, an ethnic group originating in modern-day Ukraine in the upper Volga region. He writes:

> They share a house, in groups of ten and twenty, sometimes more, sometimes fewer. Each reclines on a couch. They are accompanied by beautiful female slaves for trade with the merchants. They have intercourse with their female slaves in full view of their companions. Sometimes they gather in a group and do this in front of each other.

We should not necessarily jump to claim that these men were of a homosexual or bisexual disposition – they merely did not have the rigid constructs of sexuality that we hold today. Nevertheless, this does not mean we should disregard the topic entirely as quotes like the abovementioned show a time when such concepts of gender and sexuality were fluid and flexible before the Early Modern period when tolerance and openness begin to constrict and cease. As such, this chapter will explore the pivotal period when we see a noticeable change in the winds of tolerance, acceptance and fluidity. We shall also see how saints play a role in both sides of the coin as a symbol for fluidity as well as conformity.

A crucial concept in the history of gender is biological destiny. For centuries, medieval medicine and philosophy recognised ambivalent concepts of gendered sexuality – hermaphrodites, homosexuality, 'feminine' men – but they witnessed these within a world which firmly had two genders and two sexes; the female Eve, and the male Adam. As far back as St Augustine of Hippo we see the *City of God* refer to hermaphrodites in a list of what he calls 'monstrosities': 'Others have characteristics of both sexes, the right breast being male, and the left female, and in their intercourse they alternate between begetting and conceiving.'

He does so to define what he and his contemporaries would consider, and measure, as 'what constitutes the persistent norm or nature'. As such, venturing forth we too must understand the medieval views of sexuality in relation to the considered norm. A great example of this can be seen in turning to Anglo-Saxon society with ideas of 'manhood'. Although the term is distinctly gendered now, in Anglo-Saxon society, '*mann*' which 'man' comes from simply meant a person, and '*had*' which 'hood' derives refers to rank. As such, 'manhood' in Anglo-Saxon culture was interwoven with status and a person's ability to perform their duty. Manhood could thus be given and taken at will depending on events. The Penitentials are a list of Anglo-Saxon penances which were to be delivered for specific sins committed. Gender, sexuality, and the concept of 'manhood' are integral to these: 'If a husband is impotent and it is known, then a woman may abandon him for another.'

Here, as the man could not carry out his defined role and thus his status was damaged, then his 'manhood' was withdrawn and the woman was free to marry another. Another example is of penance is: 'He who has sex with a baedling, virile male, or animal should fast ten years.'

There is a degree of debate over what a 'baedling' was. It roughly translates to mean a hermaphrodite, but directly means 'not-man', or someone who has lost their manhood. The *Liber Monstrorum* refers to 'a person of both sexes' who is 'physically masculine yet loves female occupation, and fools around with ignorant men'. Once again, we cannot be certain, but it most probably referred to someone who did not fit the social boundaries of manhood or a woman. As such, Anglo-Saxon society had preconceived perceptions of what was a man and woman, '*maanhad*', but sex did not define them.

These ideas, of course, did not spring to life out of nowhere, but rather were built on the ideas established in the former Greco-Roman world they inherited. Here we see sexual intercourse was embedded within notions of gender: 'For it is the semen, when possessed of vitality, which makes us men, hot, well-braced in limbs, heavy, well-voiced, spirited, strong to think and act.'

There was a close association in Antiquity between masculinity and semen that was not necessarily attributed to biology such as intelligence, but it was these ideas which cemented in medieval thought the assumption that gender was strongly linked to sexuality. In medieval medicine, for example, warnings of fatiguing vitality are issued to men who partook in sexual activity. In other words, to ejaculate semen was to expel vital spirit (*pneuma*). This induced fear led to a wide variety of medical recommendations to circumvent such a damaging effect. Men were told to not have intercourse on a full stomach or in the morning on an empty stomach. Men should exercise or partake in a strenuous activity before sex and follow it with a dry massage. If, however, you fail to do so and have sex 'without restraint', you then must 'have sufficient sleep and avoid tiredness that comes from anger, pain, joy, excessively weakening activities, steam baths, sweating, vomiting, drunkenness, heavy work, becoming too hot or too cold'.

As such, a man had to ejaculate sparingly in order to save his *pneuma* and stay strong in mind, body and spirit. With this in mind, as much as we may believe that the role of a woman was to produce an heir, men were equally as responsible to use their sperm wisely to produce a healthy successor. Men would adopt a strict lifestyle with a restrained diet to build up their *pneuma* for one fertile sexual act that would take place in the evening after the woman's menstrual period. Following this, the woman should cross her legs to keep in the previous semen and spend several days in bed if she wanted to be sure of conception.

For a woman, however, medieval thinkers believed the opposite:

> The more women have sexual intercourse, the stronger they become, because they are made hot by the motion that the man makes during intercourse. Further, male sperm is hot because it is of the same nature as air and when it is received by the woman it warms her entire body, so women are strengthened by this heat. On the other hand, men who have sex frequently are weakened by this act because they become exceedingly dried out.

This is why this chapter began with a disclaimer as these ideas of sexual prohibition inherited from Greco-Roman medical texts are so far removed from our own conceptions and are almost humorous in their absurdities. Nevertheless, not only was controlled sexual activity at the forefront of ideas of gender but also moral pollution and virtue. Romans believed that chasteness or sexual moderation was not only healthy but necessary to preserve gender identity. Involvement in public service was crucial to the Roman concept of an ideal man. As much as women were excluded, so were men who were thought to have 'feminine' traits. Expending your *pneuma* therefore meant risking your participation in public order. In the same way that in Anglo-Saxon culture 'manhood' could be given and taken, masculinity in Antiquity could be lost with ejaculation. Too much ejaculation could cool a man's nature to become more feminine.

Equally, the type of sexual intercourse a man had was integral to his potential feminisation. If, for instance, he was to play a submissive role in intercourse or allow penetration in a homosexual encounter then his masculinity could be questioned. What is particularly interesting is on the latter; it was perfectly acceptable to be an active partner in a homosexual relationship, but penetration was condemned. Alongside this, oral sex with a female partner was condemned too as it inverted the social hierarchy. As such, public service was deeply interwoven into the core aspects of life in the ancient world. Fear of effeminacy was a fear of losing one's status and public image as opposed to the nature of sexuality itself.

For women, however, sexual intercourse did not debilitate them as it did men. In fact, it was believed that women had a heightened connection with intercourse and their capacity to experience and enjoy it. Tiresias, in Greek mythology, expresses this when he is transformed into a woman, and then restored as a man. Upon being asked who enjoyed sex more, he said, 'If the parts of love pleasure be counted as ten, thrice three go to women, one only to men.'

The explanations for this were, once again, connected with ideas of duty. The function of women was primarily reproductive. If men served the state through service, women did through reproduction. Nevertheless, scholars were preoccupied with the nature of the female seed. The Middle Ages inherited two prominent views of female sexuality from the ancient world. The first approach, known as the Galenic view, saw that women produced a seed like men and thus needed to be pleasured in order to produce the seed. The Aristotelian view said the opposite, that they did not produce a seed and thus whether or not the female enjoyed the intercourse was irrelevant. Considering that a book called *Everything Men Know About Women* by Dr Alan Francis published in 1989 featured 128 completely blank pages, it seems that a thousand years has done little to improve men's understanding of women and intercourse. Still, these two ideas had profound ramifications in the medieval era for attempting to understand female sexuality and sexual expression. Yet, in doing so, the church fathers strongly altered the view to interweave it with a strongly gendered emphasis. Isidore of Seville offered questionable wisdom when he wrote, 'Women are under the power of men because they are frequently spiritually fickle. Therefore, they should be governed by the power of men.'

Elaborating on this, St Ambrose further added that men had 'different customs, different complexions, different gestures, gait, and strength, different qualities of voice'. Thus, masculinity was underpinned by active participation in the world as much as in his sexual relationships. The *loci* of sexual pleasure also played into this. Medieval thinkers saw the male genitalia as the focal point of strength, muscle, power and activity while regarding the navel as the female focal point of pleasure (further highlighting their lack of understanding of women) which they viewed as passive and nurturing. As such, the church fathers of the medieval era distinctly continued the former Roman perspectives of gender and sexuality that to be active was to be male, the sex of the sexual partner was irrelevant, and, to take pleasure was virile, and to accept it was servile. They did, however, modify the Roman rule on homosexual encounters that they regarded as sinful.

It is important to recognise this difference, as a crucial influence on the transition of these ideas was faith. Associating masculinity with power now not only meant physical power but also spiritual power. Christian thinkers extended the representation of the male body to spiritual strength as much as physical empowerment – a concept especially prevalent with the rise of the warrior class and subsequent Crusades. For women, however, it was the opposite. Isidore writes the following: 'Man drew his name (vir) from his force (vis), whereas woman (mulier) drew hers from her softness (mollities).'

To contrast men who were strong, rational and spiritual, women were seen as soft and carnal. Women, according to Isidore, embodied sexuality: 'The word femina comes from Greek derived from the force of fire because her concupiscence is very passionate: women are more libidinous than men.'

As such, women were seen as temptresses who continuously reproduced Eve's initial temptation of Adam. St Jerome furthers this by warning:

> It is not the harlot, or the adultress who is spoken of, but women's love in general is accused of ever being insatiable; put it out, it bursts into flame; give it plenty, it is again in need; it enervates a man's mind, and engrosses all thought except for the passion which it feeds.

Here there is a nature of threat as much as fear. Women removed him from the rational world that defined him and his masculinity. Once again this echoes the Roman notions that man could succumb to passion and lose his masculinity. This 'hyper-sexuality' of women was a concept which would shape theological ideas in church law for centuries. The eleventh-century canon lawyer Gratian, for example, affirmed that women were more 'susceptible to sexual corruption than men' and by the later Middle Ages legal statutes demonstrate a continued belief in women as sexually voracious. This concept would later lead to assumptions that women were more likely to be witches in the Early Modern period as they were to have sexual activities with the devil and corrupt the minds of men.

On the topic of lust, many of the church fathers saw sexuality as an accident of Adam and Eve's fall, but part of God's wider plan. Although St Augustine of Hippo disagreed with this, he did agree that Adam and Eve's disobedience introduced physical consequences. With this, a biological view of Original Sin developed whereby this sin was transmitted through semen in sexual acts and then cultivated by female lust in the womb. This would lead us to believe that Augustine did not see sexuality as purely a female experience but rather could also be found in the male erection – a somewhat progressive argument: 'The genital organs have become the private property of lust. [Passion] rises up against the soul's decision in disorderly and ugly movements.'

Perhaps this alternative view came from his own experiences as a young man and his complex relationship with lust and women. He claimed that sexuality was natural to both sexes and while he did associate the male sexuality with power and the female with passivity, he did not agree that women were carnal and men were spiritual.

Medieval medicine would continue to build upon these inherited Greco-Roman and Christian understandings, much of which was underpinned by theology. Scientists of the medieval age believed that female menstruation was not only a prominent factor in defining women's social and cultural functions but also served to purify their bodies. Menstrual blood was thus impure and unrefined toxicity as it marked an inability for the body to warm blood enough to refine it – a theory originating from the cool humours of women. The nature of this led people to believe it would have differing impacts on the two sexes. For women, it was beneficial in cleansing their blood and spiritual sins, 'leaving them less polluted by harmful residues or less burdened by excess of useful residues than men'. Medical practitioners therefore emphasised the importance of menstruation and often prescribed cures for amenorrhea. For men, however, it was dangerous:

> If you knowingly go with a menstruous woman your whole body will be infected and greatly weakened, so that you will not regain your true colour and strength for at least a month, and like a liquid adhering to your clothes, this stink will corrupt a man's entire insides. [...] Do not go near a menstruating woman, because from this foulness the air is corrupted, and the insides of a man are brought to disorder.

Once again this would inform later ideas in the Age of Witchcraft in the 1600s whereby it was believed that the menstrual blood of women could cause crops to wither, wine to sour, plants to parch, trees to die, iron to corrode, and dogs to become rabid. It was a prominent factor used in the medieval period to define and distinguish between a woman and a man – men had beards, pronounced veins, and (according to Aristotle) nosebleeds, while women menstruated.

Given this is the medieval period, it would not come without its paradoxes and contradictions. Some women were able to exercise power equal to men. Adela of Blois, for example, was regarded as a lord as opposed to a lady for the power which she wielded. Likewise, there are plenty of famous saints and mystics who were women, such as Julian (Juliana) of Norwich. The twelfth and thirteenth centuries, for example, saw an exponential growth of the cult of the Virgin Mary in Europe following the writings of St Bernard of Clairvaux. Following the Black Death, many households were left headed by women which, in urban centres, gave rise to the *femme sole* law that granted certain rights to women. Due to labour shortages following the plague, many women also took up male jobs such as ploughing. Also turning tradition on its head was the church which, in a binary world between male strength and female passivity, saw the rise in a 'third gender' of male clergy. As these were men prohibited to bear arms and strength, they were regarded as men with female qualities and thus an alternate masculinity developed within the church itself. These early theories set the precedence of medieval life for centuries to come. Political activity was ultimately reserved for men. Women who did gain power were often scorned with libel about their lust such as that seen with Justinian's wife Theodora. Primarily, this was because of the definitions of gender set forth by St Ambrose, St Jerome and St Augustine, meaning women were confined to low-paying jobs that required less strength. Equally, women who were married were hindered from participating in business deals by a *femme couverte* law as all property or agreement was under the husband's name. Furthermore, despite women medically treating other women for centuries, which allowed them to be partly educated, in the fifteenth century universities and guilds became more popular, medicine became professionalised and such opportunities restricted. Essentially, as a capitalist economy grew following the period of state formation in the earlier centuries, divisions in gender, race and class became more prevalent – especially when the economy hindered women from accessing it.

Again, what is seemingly odd is that the Middle Ages are often scorned for being archaic in their universal intolerance towards people of colour, women and non-heterosexuals. The latter, however, appears to muddy the waters. As we saw from the Roman ideas of gender and sexuality, the focus was on the self as opposed to the partner and so homosexuality was moderately tolerated. Christianity thus may have emerged from a time when same-sex partnership was a common feature of everyday life and so remnants of this endure. We see elements of sexual fluidity in Viking cultures and Anglo-Saxon societies. In Muslim Iberia, for example, it is recorded that some girls dressed as boys and cut their hair short. Even in the thirteenth century after the Christian takeover it was regarded as more of a sin in Spain to be associated with a Muslim than to be in a homosexual relationship. Archives even hold erotica from the twelfth century that describe vibrant and vivid gay sub-cultures in southern Europe.

Archaeological evidence also points towards a fluidity in material culture. The Suontaka Burial in Finland, dated to around the eleventh century, contains two swords with 'male' paraphernalia yet the body is dressed in feminine clothes. A DNA test on the body showed it to have XXY chromosomes as opposed to the typical male XY or female XX – could this be a non-binary or intersex person biologically? Perhaps so, but it shows that the 'archaic' labels we place on the Middle Ages may not hold true.

While prior to the twelfth and thirteenth centuries the church was tolerant of homosexuality with lenient punishments, if they were even enforced at all, the winds changed fairly quickly. On one hand, some members of the church were accepting of gender fluidity and homosexuality, while others were equally as condemning and oppressive.

The Third Lateran Council in 1179 officially outlawed sodomy. Any cleric that practised this was to be either expelled or exiled to a monastery for penance, and lay people could even be excommunicated. At first, the enforcement of these rules was suggestive and sporadic. We see, for example, Eadmer of Canterbury preach to Anselm of Bec that young monks at Canterbury grew their hair out like girls and groomed themselves impiously with self-obsession – even engaging in minor sexual acts. He states to Anselm that the young monks should adopt a more manly bearing. As such, with this third gender of male clergy within the church, some sought to enforce gender policing. Anselm even asks William Rufus, the king of England, to convene a church council against sodomy that had 'plagued the land' so that England would not be punished. With the influential writings of theologians such as Thomas Aquinas and Bernardino of Siena, the severity of the sin was emphasised.

By the fifteenth century, church opinions were hostile towards homosexuals and harsh in their punishments. At a time when the heresy of Cathars, Hussites, Waldesians and other groups was rampant, papal inquisitions were dispersed to attack any non-conformists including Jews and homosexuals and to use any means necessary to stop this plague. In Renaissance Florence, for example, law courts 'carried out the most extensive and systematic persecution of homosexual activity in any pre-modern city' between 1432 and 1502. An abundance of archival records from such courts show that Florence had an extraordinarily high number of incidents that cited homosexual behaviour among Florentine males – seemingly the majority of the male population were convicted of a homosexual act at some point in their lives. Some characteristics of these encounters, however, point towards modernity as opposed to antiquity. Genital oral sex, which the Romans scorned for its damage to masculinity, was a frequent tradition of the Florentines. Records appear to show a fluidity in positions, roles and acts that would turn all of the abovementioned about masculinity and sexuality on its head. Florence is apparently a liberal haven whereby men both gave and received penetration, oral, and more. As such, rather than an inequality in the enjoyment of intercourse where it is neither here nor there on whether the woman has enjoyment, Florence is shown to have an ethos of mutual enjoyment in homoerotic interactions without breaking the roles of gender and its definitions. One such man convicted was Miniato di Lapo, charged in 1352 with a wicked desire 'who has practiced the vice of sodomites for a long time in the city of Florence publicly and openly with many, many men'. Not only does this show that certain men were homosexuals who frequently had active same-sex partnerships, but the emphasis on 'publicly and openly' shows the freedom that Florentines held.

The fourteenth-century statutes of the Florentine Law Courts frequently echo the law codes of Justinian by which sodomites were to be castrated, decapitated, or burnt. In truth, many of the incriminated were not punished and those who were were given fines, public humiliation, short prison sentences, or exile. If a 'sodomite' was to confess to his acts, his punishment was halved. If he turned himself in before he was caught, and named his partner, he was guaranteed immunity. This is why there are a bustling number of records in Florence as although the papal inquisition was in full swing to seek out heretics and sinners; homosexuality was so common that a mitigation of these crimes was always enforced. As a result, during the three decades between 1478 and 1502, 12,000 cases were recorded in the courts with eleven men condemned to death, but only three of these actually executed.

While many were tightening the constraints with definitions outlined by early church fathers, others were more relaxed. As with any hostility, people turn towards saints who then become symbols against oppression. Thus, with the condemnation of homosexuality and alongside the emphasis on conformity in gender and sexuality for men, women, and those who identified in between, one such saint rose above the societal confines to become known as the 'transgender saint'. Wilgefortis, known as the bearded female, was recorded as being one of seven or nine children born to a non-Christian king of Portugal, later becoming Christian with her siblings. She was promised in marriage to the king of Sicily who, at the time, was also a non-Christian. Wilgefortis, however, disapproved of the marriage and wanted to commit herself to Christ through perpetual virginity. She prayed to God for disfigurement which resulted in the sudden emergence of a full and luxurious beard and moustache. The king of Sicily, upon seeing his bearded lady, called off the wedding. Her father, however, was deeply enraged by this as it jeopardised a key alliance. Because of her pursuit of Christ, he had her crucified so that she would die in the same manner as her heavenly love. Wilgefortis, while on the cross, prayed that she would be remembered for her dedication to Christ alongside her passion to be freed from cares and worries. She would become particularly popular amongst wives who would donate a peck of oats to liberate them from abusive husbands.

Historically, however, it is difficult to place Wilgefortis. Neither records nor her hagiography define a specific date but may suggest this (perhaps it was even a fictitious legend) to be from as early as the second century or as late as the tenth. Some historians have suggested that the legend may have emerged from a reference made by Gregory the Great in the *Dialogues* of a bearded nun called Galla. Whatever the date may be, her cult was popularised after 1200 in Europe following the papal crackdown on homosexuality. From hereafter she quickly became known as the 'transgender saint' who stood as a symbol for people who did not fit the defined norm of the period. In this way, she was a liberator and often written about in reference to Galatians 3:28: 'There is neither Jew nor Greek, there is neither slave nor free, there is neither male nor female; for you are all one in Christ Jesus.'

For many, it appeared that through Wilgefortis and by extension Christ, all barriers of social class, race and sex could be overcome. Harking back to definitions of womanhood, Wilgefortis clinging to her virginity and opposing the definition that women were lustful and highly sexual beings also gave rise to the notion of *femina virilis* – a warrior maiden within the spiritual realm. By holding in her sexual desire (a concept encouraged amongst men) as well as bearing the features of a man, she herself became male through her commitment to Christ. This is also seen amongst other female martyrs like Perpetua in the third century. In a dream shortly before her death, Perpetua sees herself in a male body. Likewise, Blandina, another martyr, perceives herself as having been 'clothed' with the essence of 'athletic' Christ (male strength) and becoming like him when dying. As such, women who displayed male traits like courage, strength and restraint were seen to rise above gender transgression.

For centuries, the realm of sainthood was dominated by males who aspired to be models who embodied Christ's message. Yet, from the twelfth century, particularly amongst Benedictines and Cistercians, the concept of Christ as the 'divine bridegroom' meant women could seek a union with Christ and also achieve an added cachet in the male imagination that could lead to sainthood amongst women. Paradoxically, this then led to Christ exemplifying certain feminine traits alongside masculine. In many ways, Christ himself transcended gender and sexuality (or at least was able to interchange). Gender inversion thus developed with monks referring to themselves on occasion as women. Some women even had visions of themselves as males. This did not necessarily have any practical implications but rather served to enhance one's only sanctification. In other words, to rise up to heaven one must rise above earthly limitations and societal boundaries. This led to Orders like the Beguines emerging who were semi-religious sisterhoods that expressed a feminine love for Christ and were regarded as brides of Christ. Here the Eucharist took on a new form, one in which the consumption of bread and wine was almost a metaphor for an erotic union as much as a spiritual as men and women were wedded to Christ himself.

From 1200 to 1500 where the biology of the body took on a new theological significance, the distinction between male and female was, for many, blurred. The former definitions set forth by antiquity weakened and were replaced by distinctions that were far less clear cut. Due to such interchangeability of sex such as that seen in Wilgefortis and in Florence, men and women could experience Christ's passion in a profoundly flexible way. Even in the *Divine Comedy* there is gender fluidity in Beatrice. In *Purgatorio XXX*, Beatrice is hailed in masculine terms as 'Blessed is he who comes'. This conventionally refers to a greeting to Christ and is traditionally sung at Holy Communion but here it refers to Beatrice without any alteration to the masculine Latin ending. As such, in heaven masculine and feminine traits are complementary and simultaneous.

Despite this perceived freedom of gender and sexuality, the voice of the oppressors was far louder. As the Renaissance fed into the Early Modern Era and the age of science and colonialism unravelled, the Inquisition took on new forms underpinned by notions of racial hierarchy, whiteness and male superiority. In the face of persecution, and excommunication, this prompted Orders and kingdoms alike to draw up new laws preventing same-sex relationships. In seventeenth century Malta, for example, the Knights Hospitaller placed harsh prejudice on, and threatened to burn, any who engaged or even spoke of same-sex relationships. Once again, it all came down to power and control as the church felt caught between the perceived punishments sent by God (such as the Black Death, Reformation and Popular Revolts), and the liberty of its people.

Chapter Seventeen
The End of Sainthood

In a sparsely populated area of what is now the centre of Germany lived a young peasant who, after studying law at university, was caught in a terrific thunderstorm while on his way back home. The storm was so violent that the man believed it to be God unleashing the very heavens upon him to take his life. In desperation, he cried out to St Anne and promised that if his life was spared, he would take up the religious robe as a monk. The storm eased and as God had kept his vow, so too did this young man. Thereafter, he made his way back to his university whereby he gave away all his possessions, abandoned law, and entered the monastery at Erfurt. He believed that by taking up the life of a monk his spiritual struggles would end. But why St Anne? Well, Anne was the patron saint of miners, the profession of the young man's father, and so his experience with the saint was deeply interwoven into his life. No doubt there would have been a shrine in his home town where the young man prayed and worshipped. Little did he know at the time that the end of saintly worship and one of the most defining events in Christian history would come about by his own hand, as this young man caught in the storm was the famous Martin Luther.

In many ways, Martin was a product of the medieval era. He, like many, offered devotion to saints, and his story of taking up the cross is no different to those who, in desperate times, pleaded to God and promised to enter religious life in exchange. Yet, Martin also embodied the new humanist movement of the fifteenth century that called for a return to humility and genuine piety. It would be the combination of these two characteristics within him that would contribute greatly to the Lutheran Reformation. Martin was a model monk and quickly rose within his Augustinian order to a position of great authority. In 1511, he attained the role of a professor of philosophy at the newly established university at Wittenberg. While here, deep-seated anxiety grew within him once again that harked back to that fateful night in the thunderstorm. Martin, as a result, undertook incredibly extreme acts of penance as well as daily confessions as he believed he was unworthy of God. The self-harm he inflicted led to paintings and descriptions presenting him as gaunt, wild-eyed and suffering. He was obsessed with his own morbid condition and became preoccupied with a self-perception of inadequacy. His confessor, to instil some vigour into Martin, urged him to find spiritual peace in the Bible. And so from 1513 to 1518, Martin preached and lectured on Psalms, Epistles, Romans, Galatians and Hebrews to crowds that came to listen. The source of Martin's fear of God was found in divine justice, condemnation, judgement, and all the inner medieval workings of doom and hell. In Romans 1:17, however, he discovered 'the righteous shall live by faith' which led him to affirm that justice was defined by goodness and righteousness to those who trusted in him. A phrase from his lectures on Romans sums it up neatly: 'Always a sinner, always a penitent, always right with God.'

Here he found the peace he was looking for, but also the seeds of revolution. In his view, a Christian was not someone who did not sin, but rather a sinner who placed their faith in Christ. Pure faith was all God needed as opposed to all these works of art, theological writings, adorned statues and shrines of intercessors.

Alongside German theologians and mystics, St Augustine was one of the greatest influences on Martin. Despite asserting man's corruption and helplessness before God, thus diverting from the schools of thought established by the likes of Erasmus, Humanism played a vital role alongside the Early Church Fathers in building the theology of Martin. Greek Philology and Erasmus's New Testament both aided in cementing Martin's interpretations of the Bible. He also saw, for instance, that the New Testament bade men to 'repent', turn inward, and not 'do penance' in the sense of works of satisfaction. The issue, however, was that in order to achieve this, the whole medieval fabric of worship, penance and merit had to collapse.

Above all, indulgences were the main issue Martin targeted. In its original form, an indulgence was an exemption from penance on behalf of the penitent. A man may, for example, be permitted to replace a pilgrimage to the Holy Land with a gift of alms to the poor or church. This would establish almost an exchange rate for penance whereby people could trade and exchange pious acts with the church to reduce certain punishments. Gradually, this became out of control and Christ appeared to have a 'boundless treasure of merit' for mankind. Like a banker transferring money from a rich man to a bankrupt pauper, the pope could issue a seemingly unlimited supply of merits to repentant sinners in return for wealth. Over time, rather than paying alms to the poor in lieu of pilgrimages, payments would be made to church officials and the pope, quickly becoming an indispensable form of income to the papacy. Further distortion arose when the general populous understood indulgences to remove sin entirely and thus could be bought on behalf of those in Purgatory. Indulgences therefore quickly attached to pilgrim sites, shrines, relics and saints themselves, although parts of the church had, for a long time, criticised their use. Martin witnessed just how corrupt things had become when Prince Albert of Brandenburg became the Archbishop of Magdeburg and Mainz as well as the primate of Germany aged only 23. Albert had bought his position through bribes and fees using the Fugger banking family. To pay his debts to the bankers, he then set forth a marketing campaign on behalf of Pope Leo X's new indulgence scheme. Half of the proceeds were to go to the pope to contribute to the rebuilding of St Peter's in Rome, and the other half to Albert and his bankers. Sources describe the Dominican Tetzel going from town to town uttering, 'Place your money in the drum; the pearly gates open and in walks mum.'

Martin, still energised by his spiritual breakthrough from lecturing, immediately realised this was a cruel and blasphemous trick on the ignorant – or 'plate-lickers' as Guibert of Nogent would regard them. Martin was right in what he saw – the church was taking advantage of the poor for self-gain. Empowered, he wrote ninety-five Latin propositions attacking the abuse of indulgences. These were translated into the vernacular and distributed widely across Europe. He moved to publish a series of pamphlets, which became increasingly more aggressive as church authorities moved against him, before attacking the more general issues of church teachings and practice. If, by his understanding, faith in the word of God was all that was needed, then this pageantry of relics, saints, priests and monastic communities was a distraction and entirely in vain. Following this, he denied the primacy of the pope and the infallibility of the religious councils that had been held. In 1520, after condemnation, he was summoned before Emperor Charles V at the Diet of Worms whereby he made an emotional and infamous speech and refused to retract the outspoken attacks he had made. As a response, he was outlawed, excommunicated and exiled.

What made things different from previous calls for reform was a new technological revolution in Europe. Martin was a gifted writer and, with the growth of literacy following the invention of Printing Press, the written word could become a vehicle for mass persuasion. By 1521, over 300,000 copies of Martin's books were in circulation. What also made Martin's reforms so popular was that much of Germany was governed by local knights with loose connections to the crown, and thus the political coherence of the kingdom was tenuous at best. As such, with recent military failures and financial demands making a strain on the populace, urban centres were powder kegs ready to spark. Despite tensions between oligarchs, guilds and labourers, their hatred for the clergy, ecclesiastical tax burdens and foreign loyalties united them under Martin's banner. What drew in the hearts and minds of many was his repudiation of ecclesiastical pageantry and insistence that all believers were saints in their own rights and thus no one could improve upon the laws of Christ. Likewise, his attacks on scholastic theology and finance appeased humanists and intellectuals as well as those at the bottom of the feudal pyramid who, for centuries, sought freedom from the ecclesiastical burdens placed on them. His reforms to limit church power, harking back to the eleventh- and twelfth-century Gregorian reform movement, appealed to rulers who were tired of submitting fealty to their papal overlords. Although Martin called for spiritual reform, it quickly took on a political message as city after city declared themselves as allies of Martin's movement.

The call for reform quickly grew beyond Martin while he was in exile, since Alexander Carlstadt, another professor at Wittenberg, took the revolution into his own hands. Through him, Mass was abolished, organs silenced, relics ransacked and iconography tainted. Coming out of hiding, Martin attempted to mitigate the growing calamities through a series of sermons preaching charity and gradual reform. Despite this, a radicalism sect formed under Thomas Munzer, a Saxon priest who rejected the authority of scripture and called for Christians to take up the sword against unbelievers and heretics. Munzer believed an apocalyptic event, similar to that expected at the turn of the millennium, would soon come and cause many to suffer. He also believed Martin to be a charlatan and liar who was selling the Gospel to the ruling class. Munzer would create the first German liturgy and prepare in Allstadt for the coming Armageddon.

Reform quickly ran riot in 1524 as a series of uprisings began that called for the abolition of serfdom and the right to elect local pastors amongst other things. Though many of these grievances were social, there was a deeply interwoven religious undertone shown in the unmistakable Lutheran propaganda that depicted peasants as the chief supporters of the Gospel. Following this, hordes of peasant rebels travelled across the kingdom sacking and burning physical symbols of the medieval age such as castles and monasteries. Munzer was a prominent theologian of this revolt declaring to his armies, 'On, on, spare not, pity not the godless, strike!'

Martin, seeing how out of control the movement had become, was horrified, not least by the fact that he and his teachings were to blame. In response to the destruction of public order, Martin issued a pamphlet called 'Against the Murderous and Thieving Hordes of Peasants' whereby he urged German princes to 'smite, slay, and stab ... remembering that nothing can be more poisonous or devilish than a rebel'. Munzer was captured, tortured and beheaded in 1525. Peasants, hearing of such attacks, discredited Martin and his Gospel believing that he had truly betrayed them and what they stood for. As such, the 1520s and 1530s saw a distinct character form within Lutheranism: all sacraments aside from baptism, penance and the eucharist were abolished; the translation of the Bible and popular hymns into German was undertaken; and an instruction manual of prayer for ministers and worshippers was created to instil a new doctrine in the church. Nevertheless, some prominent features of the 'old Church' still remained. Latin, for example, still held prominence in ceremony. Martin also cared little for ecclesiastical government and thus many of the roles of episcopacy eventually disappeared and were taken over by a mix of court ministers and lawyers answerable to the local princes. Given his dependence on such German princes, Martin had to lean on the secular arm of support more than he may have wished, creating the *Summus Episcopus* whereby if the clergy was not to implement reform, then the princes were to take charge of the task. This blurred the lines between the secular and ecclesiastical and though condemning the suppression of dissent in the 1520s, he now justified it.

From the early 1520s, the Reformation surpassed the borders of Germany and distinctive forms of Protestantism emerged across the continent. Being exiled from France by royal actions against the Lutherans, John Calvin made his way to Switzerland in 1536. Educated among French humanists, the transition to the reformed faith was seamless for him. After settling post-exile in Basel, he undertook the task of producing his first summary of the Protestant faith, *Institutes of the Christian Religion,* which would become one of the most important books of the century. One of the main theological points Calvin makes within the book is that man knows himself only in relation to God and thus is an instrument of God which would mean his salvation is predetermined: 'Eternal life is foreordained for some, eternal damnation for others.'

Essentially, Calvin's theology dictated that everyday actions are fickle and rather our next life in heaven or hell is only determined by the will of God. Therefore, we should live in hope and conform as best we can to God's will, as opposed to the mysteries of the afterlife and morality. In pursuit of this conformity, Calvin set forth a doctrine for the church that governed every aspect of ecclesiastical life, underpinned by order, discipline and godly living. Under him, pastors served the church through preaching, encouragement, and rebuke for scripture. Teachers ensured doctrinal purity, deacons dealt with finances and administrative tasks, and lay elders would administer moral discipline through an ecclesiastical court whose punishments extended to excommunication. In order to ensure moral standards were upheld, spying and fault-finding were also encouraged among monks. The Church of Calvin was a rather bleak one that primarily focused on serving God and God alone; gone was the medieval pageantry of arts, theology, calligraphy, enshrinement and sainthood. Even the building that was a church was no longer a sacred dramatic space, but rather one to be used for preaching and learning as an auditorium. Despite all this, Calvin found success in Geneva primarily through the city's rejection of their overlord's authority. Yet, the idea of a 'godly commonwealth' captivated many, even if the disciplines within were restrictive. and the civic reforms of Protestantism within Switzerland became a model for reformers elsewhere on the continent. By the end of Calvin's life, Geneva was orderly, sober, and, for the most part, godly. Crime was reduced through punishment and the poor and sick were nursed and cared for. Likewise, his academy in the city made it a hub of Protestant learning in Europe, being described as 'the most perfect School of Christ that ever was on earth since the days of the Apostles'. In the meantime, Protestantism was able to gain a foothold in the northern and eastern provinces of Germany as well as parts of central and eastern Europe, partly due to the fact that Emperor Charles V was currently preoccupied in fighting Muslim armies as well as French expansion. By the time he was ready to attack the Protestants in 1546, it was too late and by 1555, the Reformation was in full swing.

Aside from the Lutheranism that encapsulated modern-day Germany, Scandinavia and parts of eastern Europe, and Calvinism that had reached Switzerland, Hungary, Poland and much of Scotland, it was England's turn to undergo a reformation that would give birth to the Anglican Church. England's reformation was perhaps one of the longest and most fragile in Europe. The Humanism of Erasmus and the work of John Wycliffe and the Lollards had a long and deep impact in England that had rendered the country almost predisposed to Protestantism. Though Lutheran books circulated and Tyndale's English New Testament appeared in 1526, their king, Henry VIII, remained a staunch papal supporter – even gaining the title 'Defender of the Faith' in 1521 for his Defence of the Seven Sacraments against Martin Luther. This meant that Protestantism made little headway for a while – until Henry sought to divorce his wife Catherine of Aragon for failing to produce an heir. The divorce, as the infamous story goes, was refused and Henry turned to cut ties with the church. In 1534, Henry declared himself the head of his own church (the Church of England), abolished papal authority, and embarked on a campaign known as the 'Dissolution of the Monasteries' whereby the many shrines of saints across England, even at Canterbury, were sacked and destroyed. Within a year, the most prominent and powerful holy seat of power in England, the archbishopric of Canterbury, that had been a beacon of faith and reform under Stephen Langton, Hubert Walter, and Thomas Becket was forever lost to the Anglican Church. The king then exercised his newly founded authority to issue The Ten Articles in 1536 that were the Church of England's first codification of doctrine. Though it originally upheld the former beliefs in purgatory, saint veneration, and relics, these were discouraged as superstition under Thomas Cromwell, the king's vicegerent in spirituals.

With the ascension of Edward VI and later Elizabeth I, England would further be tormented by successive kings and queens flipping back and forth between Catholicism and Protestantism, giving rise to campaigns against heresy, wars with Catholic countries, and widespread bloodshed.

Despite northern Europe being entrapped in the turmoil of the Reformation, the south was left largely untouched and remained strong supporters of the pope and papacy. They were, however, presented with the opportunity of a counter-Reformation in order to not succumb to the criticisms presented before them. This would be incredibly difficult, given the widespread support in Europe for Martin Luther, John Calvin and other Reformation leaders. With this in mind, the Council of Trent was held in 1545 to pacify the church and act before conciliar ideas began to spread. Led by Pope Paul III, this council was to endure until 1562 due to various interludes, including one for ten years due to a war. To say the council was problematic from the start is an understatement – only thirty-one bishops from Christendom attended and of these, only one was German; even at its largest when 270 clergymen attended only thirteen of them were German. As such, the voices of the Reformation were not particularly represented. Further issues arose from the differing motives of the council. The emperor hoped that the council would aid in tackling the practical issues arising from the wars, revolts and uprisings he faced. The pope wished for church doctrine (from hereafter we can call this Catholic) to be reaffirmed. The French, however, did not want the council to achieve anything so it could continue its war efforts while Emperor Charles was distracted. Despite this mess, there were some measures achieved: the seven sacraments were reaffirmed, as were Purgatory, transubstantiation, indulgences, Mass and the invocation of saints. The council also rejected Luther's definition between sanctification and justification by affirming that, 'Man is justified wholly by grace, and can do nothing of himself to merit justification, nevertheless he can and must cooperate with grace by freely assenting to it.'

As such, man was still a sinner as justification was not wholly necessary, yet man could be changed by justification through hope, charity and good works with the power of God. This is highly complex but it enabled the Catholic doctrine to navigate the treacherous waters of heresy to attempt a reconciliation with Protestantism.

This doctrinal work appeared to ensure that Catholics and Protestants could unite over what was deemed an unbridgeable division. The council put forward a vision for the church whereby it acted as a well-disciplined army that would have a regulated hierarchy and order. Bishops, for example, were encouraged to go out and preach but also participate in synods and councils to ensure unanimity. Likewise, religious orders were to be brought under episcopal control and only able to act with a bishop's permission. Most importantly, seminaries were to be established to ensure the clergy produced were pious, chaste, conscientious and educated. It seemed as though the council, despite its setbacks, would be successful.

Over the century, churchmen sought to implement the new authoritarian framework. A by-product of this, however, was a suffocation of the arts. In its decree on saints and relics, the church encouraged piety but scorned any abuse such as 'boisterous festivities and drunkenness' at festivals, saints' days, or Translations. Likewise, the prohibition of 'unusual images' was particularly used to attack religious paintings in the 1570s to exclude anything 'superstitious, apocryphal, false, idle, new, or unusual'. Worship was directed away from saints and towards parish churches with any activity outside of the parish church discouraged. Many painters found themselves put before the Inquisition for their deviation from the spiritual. Michelangelo's Sistine Chapel was attacked for its inclusion of classical figures, while characters in his *Last Judgement* were covered to circumvent their nakedness. As such, the worship of saints only truly remained in France, Spain and Italy – where it was a shell of its former self. Yet, perhaps the most remarkable impact of the Council of Trent was the renewed primacy it gave the papacy. To a certain extent, Martin Luther had saved the pope as he was now entrusted with promoting and commanding proceedings and leading the way for change; the pope was now a symbol of unity in Christendom and only he could coordinate missionary efforts from the New World in the West to the ancient civilisations of the East.

This would only last for a time, as a cloud of war and disunity would settle across central Europe. Just as our story began with the sack of Rome, so too does it end with it. Italy, in the sixteenth century, was a fragmented region, divided into several independent city-states and territories. At the centre of this complex web of alliances and rivalries was Rome, the seat of the papacy and a symbol of religious and political authority. In 1526, Charles V, the Holy Roman Emperor, faced off against a league of Italian states known as the League of Cognac, which included Pope Clement VII, the Republic of Venice, and the Kingdom of France. The emperor's forces, led by the Constable of Bourbon, marched towards Rome seeking to assert their dominance in Italy. Despite the pope's attempts to negotiate a peaceful resolution, the Imperial army arrived at the gates of Rome in April 1527. The defenders of the city, comprising both mercenaries and papal troops, were ill-prepared and heavily outnumbered. Their morale was further weakened by the fact that they had not been paid for months. On 6 May 1527, the Imperial army launched a full-scale assault on Rome. The city's defences were breached, and a brutal and chaotic scene unfolded as the soldiers rampaged through the streets, pillaging and destroying property, desecrating churches and committing acts of violence against the civilian population. Pope Clement VII sought refuge in the fortified Castel Sant'Angelo, along with a small number of loyal cardinals and officials. The siege of the castle lasted for six months, during which the pope and his defenders endured great hardship as prisoners. He was able to escape to Viterbo, but returned to a destitute Rome in October 1528. Ultimately, in June 1529, Clement VII negotiated a surrender and paid a substantial ransom to secure his release. The Sack of Rome had profound consequences for Italy and Europe as a whole. It shattered the illusion of Rome's invincibility and marked the decline of the Italian Renaissance as a dominant cultural and artistic force. It also acted as a prelude to the Wars of Religion that would endure for centuries. Equally, the pope's reliance on foreign powers for protection exposed the vulnerability of the church and undermined its moral authority to a point which it could never truly recover from. The world hereafter would drastically change as power, wealth, and empire would surpass piety. Thus, as our story began with the Sack of Rome and the beginnings of a New World, here we find the end of our tumultuous age and the birth of the Early Modern World.

Following Martin Luther, the world of saints was not entirely destroyed but most definitely degraded. In parts of Europe and the wider world that remained Catholic, the idea of saints continued, but in a far lesser form than before the Reformation. Although the Reformation did not, in theory, deny the significance of the saints as historical witnesses to the power and grace of God, it did eliminate their veneration and remove their images and relics from churches and homes.

In many ways, the Reformation also changed the type of person to become a saint. As opposed to pious kings, idolised bishops, and warriors who swapped sword for Bible, there was a rise in reformist saints who fought back against the destruction caused by the Reformation. As formerly witnessed during Arab and Viking attacks of the Early Medieval period, this was a distinct tactic utilised by the Papacy to reignite religious fervour in deeply unstable times. Yet in the post-Reformation age, these saints would only be recognised by certain sects of Christianity in certain countries. This is why, in today's world, we bear witness to saint's days that are confined to the Roman Catholic church, Orthodox Church, Anglican Church, Coptic Church, and so on. Due to this diversity of Christianity, the pursuit of a counter-offensive could never achieve the level of security and confidence the Church once had. Equally, as the Age of Enlightenment ushered in a scientific mind, the world no longer had a place for the mystical and faithful and thus there was a steep decline in the veneration of people, even within the Roman Catholic Church.

Of course, in Catholic countries where religion has retained an important role, the veneration of saints still remains. Even today you will find pilgrims along the Camino de Santiago visiting relics dotted along the ancient pilgrim route, but by no means does it begin to emulate the spiritual systems of the eleventh, twelfth, and thirteenth centuries. Even within nations steeped in Christian traditions, we witness a discernible decline. In May 1978, a substantial 90.5 per cent of Spaniards identified themselves as Catholic. However, fast forward to

October 2021, and this proportion had dwindled to 55.4 per cent, as reported by the CIS, Spain's esteemed sociological research institution. Similarly, the trajectory of Christianity in France has been one of gradual descent since the 1980s. A survey conducted in 2021 revealed that more than half of the French populace no longer hold faith in God or regard Christianity as pertinent. The percentage of individuals receded from 81 per cent in 1986 to a mere 47 per cent in 2020.

And so now we find ourselves with saints as endangered species, mere shadows of their former selves, destined to fall into disrepair despite the power they hold as symbols of the past.

Further Reading

This history of the Middle Ages could not be possible without the vast work and discoveries made by historians in the last century. Each chapter has relied on a plethora of hagiographies, journal articles, books, manuscripts, Bible excerpts, and much more. As such, I have curated the resources used to guide readers to explore more about the relationship between saints and the Middle Ages:

'Customary of the Shrine of St Thomas', Add. MS 59616, f. 9

Acta Sanctorum, October, vol. 1, edited by J. Ghesquiero (Antwerp, 1765)

Aird, William M., *The Boundaries of Medieval Misogyny: Gendered Urban Space in Medieval Durham* (Cardiff University, 2008)

Airlie, Stuart, 'Charlemagne and the Aristocracy Captains and Kings' in *Power and Its Problems in Carolingian Europe* (Taylor and Francis, 2012)

Alighieri, Dante, *The Divine Comedy*, Translated by Henry Wadsworth Longfellow, (Canterbury, Canterbury Classics, 2013)

Andrea Berto, Luigi, '"Utilius est veritatem proferre", A Difficult Memory to Manage: Narrating the Relationships between Bishops and Dukes in Early Medieval Naples' in *Viator*, vol. 39, no. 2

Anna Komnene, *The Alexiad*

Arcoid, *The Saint of London: The Life and Miracles of St Erkenwald*, ed. E. Gordon Whatley, (New York: Medieval & Renaissance Texts and Studies, 1989)

Augustine, *City of God*

Augustine, *Confessions*

Barrett, James H. 'What Caused the Viking Age?' *Antiquity*, vol. 82, September 2008, p. 671–685

Barrow, J.S., 'Ideas and Applications of Reform' in *The Cambridge History of Christianity* (Cambridge University Press, Cambridge, 2008)

Bartlett, Robert, *Medieval and Modern Concepts of Race and Ethnicity* (Duke University Press, 2001)

Bernard of Angers, *The Book of Sainte Foy*, translated by Robert Clark and Pamela Sheingorn, (Philadelphia, 1994)

Black, Antony, *Political Thought in Europe, 1250–1450* (Cambridge University Press, 1982)

Booker, Courtney M. 'The Public Penance of Louis the Pious: A New Edition of the Episcoporum de poenitentia, quam Hludowicus imperator profesus est, relatio Compendiensis (833)' in *Viator*, vol. 39, no.2

Boon, Jessica A., 'Medical Bodies, Mystical Bodies: Medieval Physiological Theory in the Recollection Mysticism of Bernardino de Laredo' in *Viator*, vol. 39, no.2

Boserup, Ester, *Population and Technological Change: A Study of Long-term Trends*, (University of Chicago Press, 1981)

Brown, Peter, 'A Dark Age Crisis' in *The English Historical Review* (Oxford University Press, Oxford, 1973)

Bull, Marcus, *The Roots of Lay Enthusiasm for the First Crusade* (Wiley, 1993)
Bull, Marcus, *Tale of Beryn The Miracles of Our Lady of Rocamadour: Analysis and Translation* (Woodbridge, 1999)
Bullough, Donald, 'Charlemagne's Men of God' from *Charlemagne: Empire and Society* (Manchester University Press, Manchester, 2005)
Burgtorf, Jochen; Crawford, Paul; Nicholson, Helen, *The Debate on the Trial of the Templars, 1307–1314* (Farnham, Ashgate, 2010)
Burton, Thomas, *Chronica Monasterii de Melsa*, ed. E.A. Bond, RS, vol. 43, 1868
Calendar of the Liberate Rolls, London, 191664, vol. 2
Callahan, Daniel, *Ademar of Chabannes, millennial fears and the development of Western Anti-Judaism* (Cambridge University Press, Cambridge, 2009)
Cartulario del 'Sant Cugat' del Valles, edited by J. Rius Serra, vol. 2, (Barcelona, 1945–47)
Cobb, Paul, 'The Empire in Syria, 705–763' from *The New Cambridge History of Islam* (Cambridge University Press, Cambridge, 2010)
Councils & Synods, with other Documents Relating to the English Church, edited by F.M. Powicke and C.R. Cheney, (Oxford: Clarendon Press, 1964–1981)
Cowdrey, H.E.J., *Pope Urban II's preaching of the First Crusade* (Oxford, 1970)
Devisse, Jean; Mollat, Michel, 'The Shield and the Crown' in *The Image of the Black in Western Art*, vol. II, edited by David Bindman and Henry Louis Gates Jr, 31 (Massachusetts, Harvard University Press, 2010)
Devisse, Jean; Mollat, Michel, 'The Appeal to the Ethiopian' in *The Image of the Black in Western Art*, vol. II, edited by David Bindman and Henry Louis Gates Jr, 83, (Massachusetts, Harvard University Press, 2010)
Dixon, W.H., *Fasti Eboracensis* (London: 1863)
Douie, D.L., 'The Canonization of St. Thomas of Hereford', *Dublin Review*, vol. 229, no. 469 (1955), p. 276
Draper, Peter, 'Bishop Northwold and the Cult of Saint Etheldreda' in *Medieval Art and Architecture at Ely Cathedral*, BAACT, vol. 2, 1979
Dugdale, William, *The History of St Paul's Cathedral in London from its Foundation*, 2nd edition, London, 1716
Duggan, A.J. 'Canterbury: The Becket Effect' in *Canterbury: A Medieval City*, ed. C. Royer-Hemet, (Newcastle-upon-Tyne, 2010)
Einbinder, Susan L., 'Recall from Exile: Literature, Memory and Medieval French Jews', *Jewish Studies Quarterly*, vol. 15, no. 3 (2008), pp. 225–240
Einhard, *Life of Charlemagne*
Fawtier, Robert, *The Capetian Kings of France* (Palgrave Macmillan, 1969)
Finucane, Ronald C. *Miracles and Pilgrims: Popular Beliefs in Medieval England* (Palgrave Macmillan, 1995)
Frassetto, Michael, *Christians and Muslims in the Middle Ages: From Muhammad to Dante* (Washington, DC: Lexington Books, 2019)
Fredona, Robert, 'Carnival of Law: Bartolomeo Scala's Dialogue De legibus et iudiciis' in *Viator*, vol. 39, no. 2
Gabriele, Matthew, 'The Provenance of the Descriptio qualiter Karolus Magnus: Remembering the Carolingians in the Entourage of King Philip I (1060–1108) before the First Crusade' in *Viator*, vol. 39, no. 2
Gabriele, Matthew; Stuckey, Jace, *The Legend of Charlemagne in the Middle Ages: Power, Faith, and Crusade* (Palgrave Macmillan, 2008)

Garrison, M., 'The Franks as the New Israel Education for an identity from Pippin to Charlemagne' in *The Apocalypse in the Early Middle Ages* (Cambridge University Press, Cambridge, 2014)
Gaunt, Simon; Pratt, Karen, *The Song of Roland, and Other Poems of Charlemagne* (Oxford: OUP Oxford, 2016)
Green, Karen, *Virtue Ethics for Women 1250–1500* (Springer Science & Business Media, 2011)
Guibert of Nogent, *Monodies Book 1*
Guibert of Nogent, *Monodies Book 2*
Guibert of Nogent, *Monodies Book 3*
Hable Selassie, Sergew, *Ancient and Medieval Ethiopian History to 1270* (Addis Ababa: United Printers, 1972)
Hahn, Wolfgang, 'Late Antiquity Trading Gold in South India', *Revue Numismatique*, vol. 6, no. 155 (2000)
Haney, Kristine Edmondson, *The Winchester Psalter: An Iconographic Study*, (Leicester: Leicester University Press, 1986)
Harris, Jennifer A., 'The Fate of Place in the Twelfth Century: Creation, Restoration, and Body in the Writing of Bernard of Clairvaux' in *Viator*, vol. 39, no. 2
Haseldine, Julian, 'Friendship, Intimacy and Corporate Networking in the Twelfth Century: The Politics of Friendship in the Letters of Peter the Venerable', *The English Historical Review*, vol. 126, no. 519 (April, 2011)
Head, Thomas 'I Vow Myself to Be Your Servant: An Eleventh-Century Pilgrim, His Chronicler and His Saint', *Réflexions Historiques*, vol. 11, no. 3 (Fall 1984)
Heng, Geraldine, *The Invention of Race in the European Middle Ages* (Cambridge: Cambridge University Press, 2018)
Henry of Avranches, *Shorter Latin Poems*
Henze, Paul, *Layers of Time: A History of Ethiopia* (London: C. Hurst & Co Publishers Ltd, 2000)
Holtzmann, Walther, 'Decretales Ineditae Saeculi XII', *Biblioteca Apostolica Vaticana* vol. 4, no. 36, (1982)
Immonen, Teemu 'A Saint as a Mediator between a Bishop and His Flock: The Cult of Saint Bononius in the Diocese of Vercelli under Bishop Arderic (1026/7–1044)' in *Viator*, vol. 39, no. 2
Jones, C.W., *The Nicholas Liturgy and its Literary Relationships (Ninth to Twelfth Centuries), with an Essay on the Music by Gilbert Reaney* (Berkeley, 1963)
Jones, Dan, *Powers and Thrones: A New History of the Middle Ages* (New York: Viking, 2021)
Jones, Gwyn, *The Norse Atlantic Saga, Being the Norse Voyages of Discovery and Settlement to Iceland, Greenland, and North America* (Oxford University Press, 1986)
Kennedy, Hugh, *The True Caliph of the Arabian Nights* (History Today, 2004)
Kennedy, Hugh, 'Sicily and al-Andalus under Muslim rule' from *The New Cambridge Medieval History Vol III* (Cambridge University Press, Cambridge, 2011)
Kennedy, Hugh, 'The Muslims in Europe' from *The New Cambridge Medieval History Vol II* (Cambridge University Press, Cambridge, 2015)
Kitzinger, Ernst, *The Cult of Images in the Age Before Iconoclasm* (Dumbarton Oaks Papers, Cambridge MA, 1954)
Knowles, David, *The Monastic Order in England, 943–1216* (Cambridge, 1941)
Koopman, Rachel, *Wonderful to Relate: Miracle Stories and Miracle Collecting in High Medieval England* (Philadelphia: University of Pennsylvania, 2011)
Lange, Dierk, *The Almoravid Expansion and the Downfall of Ghana* (De Grutyer, 2009)

Lerner, Robert E., *The Age of Adversity: The Fourteenth Century* (Cornell University Press, 1968)
Licence, Tom, *Bury St Edmunds and the Norman Conquest* (Woodbridge: Boydell & Brewer, 2014)
Licence, Tom, *Herman the Archdeacon and Goscelin of Saint-Bertin: Miracles of St Edmund* (Oxford: Oxford Medieval Texts, 2014)
Liutprand of Cremona, *The Embassy to Constantinople*
Loud, G.A., 'Southern Italy in the Tenth Century' from *The New Cambridge Medieval History Vol III* (Cambridge University Press, Cambridge, 2011)
Luscombe, David, 'The Papacy, 1024–1122' from *The New Cambridge Medieval History Vol. IV* (Cambridge University Press, Cambridge, 2015)
Malthus, Thomas, *An Essay on the Principle of Population* (Oxford World Classics, 1798)
McGuire, Brian Patrick, 'Friends and Tales in the Cloister: Oral Sources in Caesarius of Heisterbach's Dialogus Miraculorum', *Analecta Cisterciensia* 36 (1980)
McNamara, John, 'Problems in Contextualizing Oral Circulation of Early Medieval Saints' Legends' in *Telling Tales: Medieval Narratives and the Folk Tradition*, edited by Francesca Canade, Sautman, Diana Conchado, and Guiseppe Carlo Di Scipio (New York, 1998)
Middleton, John, *World Monarchies and Dynasties* (Routledge, 2004)
Mineo, Claudia, 'The Economy of Justice: Privileges, Litigation, and the Distribution of Land in Sixteenth-Century Castile' in *Viator*, vol. 39, no. 2
Morgan, Penelope, 'Effect of the Pilgrim Cult on Hereford' in *St Thomas Cantilupe, Bishop of Hereford: essays in his honour*, ed. M. Jancey, (Hereford, 1982)
Myhre, Bjørn, *The Iron Age* (Cambridge University Press, 2003)
Nithard, *The Histories*
Noble, Thomas F.X., Smith, Julia M. H., 'Slav Christianities, 800–1100' in *The Cambridge History of Christianity* (Cambridge University Press, Cambridge, 2008)
Odner, Knut, 'Ethno-historic and ecological settings for economic and social models of an Iron Age society: Valldalen, Norway' in David L. Clarke (ed.), *Models in Archaeology*, (Methuen & Co, 1972)
Odo of Cluny, *The Life of Gerald of Aurillac*
Orderic Vitalis, *The Ecclesiastical History*
Ozment, Steven, *The Age of Reform, 1250–1550: An Intellectual and Religious History of Late Medieval and Reformation Europe* (Yale University Press, 1980)
Petry, Carl, 'The Ism'l Da'wa and the Fatimid caliphate' from *The New Cambridge History of Egypt* (Cambridge University Press, Cambridge, 2008)
Price, Neil, *Children of Ash and Elm: A History of the Vikings* (Basic Books, 2020)
Price, Neil, *The Viking Way: Religion and War in Late Iron Age Scandinavia* (Oxbow Books, 2019)
Procopius, *The Secret History*
Pyun, Kyunghee, 'Foundation Legends in the Illuminated Missal of Saint-Denis: Interplay of Liturgy, Hagiography, and Chronicle' in *Viator*, vol. 39, no. 2
Reginald of Durham, *Reginaldi Monachi Dunelmensis Libellus de Admirandis Beati Cuthberti Virtutibus Quae Novellis Patratae Sunt Temporibus* (Durham: Surtees Society, 2007)
Reuter, Timothy, 'Introduction: Reading the tenth century' from *The New Cambridge Medieval History Vol III* (Cambridge University Press, Cambridge, 2011)
Riddle, John, *A History of the Middle Ages, 300–1500*, (Rowman & Littlefield, 2008)
Robinson, Chase, 'Pre-Islamic Arabia' from *The New Cambridge History of Islam* (Cambridge University Press, Cambridge, 2010)

Robinson, Chase, 'The rise of Islam, 600–705' from *The New Cambridge History of Islam* (Cambridge University Press, Cambridge, 2010)
Roesdahl, Else, *The Emergence of Denmark and the Reign of Harold Bluetooth* (Routledge, 2008)
Roesdahl, Else, *The Vikings* (Harmondsworth: Penguin, 1991)
Rymer, Thomas, 'Foedera, Conventiones, Literae et cuiuscunque generis', *Acta Publica*, vol. 1, (London 1704–17)
Salisbury, Joyce, 'Gendered Sexuality' in *Handbook of Medieval Sexuality* (Taylor & Francis, 1996)
Salvian of Marseilles, *On the Governance of God*
Sawyer, Peter, *The Oxford Illustrated History of the Vikings* (Oxford University Press 2001)
Sawyer, Peter, *The Viking Expansion* (Cambridge University Press, 2003)
Sergi, Giuseppe, 'The kingdom of Italy' from *The New Cambridge Medieval History Vol III* (Cambridge University Press, Cambridge, 2011)
Sharpe, John, *The Viking Expansion: Climate, Population, Plunder* (University of Montana, 2002)
Sharpe, Richard, 'The Setting of St Augustine's Translation, 1091' in *Canterbury and the Norman Conquest,* (Bloomsbury Academic 1995)
Sigal, Pierre-Andre, *L'homme et le miracle dans la France medievale, XIe–XIIe siècle* (Paris, 1985)
Sindbæk, Søren M., 'Networks and nodal points: The emergence of towns in early Viking Age Scandinavia', *Antiquity* vol. 81, January 2015, p. 119–132
Smalley, Beryl, *The Study of the Bible in the Middle Ages* (Basil Blackwell, 1989)
Smith, R.A.L., *Canterbury Cathedral Priory* (Cambridge, 1943)
Smith, R.A.L., *Collected Papers* (London, 1947)
Southern, R.W., *Saint Anselm and His Biographer: A Study of Monastic Life and Thought* (Cambridge, 1963)
Spencer, B., 'Pilgrim Souvenirs', in *Medieval Waterfront Development*, edited by G. and C. Milne, London and Middlesex Archaeological Soc., Special Paper no. 5 (London, 1982)
Spencer, B., 'Medieval Pilgrim Badges', *Rotterdam Papers*, vol. 1 (1968)
Stanley, A.P., 'The Shrine of St, Thomas of Canterbury' in *Historical Memorials of Canterbury*, 12th edition, (London, 1891)
Strayer, John, *Medieval Statecraft and Perspectives of History: Essays* (Princeton University Press, 2015)
Strayer, John, *The Reign of Philip the Fair* (Princeton University Press, 2019)
Suger, 'De Administratione' in *Selected Works of Abbot Suger of Saint Denis*, translated by Richard Cusimano, and Eric Whitmore, 81, (Washington DC: The Catholic University of America Press, 2018)
Suger, 'The Book of Accomplishments during his Administration' in *Selected Works of Abbot Suger of Saint Denis*, edited by Richard Cusimano and Eric Whitmore, 208 (Washington DC: Catholic University of America Press)
Swanson, R., *Religion and Devotion* (Cambridge European Medieval Textbooks, 2008)
Thomas of Monmouth, *The Life and Miracles of St William of Norwich*, (Cambridge: Cambridge University Press, 1896)
Urry, William, *Canterbury Under the Angevin Kings* (London, 1967)
Walberg, Emmanual, 'Date de la composition des recueils de Miracula Sancti Thomae Cantuariensis', *Le Moyen Age*, vol. 22, (1920): 259–274
Walter of Coventry, *The Historical Collections of Walter of Coventry*, ed. W. Stubbs, RS, vol. 58, 1872

Webb, Diana, *Pilgrims and Pilgrimage in the Medieval West* (London: I.B. Tauris Publishers, 2001)
Webster, Paul; Gelin, Marie-Pierre, *The Cult of St Becket in the Plantagenet World, c,1170–1220* (Woodbridge: Boydell Press, 2016)
William of Malmesbury, *Vita Sancti Wulfstani*
Woodruff, C.E., 'The Financial Aspect of the Cult of St Thomas of Canterbury', in *Archaeologia Cantiana*, vol. 44 (1932)
Yarrow, Simon, *Saints and their Communities* (Oxford, OUP, 2006)
Yates, Nigel, 'The Fabric Rolls of Hereford Cathedral, 1290/1 and 1386/7', *The National Library of Wales*, vol. 18 (2004)
'Monasterii de Wintonia', in *Annales Monastici*, vol. 2, ed. H.R. Luard, RS, vol. 36, 1865
'Opus De Miraculis Sancti Aedmundi by Abbot Samson' in *Memorials of St Edmund's Abbey*, vol. 1, edited by Thomas Arnold (Cambridge University Press: 2012)

Index